who printed it)

Financial
Planning
for
New Businesses

Financial Planning for New Businesses

Victor Durkacz

Ian Currie

Anne Phillips

Senior Members of the Business Services Department, KMG Thomson McLintock Chartered Accountants, Edinburgh

JOHN WILEY & SONS
Chichester · New York · Brisbane · Toronto · Singapore

Library of Congress Cataloguing-in-Publication Data

Durkacz, Victor Edward.
  Financial planning for new businesses.

  Includes Index
  1. New Business enterprises——Finance. 2. New
business enterprises——Great Britain——Finance. 3. Tax
planning——Great Britain. I. Currie, Ian. II. Phillips,
Anne. III. Title.
HG4027.6.D87   1985   658.1′5   85–17927
ISBN   0 471 90843 6 (pbk.)

British Library Cataloguing in Publication Data:

Durkacz, Victor Edward
  Financial planning for new businesses.
  1. Corporate planning
  I. Title   II. Currie, Ian   III. Phillips, Anne
  658.4′012   HD30.28

  ISBN 0 471 90843 6

Printed and bound in Great Britain

Acknowledgements

The authors would like to acknowledge the help received from the partners and staff of KMG Thomson McLintock, Edinburgh, and also from Mary, Robert and Elizabeth, our respective spouses.

Contents

I   Introduction   1
II   The business plan   5
III Tax planning   105
IV   Sources of finance   219

Appendices
  A National Insurance Contributions   246
  B Personal Allowances   248
  C Income Tax Bands   249
  D Corporation Tax   250
  E Capital allowances   251
  F Car and fuel benefits   252

Index   253

I Introduction

This book is a layman's guide to financial planning for starting in business and for expanding an existing business. The points it makes are simple and very practical. New businessmen and women who read it and apply its suggestions should greatly increase their chances of surviving the vulnerable early years of their venture.

Some will find that, after careful consideration, their proposed business is just not viable. They will then go back to the drawing board and produce a viable business plan, or scrap the project altogether. Either way, they will have been saved from possibly serious financial loss, and from contributing to the unacceptable level of start-up failures.

The authors are an experienced team of new business accountants, who have brought together the most important points for small businessmen to consider when planning a new venture. 'The Business Plan' is a step-by-step guide to putting together a new business proposal and projecting profits and cash flow for the critical first year. Very often the plan is used as a basis for raising finance, though even where securing finance is not a problem the preparation of a detailed business plan is still an essential discipline. There is, of course, no single way to produce a business plan, and its format will depend on the nature of the business and the sources of possible finance. However, the suggestions in this book are based on the experiences of small-business start-ups, and the underlying principles can be adapted to most situations.

Nowhere is the UK tax system more complex than in the rules for taxing new businesses. Part III — 'Tax Planning' — explains the principles at work, and gives many practical examples of how the tax burden can be minimized. It even shows how the tax rules can be used to provide a cash-injection into new businesses in some circumstances.

The last section — 'Sources of Finance' — summarizes the sources of finance open to new businesses, and gives some practical tips on how these should be approached.

Whilst you will find many useful ideas in the text, it is important not to treat it as a Do-It-Yourself manual for starting in business. There can never be a substitute for the advice of an experienced new-business accountant or lawyer, who will tailor-make his advice to your particular needs. Remember also that nowadays most lawyers and accountants are sympathetic to the aims of small businesses and understand their financial constraints. Very often they will not charge for an initial consultation and some may also be prepared to restrict their fee in the first year. Reading this book will help you understand what your financial adviser can achieve for you, and will help you to get the most out of his expertise.

II   The Business Plan

Chapter 1

Introduction

Before going into the step-by-step approach to preparing a business plan you should first of all ask yourself why such a plan is required. What advantages do you think you will gain from preparing it? The major reason for preparing a business plan is to provide a document of some type to give to your bank manager when you are looking for either initial finance or additional finance. This is the case whether you are looking for an increase in present overdraft facilities or require a large additional facility by way of a long-term loan. It may be that you are approaching a different finance source, such as a merchant bank, a venture-capital company or a government agency, and a plan will also be required for this.

Given that this is the major reason for preparing the plan, you must then decide how you wish to present your case. The overriding aim must be that the plan should present your best estimates for the future and that these estimates should be actually achievable by your business. To you it may be self-evident that your ideas are an interesting investment opportunity. The object of the plan is to get this message across to the expected source of finance.

There is therefore no room in such a plan for gimmickry or misguided humorous statements. These would only divert the reader's attention from the main purpose of the plan. The person reading it is a representative of your source of finance. His name will be on the line if things go wrong. He is looking for facts and realistic assumptions which will convince him that this project is one which he can recommend to his firm for investment.

The plan should be prepared by you with the help of your accountant or other financial advisor. But it is important that your philosophy for your business must show through. Too often such plans are prepared by the accountant with the help of his client, and this can be fairly obvious to the reader. The preparation of the projections, the printing and physical putting together of the plan can be best done by the accountant and his staff. But explaining the underlying concept is best left to you — it is your idea after all, not your accountant's.

In most cases it will be reasonably simple for the reader to check all the figures and assumptions. What he cannot check is the personality of the person operating the business. Therefore your plan should give a full description of yourself and your key staff. This should include details of any previous businesses operated by you and their outcome. Most of all, the attitude that should shine through the plan is a positive wish to succeed and a realistic appreciation of all the possible problems of your type of business.

You should also point out to your reader that although the major aim of the plan is to raise finance, your planning will not stop there. You should give specific details of how you intend to make sure that the reality of the situation will be examined. You should therefore give an account of the detailed steps you will take to monitor your forecasts. This will usually mean preparing monthly figures and comparing these with budgeted figures.

You should also tell your reader what you will do if your original forecasts are not met; for example, if your sales are less than those projected or less profitable than anticipated. At all times you should let your reader see that the plan is not solely a document used to raise finance which will be put in the waste-bin as soon as you get the money; it is also a plan of how the business will actually be run. You may intend to use your accountant to monitor the forecasts and set up a system of monthly reporting. If this is the case it should certainly be noted in the plan.

As well as being a document prepared to raise finance a properly prepared business plan will concentrate your mind on the reason for setting up business. Before writing it you may think you have sufficient finance and no external finance is required. After preparing the plan you may find that this is not the case. Preparing the plan may also bring to your attention aspects of the business to which you have not given enough consideration. For example, are you a multi-product or a single-product business? While preparing the plan it may become obvious that you should increase or decrease your range of products. This may be due to certain products being unprofitable. On the other hand, you may find you are spreading your talents over too many products and not concentrating enough time on the important ones.

As long as you are in charge of preparing your own business plan it will be a comprehensive, well-thought-out document, presenting your business as you see it. It is therefore a useful exercise for every businessman to carry out. It should not merely be brought out and dusted down any time finance is required.

Chapter 2

Collating all the Relevant Information for the Business

2.1 SALES PRICING

The business will produce either goods for sale, services for sale or a combination of both. Market research of some kind for both types of sale is essential. Even a one-man business doing building repairs must decide on which areas of a town offer the best opportunities. He must also decide who his competitors are in this chosen area and how much they charge for similar work. Do they charge purely on an hourly basis or do they charge for time plus materials? If they charge for the materials, how much do they mark up the price of the materials used? A large competitor may add only a small mark-up to materials used. He may be buying the materials at a cheaper price because of a discount for large orders. The one-man business usually buys the materials at a cash-and-carry and will normally be paying more for them than competitors. If he adds a larger profit percentage to his materials his customers may wish to buy the materials required themselves and only pay him for the time he takes to do the job.

He will also have to decide what his rate per hour should be. This should be lower than his larger competitors since they will have greater overheads. If his total sales estimated for the year are below the VAT threshold he will not require to register for VAT and therefore he will not charge VAT to his customers. This could help him to compete. Of course, if there are other one-man businesses in the area he should try to find out their charge-out rates and slant his rate to compete with them.

A small shop which is open for extended hours, say 8.00 a.m. to 8.00 p.m., can afford to charge prices substantially higher than, say, a supermarket, which has normal opening hours. This applies especially in areas which are densely populated and where there are no similar shops nearby. It can also apply to heavy or bulky goods which customers are not prepared to carry for a long distance.

There may be similar small shops in the same area and price-competition may be extremely keen on certain articles. Are these goods worth stocking at all? Or if they are not stocked will customers go to the other shops and, while there, buy all the rest of their shopping?

The article being sold may be unique to you. In this case the price is dependent on how much the customer will pay before he either decides to make it himself or to do without it altogether.

Market research is therefore vital. A larger business may use a specialist market-research consultancy. A smaller firm will use its own common-sense approach and investigate fully the area in which it is 'setting up shop'. It will also investigate in depth the items it is selling. This can often be done by studying trade magazines which may also yield good ideas on other aspects of the business. They will give a general idea of discounts offered to larger purchasers, competitors' charges for carriage and post-age, minimum amounts that one can order, and other practical points. The small trader can also do his own market research by 'knocking on doors'. This is time-consuming but can give a good idea of the size of the market, the prices at which products can be sold and the possible product range.

Pulling together all the information gained through his market research the trader should have a general idea of what he should sell and the price he should sell it at.

Whilst carrying out market research it sometimes comes to the trader's notice that there is a large gap in the market for another product which he was considering stocking only as an extra. This can be an unexpected bonus and makes his market research more worthwhile. It would not be the first time that a profitable product has been discovered by accident.

2.2   COSTING OF ALL INPUTS

Having arrived at your pricing strategy, the cost of goods or services to be sold should be examined. If the business is purely marketing (i.e. buying an article and reselling it) then this is reasonably simple. You must decide what quality of product you require for resale and try to purchase it at the lowest possible price. The usual method is to buy in such large quantities that you obtain a reduction in price. The second is to make early payment for goods and obtain a discount for so doing. This second method is really a financial decision which depends on the availability of funds. It should therefore not be taken into account when calculating the costing of goods purchased.

Where services are to be sold the cost of these services can be easily estimated. This will normally be the wages of the employees plus wage-related costs (i.e. National Insurance paid by the employer and pension contributions paid by the employer). There may also be the cost of travelling to the place where the work is done and any incidental materials which are not separately charged. If machinery is used then some allowance for that machinery should be included.

Cost of services	£
Employee's wage for week of 40 hours	80.00
Employer's National Insurance contribution	8.40
Employer's pension contribution	8.00
Total weekly cost	96.40
Basic cost per hour	2.41
Travelling time — 1 hour per day	
Cost of travel per day	4.00
Machinery costs not separately charged per day	3.00
Total weekly cost (as before)	96.40
Travelling cost (five-day week)	20.00
Machinery costs	15.00
Total costs per week	131.40
Total chargeable hours (as before)	40
Travelling time	5
Net chargeable	35
Total cost per chargeable hour	3.75

Where a combination of services and goods are sold then a combination of the above will be used. The only difference may be that the goods sold may be sold at cost or cost plus a small percentage to cover handling charges. This would be the case in, for example, a builder doing a small repair job or a decorator.

Where a manufacturing process is involved the costing is much more complicated. In this case you have to estimate what the sales per period will be. You then calculate the costs involved in producing that output. These costs include raw materials, machinery, running costs, the cost of the factory, cost of labour, maintenance costs for the machinery and depreciation (i.e. writing off the cost over a fixed period) of both machinery and the factory.

These costs will be either fixed or variable. Fixed costs will be incurred whether goods are being produced or not, and variable costs will be incurred in proportion to the quantity of goods produced. Examples of fixed costs are all the costs of the factory such as rates, rent, repairs to buildings and depreciation of buildings. Variable costs are raw materials used in the production process, Labour, costs of operating the machinery and possibly depreciation of that machinery.

By calculating all these costs for each period you arrive at the total cost of producing the number of goods required in that period. By dividing the total costs by the total number of goods you arrive at the cost per article. You can then compare this with the price at which the article is to be sold. You can also use this figure as a basis for your pricing policy.

Cost of Manufactured Goods	
Number of items to be sold	1000
Cost of Manufacture	£
Variable Costs	
Raw materials	2000
Wages	1000
Machinery costs (excluding depreciation)	500
Depreciation of machinery	200
Total variable costs	3700
Fixed Costs	
Rent	350
Rates	200
Building repairs	150
Building depreciation	100
Total fixed costs	800
Total manufacturing costs	4500
Cost per item to be sold	4.50
Sales price per item	9.00
Profit per item	4.50

At this stage you will have an idea of your gross profit per article. This is the difference between the sale price of an article and the cost of either producing it or purchasing it. The total gross profit for the total number of articles to be sold must obviosly, over a longer period, be sufficient to cover all the other costs of the business. You should then go ahead and calculate these other costs.

Distribution might well be a significant additional cost. You may use outside hauliers to deliver the produce or use your own fleet of trucks and vans. You can calculate the cost of outside hauliers simply by using their rates for the distances involved and for the quantity or weight of your products. Costing the use of your own vehicles can be more difficult. In this case you should estimate the number of vehicles required and then the cost of running them and paying the wages of their drivers. Other costs to be calculated include administration, finance and other overheads. The detailed costing of these will be covered in a later section. The main point of this section is to arrive at methods for obtaining the cost of all these items in reasonable detail.

Chapter 3

Taking a Forward View

3.1 MARKETING

Marketing is not the same as selling. It is a much broader subject. It includes (a) knowing your market, (b) knowing your project, (c) considering all types of advertising and sales promotion, and (d) the actual selling of the product.

KNOWING YOUR MARKET

You should try to look at your market from the point of view of your customer and decide what goods your customers will wish to buy. You should also ask whether such aspects as quality of service, speed of delivery or packaging are important. If you sell only one product are there other ancillary or complementary products the customer would like to buy? If the market for the product is dying because of a new product, you may wish to investigate the possibilities of that other product. If larger companies are already producing a product an incomer to that market will have to be very special to compete. This is not to say that some small businesses cannot profitably compete with larger ones. If they can it is usually because of some difference in the product or service. It can also be dangerous to produce one product which is highly specialized. Although this product is at the moment irreplaceable there may come a day when it is superseded by new technology. When this happens the business has then no product to sell. On the other hand, it is tempting to produce a whole range of articles. Against this must be weighed the effort required to sell all these articles, particularly when some of them have direct competition in the market already.

Knowing your market also means knowing the strength and size of one's competitors, and knowing why they do not already produce some of the articles which you intend to produce. If you cannot produce an article more cheaply than it can be bought from a competitor then it is obviously not a good idea to produce it yourself. The only reason for producing such an article yourself would be if you thought you could ensure a higher level of quality control.

Certain of your competitors may be in other markets as well as the one you are in. If this is the case you should attempt to find out which is the most profitable part of such firms. Ask yourself whether you should be in that market sector only, or if this would leave you vulnerable to changes in customers' tastes. This may be the reason why your competitors are spread over two or more market sectors. Again, your market may be local compared with your competitors' national market, and they might be unable to relate to individual localities. If the local market is large enough it may be adequate for your business, though this, of course, restricts the number of customers, and total dependence on one area or industry can be dangerous.

KNOWING YOUR PRODUCT AND HOW TO PRICE IT

You must know your own product and why your customers will buy from you and not from your competitors. This is especially true in the smaller business, which is proprietor-owned and managed. The owner is identified with his product and business, whether it be a service, manufacturing or retail business. He must therefore be absolutely sure that he knows every detail of the products, what they are used for, and who his customers are.

In pricing policy, costs are very important, but there is usually no point in starting from the cost of production. The first figure used in pricing should be what competitors are charging. You should work back from that figure, calculating whether the business can make a profit by selling the article at that price. You can then work out your total cost of producing the article (labour, materials and overheads) and compare this with your competitors' selling price. Then you should consider whether the product could be sold at a cheaper price and still make a profit. You must also consider whether it would still sell at a higher price, due possibly to some 'improved' feature. In other words, the main question in pricing is to find out what the market will pay for your product.

CONSIDERING ALL TYPES OF ADVERTISING AND SALES PROMOTION

Techniques of advertising and promotion really depend on the scale and type of your market. The best advertisement for any product is the word-of-mouth appreciation of the product by a satisfied customer, though this is only effective in a small, localized market. It does not readily translate to a national market. Good advertising depends on where it is placed, when it is placed and the manner in which it is written. In local conditions it is sometimes as well to use a local weekly newspaper. Alternatively, it can be useful to deliver leaflets to identified customers. On a larger scale you must decide which newspapers your customers are likely to read, and advertise in these on a regular basis.

Depending on your product, it may also be useful to advertise regularly in the relevant trade journals. Other promotional activities can also be useful so long as they are appropriate to the product and the scale of the market. You could have a distinctive logo appearing on everything connected with the business, from packaging, letter heads and other stationery, to vehicles. Consider appearing at sales exhibitions, or handing out free pens, keyrings, etc, with your name on them. Firms which employ delivery drivers should always ensure that their drivers are courteous to other drivers and even help them if necessary. This can create a good impression of the firm itself and can actually bring in business. If this attitude is spread throughout the business as a whole it can do wonders for your image, whether the business be large or small, or trading nationally or locally.

SELLING THE PRODUCT

Your strategy will depend largely on whether the firm is large enough to employ salesmen. If it is not, then you will be the person who carries out the selling.

Effective selling is a profession like any other, and requires much skill acquired over a period of years. The skills required should *never* be underestimated. You cannot expect to become an effective salesman overnight, and you should learn all you can about selling by reading and attending courses. You should role-play sales interviews with your staff or even with your spouse, getting them to ask you awkward questions. Only with practice will you come across to customers as natural and sincere.

A good salesman is sincere and enthusiastic. The customer must feel that the salesman wishes to sell him the article. He must also feel that the salesman's description of the article and all its good points is true. Above all, a good salesman actually *listens* to what his customer says and adapts his presentation accordingly. The importance of good selling techniques cannot be overemphasized. There is no point in producing articles unless they are sold, and sold at a price which gives the seller a profit, and there are no articles which can be sold without some form of sales effort.

3.2   FORECASTING MARKET SIZE AND SHARE

Having gained sufficient background information to forecast the market size the next stage is to calculate your potential share of that market. From your market research you should have a good understanding of your market and whether there is any possibility of expanding it.

You will also have an idea of the growth rate of your market and whether you want to attack, the top end with expensive high-quality goods and services, or the bottom end, where low price is the major selling factor.

You will also have worked out the size and strength of the competition, and how much of the market he can reasonably hope to obtain. This will allow you roughly to forecast your own growth rate. Will it take one or ten years before you reach the percentage share of the market you would like? Will you go on growing in that market and will that market continue to grow or contract?

3.3   FORECASTING MANUFACTURING CAPACITY AND CAPACITY TO PROVIDE SERVICES

In a manufacturing business the owner will know the number of articles he hopes to sell and therefore must produce. From this information he must work out what manufacturing capacity he needs. This leads on to the basic questions of how can the required number of articles be made in one month, and how much stock will need to be held at any time to fulfil the orders forecast.

The choice of machinery is obviously a central decision. In some cases this may be specially built and may possibly be automatically controlled. The number of machines required must be estimated as well as the floor space for production and ancillary areas for administration. The number of vehicles required for deliveries or collections of raw materials must also be forecast. Will the customer collect or receive deliveries? Will a good location significantly reduce transport costs?

In a service industry, having forecast the level of service required the problem of how to organize the provision of services must be tackled. Will service personnel work from a central point where spare parts are stored and from where they can be effectively supervised? Will they each work independently from their own homes and be brought together regularly for meetings to discuss strategy and problems? What tools, machines, vehicles, etc. will they require and how many of each? Will these be shared or will each operative require his own? Will the vehicles require a radio-telephone system?

All these questions will require to be thought through and used to estimate the business's capability to live up to projected capacity.

3.4   FORECASTING EMPLOYEE NUMBERS AND COSTS

In both manufacturing and service businesses a forecast will then be required of employee numbers and grades and the various costs relating to their employment. This number should include all the staff, from shop-floor operatives to administration staff, accountancy staff, sales staff and personnel officers. The costs should include an allowance for any increases projected in wage rates in the period covered by the plan. They should also include the present National Insurance rates and an allowance for any known or expected increases. Costs of any actual proposed staff superannuation schemes must be included.

There may also be other perks, e.g. cost of luncheon vouchers or a canteen, use of the firm's cars for personnel, etc. When working out all employee costs it should be remembered that even in the best-run business there will be free time for employees as well as holidays. There may also be the necessity at some periods to work overtime, which will be paid for at higher rates. All these aspects must be considered when forecasting the employee costs.

3.5   FORECASTING   STOCKHOLDING   FACILITY   FOR FINISHED GOODS AND PURCHASES

In a manufacturing business an estimate of the maximum area required for raw materials should be made, as well as an estimate of the maximum area required at any one time for finished goods and packaging materials. The factory space must obviously be large enough for these as well as for the manufacturing process and other ancillary areas. The layout of the goods-inward department and the goods-outward department and their relation to the production area should be carefully planned. These departments must be costed, and included in these costs will be all material-handling devices. These can be purchased outright, bought on hire purchase or leased, depending on the businesses cash-flow requirement and tax position.

In a marketing or retailing business an estimate will be necessary of the area required to store the maximum number of articles required at any one time. Depending on the size of the operation, this can range from a small shed with a fork-lift truck to a large warehouse with a range of mechanical handling devices.

In both types of business the maximum number of articles or materials for which you require space will depend on several factors. What is delivery like from suppliers of your materials? What is the most cost-effective quantity of raw materials or finished articles to buy at any one time? On your sales side how much stock do you wish to have on hand at any time? Do you want one month's supply to fulfil orders or two months, or more?

Once you have completed forecasting all the above aspects of your business you can then go ahead and calculate the detailed figures required to make up your business plan.

Chapter 4

Calculating the Necessary Figures

4.1 TOTAL EXPECTED SALES

Having obtained all the information you require for pricing your sales or service outputs and forecasting total sales you now have to calculate the total value of sales. You first need to estimate the months of the year in which your sales will be made. By estimating the credit terms you can calculate when the payments will be received. In a service business you may have estimated, for example, that in January you will sell 500 hours of labour at £10 per hour, and if that is all you are selling your total sales will be £5000 (500 × £10). On the other hand, if you are selling a single product you may have estimated, for example, that in January you will sell 200 articles priced at £5. Your total sales would therefore be £1000 (200 × £5).

Complications will arise when you sell a number of different articles, or if you sell a combination of labour and materials. You then have to estimate how many of each article at each separate price or how many hours of labour you will sell. You must also estimate the relationship between hours worked for a customer and materials used, if indeed there is such a relationship. You would then calculate the total value of each article sold, of labour sold and of materials sold. The sum of all these totals will be your total sales.

If your sales are on a cash basis then the payment for your total sales will be received in the month they are sold. If the sales are on a credit basis then a conservative estimate of the time taken to collect debts must be made. For example, if you think your customers will take two months' credit the goods and services you sell in January will be paid for by your customers in March (i.e. two months later). You will require details of the timing of transactions to prepare the cash-flow part of the business plan.

4.2   VAT ON SALES

As will be seen in the taxation section of this book, VAT can be quite a complicated tax and is worth careful consideration. At this stage you will know your estimated total sales, and can therefore take a view as to whether or not you will be VAT-registered.

If you are under the VAT threshold then VAT does not apply to sales. On the other hand, if you are over the limit then in all your calculations you must extract the VAT element. Taking a VAT rate of 15% as the standard rate for taxable goods and/or services you must calculate the VAT included in your estimated gross sales. If all your sales are taxable this calculation is relatively simple, since the VAT included in your gross sales will be 15/115ths of those sales (or 3/23rds). In certain cases you will be selling items or services which are taxable at the zero rate and perhaps some which are exempt from VAT.

From your estimates calculated to date you will know the monthly and yearly totals of all the differing types of sales. You should therefore know the actual total of taxable sales for each period and be able to calculate the VAT on this figure. This will be shown as a deduction from total sales, leaving what are known as net sales.

VAT Calculation for Vatable and Non-vatable sales			
	SALES		TOTAL
	VATABLE	NON-VATABLE	SALES
	£	£	£
Gross Sales	3450	2000	5450
VAT (15/115 × Gross Sales)	450	–	450
Net Sales	3000	2000	5000

This applies whether you are selling goods or services or a combination of both. This is necessarily an extremely simple explanation of VAT on sales but it is all that is required at this stage. The complications of this tax will be explained in a later section.

4.3   COST OF SALES

The next problem is working out the cost of sales. In a marketing operation you will have forecast the cost of purchasing the articles you sell, and you will know the discounts receivable for purchasing large quantities. You will have decided what the price will be of the number of articles you wish to sell each month, and you will know if the goods purchased are subject to VAT. With sales in January of, say, 200 articles purchased at £3 each, the total cost of sales will be £600 (i.e. 200 × £3). This assumes that the £3 used includes delivery charges to your warehouse. In a service operation our cost of sales will include both labour costs and material costs. You will have estimated already on the sales side the number of hours you will sell and the materials you will sell. The costing of these materials will be straightforward because you will normally have calculated the sales price as cost of materials plus a percentage mark-up (to cover handling or to yield a profit on these).

Labour costs are more difficult. When you forecast the capacity you required to provide the services you estimated you would sell, you would also forecast the various grades of staff who will be paid at differing rates. They may also have differing holiday entitlements and benefits-in-kind, such as a company car.

The individual salary costs together with associated staff costs should be calculated on a monthly basis. Remember that different parts of these costs will be paid at different times. The salaries or wages for January will be paid in January; the National Insurance and Income Tax deducted from wages or salaries will be paid halfway through February. Pension-scheme contributions may be paid quarterly or yearly. Every part should be calculated monthly and the time of payment of each noted. It will then be easier to work out the total monthly salary costs, and when those costs will be paid (or how much will be paid each month).

In a production or manufacturing business calculating the costs of production will be an additional complication. This will include all costs, from raw materials through to factory costs.

You will have forecast already the materials required and their cost, and all the costs of operating the factory, including labour costs. You must now forecast when all of these costs will be payable. This will include calculating whether it is worthwhile paying in cash to obtain a cash discount or to pay later and forego such discounts. Having done this you should then note separately the costs of each part. These factory costs will be all the costs which you incur in operating the factory to produce the articles which you sell, including maintenance and depreciation of machinery, power to drive the machinery and any materials or consumables required to operate the machinery, etc. You should also estimate, as in all cases, when each of these costs will require to be paid.

You should now have, both on a period basis and for the year, the total sales figure and the total VAT (if any) on that figure, giving you the total net sales. You also have on the same basis the total cost of sales figure (excluding VAT where relevant). The cost figures should, where VAT is applicable, be calculated net of VAT, if you are going to be VAT-registered. Deducting the cost of sales from the net sales you arrive at your gross profit, also on a period basis and a yearly basis.

4.4 GROSS PROFIT

The gross profit figure must at least cover all the other costs you incur. A useful exercise now is to divide this gross profit figure for each period, and for the year, by the net sales for each period and for the year and multiply the result by 100. This gives you the gross profit percentage. It is interesting first of all to find out whether this percentage is consistent over the whole year or if it varies in some months. If it varies then you should check over your figures again carefully to make sure they are correct. If they are correct you should then try to identify reasons for the variations. For example, it may be that once you are selling a certain number of articles you achieve your maximum gross profit percentage. Usually, the smaller the number of items produced, the greater is the individual cost of each item and thus less profit is made.

		ONE £	TWO £	THREE £	FOUR £
Calculation of Gross Profit Percentage					
			MONTH		
(A)	Sales	1000	2000	2500	3500
(B)	Cost of Sales	750	1200	1375	1925
(C)	Gross Profit	250	800	1125	1575
(D)	Gross Profit Percentage	25%	40%	45%	45%

(C) Gross Profit = (A) Sales less (B) Cost of Sales
(D) Gross Profit Percentage = (C) Gross Profit Divided by (A) Sales multiplied by 100.

There can be other reasons for varying gross profit percentages, and all aspects should be investigated. In your previous market research you may have heard quoted by competitors the gross profit percentage for your type of business. You should compare your percentage with this figure. Again, if there is a large difference you should investigate this. If, for example, you are estimating a much higher gross profit percentage you should make sure that all your figures are correct and you have not omitted any major costs. You should also make sure that your sales price or prices are realistic and achievable. On the other hand, if your gross profit percentage is much lower you must make sure your estimated sales price is high enough, and that you have not been too pessimistic about your costs. You may be estimating too many employee-hours to make each article or too high a price for materials used, or possibly too high a quantity of materials used.

Most accountants in professional firms deal with a range of businesses in quite a number of varying industries. They will have at least a general idea of the gross profit percentage achieved by these businesses and should be able to verify that the figure you arrive at is reasonable. This is another good reason for using the services of a professional accountant before you commence business, even if you have complete confidence in your own ability to produce all the figures you need for a business plan.

If you are satisfied with your gross profit percentage you should then go on to work out the other costs of the business. These are distribution costs, administration costs and finance costs. You should commence with distribution costs, as these are most closely related to the sales of your product or products.

4.5   DISTRIBUTION COSTS

Obviously, distribution costs only concern businesses which are selling products. They may include the cost of carriage from the factory (or warehouse) to the customer. This will be either the simple cost of hiring outside hauliers to the more complicated costs of using your own vehicles. When calculating the latter you should include wage costs of delivery drivers, running costs of vehicles and the actual capital cost of the vehicles. The capital cost of the vehicle will be written off (i.e. depreciated) over the expected life of the vehicle. The running costs of the vehicles will include fuel, road tax and insurance, and repair costs. You may decide if you are to set up your own repair shop for vehicles or use an external vehicle-repair facility. If you use a contract hire facility all your vehicle costs, apart from petrol, will be known and fixed.

All these costs will be related to the number of articles you have forecast you will sell. The area you will be selling into will also be considered. In other words, you must forecast in each period the number of articles to be delivered to each destination, and from this you can calculate the number of vehicles required or the costs of hiring outside hauliers.

Even in a one-man business covering a small area with one van the costs of running and maintaining that van must be calculated. You will also have to decide over what period of time that van will be written off. By adding these two amounts together you will obtain total distribution costs for that one-man business.

Distribution Costs Calculation	
One-man Business	YEAR
	£
Fuel costs	900
Repair costs	350
Road tax	100
Van insurance	150
Van depreciation (see below)	1000
	————
Total costs of van	
(i.e. total distribution costs)	2500
	════
Van Depreciation	
Purchase Price of Van	4000
	════
Number of years over which to be written off	4
	————
Depreciation per year (4000/4)	1000
	════

Some businesses employ salesmen who sell from their vans. Again, the total costs of these vans and the salesmens' salaries will be the total costs of distribution. The larger the business or the wider the area to which the products are to be delivered, the more complicated the calculation of distribution costs will become. You must be sure that your calculations cover all the related distribution costs and that no aspect is omitted. For example, where salesmen sell from vans, the cost of training these salesmen can be treated as a distribution cost.

4.6   ADMINISTRATION COSTS

Administration costs cover all the other costs relating to the running of the business, except financial costs, which are dealt with separately. (It is a debatable point sometimes whether the cost of sales staff should be included in distribution costs or administration costs. Whatever happens, you must make sure they are included under one of these categories.)

Administration costs will cover the costs of all staff not directly included in production costs or distribution costs. It will include the cost of running the office — from stationery and telephone to rates and heat and light. It will cover any other expenses, such as lawyers', surveyors' and accountants' fees. There will, of course, be grey areas where costs are partly production costs, partly distribution and partly administration costs. Warehouse costs are an example. These are often treated as part of distribution costs, since the major task of the warehouse would appear to be to store goods prior to distribution. But the warehouse may also be the initial storage area for raw materials, and therefore part of the cost should be attributed to production costs.

ADMINISTRATION COSTS	MONTH ONE
OFFICE COSTS	£
Rent	200
Rates	150
Salaries	300
Employer's National Insurance	31
Stationery	50
Postages	35
Telephone	64
Heating and Lighting	120
PROFESSIONAL FEES	100
TOTAL ADMINISTRATION COSTS	1050

Both distribution costs and administration costs should be calculated net of VAT. You should at the same time calculate VAT payable on them whether or not the business is registered for VAT. If the business is registered it will be able to reclaim the VAT for the cash-flow projections. If, on the other hand, the business does not require to register for VAT it is useful to show a separate figure in the accounts for VAT which is not able to be recovered. This VAT-irrecoverable figure is another cost of the business.

4.7 FINANCIAL COSTS

The next aspect to consider is how the business is to be financed and the cost of this finance. This depends very much on the size of the business and the financial position of the owner(s) of the business. The business may be financed by the capital of the owner, by an overdraft facility from a bank, by a loan from a bank, by a loan from another financial organization, by some form of share capital or by a combination of some of these.

From the cash-flow forecast it will be apparent how much finance the business requires and a decision can be taken on the most suitable financial sources. The anticipated cost of finance can then be calculated. In the simplest case of the business being financed by your own capital you may put through a charge for interest on that capital either on the basis of commencing with a sum of capital (say, £10 000) and calculating interest on that at a certain rate (say, 5%). In this case your total finance cost for the year would be £500 (£10 000 at 5%) or £42 per month. An alternative is to provide interest on the balance of your capital account at each month-end in the following month. Assume, for example, that you pay in £10 000 to the business and make a profit in the first month of £1000, and take out of the business in the first month £600. The balance on your capital account at the end of the first month would be £10 400 (£10 000 plus £1000 minus £600). You would provide in the second month interest at a certain rate (say, 5% again) on this for one month. In this case the amount would be £43 (£10 400 at 5% divided by 12) and this would be the total finance cost for the second month. This would be continued on a similar basis for the whole year.

Similar types of calculation are required in other cases, for instance where interest is payable quarterly but accumulated on a monthly basis on bank overdraft, or where interest and capital are paid quarterly at

FINANCIAL COSTS CALCULATION WITH AN OVERDRAFT FACILITY		MONTH			
		ONE £	TWO £	THREE £	FOUR £
(A)	Overdraft per cash flow (before financial costs)	1000	1500	1200	1050
(B)	Interest on overdraft	0	13	19	15
(C)	Interest payable quarterly				32

(A) *Overdraft.* The final balance on the cash-flow projection each month excluding any overdraft interest.

(B) *Interest on Overdraft.* Calculated on balance at end of previous month at (say) 15% for one month, i.e. figure in month two is £1000 × 15% divided by 12 (1000 × 15/100 ÷ 12).

(C) *Interest payable.* Payment made of first three months' interest in month four (i.e. 0 + 13 + 19 = 32).

fixed amounts or variable amounts on a bank loan. Every type of finance will be subject to an agreement as to how and when interest and capital are to be paid. You must calculate these amounts in total for the year and also know when they are payable.

As will be seen from the above example, the actual calculation of these figures can be extremely complicated, and they are more easily calculated by means of a computer program than manually. The assistance of an accountant familiar with computerized forecasting will be invaluable. Alternatively, if you wish to do all the work yourself he can at least explain how to calculate the financial costs for whatever type of finance you are seeking.

You have now calculated all your costs and also you know or have estimated when all these costs will be incurred. You can now calculate your net profit.

4.8   NET PROFIT

You have now calculated all your costs and you have estimated when they will be incurred, so you are able to calculate your net profit. This is arrived at by deducting the total of all costs (distribution, administration and financial costs) from your gross profit. The resultant net profit is the reward for all the effort you put into the business. This net profit is subject to taxation in one form or another. In a limited company it is subject to Corporation Tax and for sole traders and partnerships it is subject to Income Tax. The calculation of this taxation charge is explained in Part III of this book. The taxation charge should be calculated and deducted from net profit to give the profit after taxation, which is the amount you will earn for your year's work.

You will have a general idea of the amount of money you wish to earn from the business and take out of it in each period and in total for the year. At this stage you will treat this figure as drawings and deduct it from the figure arrived at for profit after taxation. You will then, after all this effort, arrive at the final surplus or deficit of the business for the year as a whole.

This will apply in all types of businesses except limited companies. Normally, if you decide that your business is to be a limited company you will be a director of that company. In this case your 'drawings' will be a salary, and as such subject to Pay As You Earn taxation and National Insurance. It will be included in administration costs under the heading 'Directors remuneration'. But for the purposes of this exercise it is probably better to omit this figure until you have calculated your profit after taxation, unless you have a definite view of what your salary must

CALCULATION OF FINAL SURPLUS/DEFICIT FOR YEAR	£
Gross Profit	55 000
Distribution costs	15 000
Administration costs	5 000
Financial costs	2 000
Total costs	22 000
Net Profit before taxation	33 000
Taxation	8 000
Net profit after taxation	25 000
Drawings required from business	15 000
Surplus/(Deficit)	10 000

be. You can then add in a reasonable figure for salary and rework your figures to arrive at the new profit after taxation figure.

Now that you have arrived at your yearly surplus or deficit you can consider if that figure is acceptable to you. You may decide that your sales target is too high or too low, and if so you may wish to rework the figures with differing numbers for sales, values of services or a different mix of products sold, etc. It is merely a case of doing part of the calculations again and replacing figures already used with these new figures — a computer program will be invaluable here. Substituting figures will affect all or at least some of the other figures; for instance, more sales will mean higher distribution costs or a larger stockholding will require more finance, and so on. If the forecasts are set up on a computerized spreadsheet it is easier to make changes without the effort required to change a manual forecast. If the relationships of, say, sales numbers with distribution costs are incorporated into the computer model, then any change to sales numbers will automatically be carried through to distribution costs and right through to your final surplus or deficit. In this way you can experiment until you arrive at a reasonable level of sales and final surplus.

The forecast must now be put together in a logical manner and a detailed explanation of the mechanics of this is given in the next chapter.

Chapter 5

Putting Together the Forecast

5.1 PROFIT AND LOSS ACCOUNT

The normal order of layout for the forecasts is to have the profit and loss account first, then the cash flow projections and finally the balance sheet. All these parts are important in their own way. The profit and loss account shows the actual financial result of the period without taking into account whether the income shown has actually been received or the expenditure has actually been paid. It includes what are known as (a) 'accruals' and 'creditors' and (b) 'prepayments' and 'debtors'. Accruals can best be described as items of expenditure relating to an accounting period which are not paid until after the end of that period. A simple example is the expenditure incurred on gas for heating premises. The expenditure is being incurred on a daily basis but the bill is received for it (and in fact payable) every three months. Therefore in a commencing business at the end of month one you will accrue an estimated one month's expenditure, two months' expenditure at the end of month two and three months' expenditure at the end of month three.

Your purchases of materials or goods for resale may be on credit terms. If the period of credit is one month then each month-end you will accrue the one month's purchases for which you have not paid. This type of accrual is normally termed a creditor, and the term 'accrual' is reserved for expense items which are more likely to be estimated.

Thus at each period-end there will be a great deal of differing creditors and accruals, and these all require to be calculated before the profit and loss account can be compiled. There may also be pre-payments. These can be items of expenditure which are paid in advance of the date on which the expenditure is incurred. A simple example is rent, which is often paid in advance, or insurance premiums, which are also paid in this way. At the end of month one you may in fact have paid a full year's insurance premiums but you will only have benefited from one month's insurance. You have therefore pre-paid eleven months or 11/12ths of the total at the end of month one.

You may allow your customers one month's credit before they pay you. If so, you must at the end of month one pre-pay the amount due to you for sales made in the month for which your customers have not paid. This type of pre-payment is normally termed a debtor. You must calculate this for every month-end so that your total sales made in the month are shown. There are normally far fewer pre-payments than accruals, but they must all be calculated accurately in order that your profit and loss account figures will be correct. One other item which affects your profit and loss account is stock. This can be a very material figure in some businesses, and you must calculate it as accurately as possible for each month-end. In an ongoing business, stock is physically counted at least each year-end, and an accurate estimate is made for the other period-ends. Stock can consist of three categories:

(1) Stocks of raw materials (i.e. items purchased for manufacture).
(2) Work in progress.
(3) Finished goods or goods purchased for resale.

The valuation of stock can, however, present some problems. Valuation of raw materials not as yet used for manufacture is relatively simple, as these will be valued at the cost which you pay for them. The valuation of items purchased for resale are treated in the same way. But problems arise in the valuation of work in progress and finished goods.

First, you must identify the various component parts of work in progress. These may be raw materials, labour costs, costs of machinery, etc. At each month-end each item being manufactured will be at a different stage of manufacture, and this stage will be costed. This is reasonably simple if only one type of item is being produced. It is then easier to spread all the manufacturing costs over the production of that one item according to numbers produced. If a series of different items are produced which take different times and different quantities of material to produce, then it is more difficult to value these. Nevertheless, some formula is necessary to cost each item at each stage of its manufacture. In your forecasting you must therefore estimate for each item the stage of its manufacture and its cost at that stage. You must also estimate the numbers at each stage at each month-end. By multiplying the numbers of each article at each stage by the cost at that stage and adding together the

```
                              DIAGRAM ( 1 )
                              -------------------

                          PROFIT and LOSS ACCOUNT
                          ---------------------------
```

	MONTH		
	ONE	TWO	TOTAL
SALES	2300	3450	5750
Less.VAT on SALES	300	450	750
	-----	-----	-----
NET SALES	2000	3000	5000
	-----	-----	-----
Cost of Sales			
MATERIALS	500	700	1200
Opening Stock	0	100	0
	-----	-----	-----
	500	800	1200
Closing Stock	100	200	200
	-----	-----	-----
	400	600	1000
LABOUR	250	350	600
FACTORY COSTS	150	210	360
	-----	-----	-----
	800	1160	1960
Opening Work in Progress	0	200	0
	-----	-----	-----
	800	1360	1960
Closing Work in Progress	200	300	300
	-----	-----	-----
	600	1060	1660
Packaging Costs	150	210	360
	-----	-----	-----
	750	1270	2020
Opening Finished Goods Stock	0	50	0
	-----	-----	-----
	750	1320	2020
Closing Finished Goods Stock	50	270	270
	-----	-----	-----
TOTAL COST of SALES	700	1050	1750
	-----	-----	-----
GROSS PROFIT	1300	1950	3250
	-----	-----	-----
Gross Profit %	65	65	130
	-----	-----	-----
Distribution Costs	500	750	1250
Administration Costs	400	400	800
Finance Costs	0	125	125
	-----	-----	-----
TOTAL COSTS	900	1275	2175
	-----	-----	-----
NET PROFIT	400	675	1075
	-----	-----	-----
TAXATION	?	?	?
	-----	-----	-----
PROFIT after TAXATION	?	?	?
	=====	=====	=====

resultant figures you will arrive at a total work in progress at each month-end.

The other category of stock is finished goods. This is simply the stage of goods after the final stage of work in progress. If you have already calculated the cost per item for work in progress it is a simple task to add to that cost the other costs of preparing the item for distribution to your customers. These costs will normally only be the labour involved in moving the articles to your finished goods store, the labour costs of packing the articles and the actual cost of packing materials.

You will now have total figures for each period-end for each category of stock and can now proceed to complete your profit and loss account. Diagram 1 is one layout for this account, and it should be compiled on a period or monthly basis. At this stage, no figures for taxation or profit after taxation need to be entered. On the diagram calculations are kept fairly simple by assuming that all sales are subject to VAT at an assumed rate of 15% (the current standard rate). Line 1 is the total gross sales per month as estimated by you. VAT on these sales is calculated at three twenty-thirds of these gross sales. By deducting this VAT figure from the gross sales you arrive at the net sales figure.

If the business is a retail business then the total cost of sales will be the cost of purchases adjusted for movement on stock in the period. For example, in a commencing business if you buy £2000 worth of goods in month one and have a stock valued at £500 at the end of month one, your cost of sales for month one will be £1500 (£2000 less £500 stock increase).

In a manufacturing business the cost of sales will be calculated as shown in the diagram. You commence with the materials purchased and adjust this figure for the movement on stock of raw materials (i.e. lines two, three and four). In month one you purchased £500 of materials and at the end of that month had a stock of £100 of materials. This means you had only used £400 of materials (£500 less £100). Similarly, in month two you purchased £700 of materials and again your stock of materials increased by £100 (£200 less £100). This means you have used £600 of materials (£700 less £100).

The above method would be used to calculate these figures if you were calculating them after the end of the period in question. But when you are carrying out a forecasting exercise they will require to be done as follows.

Going back to the diagram, you have projected sales of £2300 gross and have calculated the raw materials required to produce these sales at £400 for month one. You have projected the stock you will require at the end of month one as £100. You have no opening stock, and therefore to arrive at this situation you must purchase materials of £500 (£400 plus £100). You then go on to month two, where you estimated you required materials of £600 to produce sales of £3450. You have projected your stock requirement at the end of month two at £200, which is £100 more than at the beginning of that month. You will then require to buy £700 of raw materials (£600 plus £100) to achieve this result.

You then add the two other components to the materials consumed to obtain your work in progress cost. These are labour and factory costs. You will have projected the labour costs you require to produce the number of goods sold and also the relevant factory costs for that number. If the factory costs are numerous (i.e. quite a few expense headings) it is preferable to prepare a separate schedule for these, and to transfer the total of this schedule to your profit and loss account as total factory costs. The work in progress which you estimate to be in stock at the end is deducted to give the cost of work in progress sold. You then add the packaging costs, and after adjusting for the movement on finished goods stock you arrive at the actual total cost of sales.

As will be observed, the first figure which is used is the total cost of sales. This forecasted figure is entered and you work backwards from it. You then enter your estimated finished goods stock which you think you will require at the end of month one. Because this is the commencing period there is no figure of finished goods at the start of the period. Therefore by adding your total cost of sales to your finished goods stock at the end of the period you arrive at the total cost of finished goods produced in the period. You then enter your packaging costs which you have estimated, and by deducting this from the total costs of finished goods produced in the period you obtain the cost of items sold.

You now enter your estimated closing work in progress and again there is no opening work in progress. You add this closing work in progress to the figure obtained for cost of items sold to arrive at the total costs of all production for that period. It is now a case of repeating this process for the twelve months.

The profit and loss account to the cost of sales stage is now complete. You deduct the cost of sales from net sales to arrive at the gross profit. By dividing this gross profit by net sales you arrive at your gross profit percentage.

You can now enter your estimates for distribution costs and administration costs. If the individual headings in the last two categories are numerous it is better to prepare separate schedules of these and enter the total distribution costs or total administration costs in the profit and loss statement.

As noted before, it is necessary to compile your cash-flow forecast before you can calculate your finance costs. It is only when you arrive at the figure of finance required in that cash flow that you can calculate what type of finance you need and how much it will cost. You will therefore calculate the profit and loss account as far as administration costs at this stage, and after you have compiled your cash-flow projections you can complete the profit and loss account.

As noted before, the profit and loss account has been kept simple by assuming all sales to be subject to VAT at the same rate. If this is not the case and some sales are subject to VAT and others are not, then complications can arise. The best way to deal with this is to produce a separate schedule showing the different items sold or groups of items sold. You can then show a deduction of VAT from those items which are subject to VAT, and for those which are not subject to VAT the gross and net figure for sales will be the same. Adding together all your gross sales will give total gross sales for your profit and loss account. Adding together all your VAT deductions will give a total of VAT on sales. When you add together all your net sales it should agree with the figure you arrive at by deducting your total VAT from your total gross sales. This is shown in Diagram 2 and will be compiled for each period.

```
                        DIAGRAM( 2 )
                        ------------------
              EXAMPLE OF BUSINESS WITH SALES AT DIFFERENT VAT RATES
              ---------------------------------------------------------

                                       MONTHS
                                       ----------
                                   ONE     TWO    TOTAL
                                   ----    ----   ----
      Gross Sales of A             575     690    1265
              VAT                   75      90     165
                                  -------------------------
      Net Sales of A               500     600    1100
                                  -------------------------
      Gross Sales of B             600     700    1300
              VAT                     0       0       0
                                  -------------------------
      Net Sales of B               600     700    1300
                                  -------------------------
      Gross Sales of C             345     230     575
              VAT                   45      30      75
                                  -------------------------
      Net Sales of C               300     200     500
                                  -------------------------
      Gross Sales of D             300     400     700
              VAT                     0       0       0
                                  -------------------------
      Net Sales of D               300     400     700
                                  -------------------------

      Total Gross Sales           1820    2020    3840
      Total VAT                    120     120     240
                                  -------------------------
      Total Net Sales             1700    1900    3600
                                  =========================
```

5.2   CASH FLOW

CREDIT CONTROL

One of the most important aspects of the cash flow of your business is the collection of cash from your debtors, or 'credit control', as it is known. It is therefore useful to think carefully about this aspect before considering the mechanics of the cash-flow statement.

The main source of your income will be from your trade debtors. This income only benefits you when it is eventually lodged in your bank account. Up to that moment you are actually financing your customer's business. This has two consequences — it costs you money and it increases your overdraft requirements. If, for example, a customer owes you £10 000 and takes two months longer to pay than was agreed, the cost to you will be £10 000 multiplied by whatever interest rate you pay on your overdraft for two months. Taking an interest rate of 15% the cost will be £250 (i.e. £10 000 × 15/100 × 2/12). Obviously, if you allowed a number of customers to do this the result would be very expensive to you. If you are estimating that all customers will pay in two months and in fact they take more time, your overdraft will be larger than you anticipated. Suppose you estimate that your overdraft will be £20 000 at the end of month two because all your customers will pay within the two-month period. Suppose that one customer takes four months to pay the £10 000 he is due. Your overdraft at the end of month two will be £10 000 more than anticipated. At the end of month three it will also be £10 000 more. It will be month four before your overdraft will be at the originally estimated figure, after he has signed his cheque, forwarded it to you and you have lodged it in your bank account.

There is another aspect which may not be evident at first glance. It is a general rule of business that the longer a person takes to pay an account the less likelihood there is of that account being paid at all. This would result in a bad debt, and the incidence of bad debts starts an extremely vicious circle which evolves roughly as follows:

(1) Your overdraft increases because your customers are not paying on time.
(2) You apply to your bank for an increase in your overdraft facility to cover the increasing overdraft.
(3) The first application for an increase is granted by your bank.
(4) Some months later your customers are becoming even slower to pay and more accounts are being written off as bad debts. This further increases your overdraft.
(5) You apply to the bank for another increase in your overdraft facility.
(6) The bank asks to see up-to-date accounts of your business before granting a further increase. These accounts are now showing bad debts being written off.
(7) The bank refuses to grant an increase in given overdraft facilities unless you can improve your credit-control procedures. The bank

will also require to see regular (probably monthly) reports to prove that you have done what they asked.

You are therefore eventually forced to implement credit-control procedures by the bank when the simple and most efficient way to make sure that your credit control is in order is to set up such procedures as soon as you commence business. The answer is to set up a very tight methodical system of credit control from the very beginning. This may seem slightly self-defeating if you are breaking into a new market and you are trying to entice new customers away from competitors. It is nevertheless true that business taken on is worse than useless if it entails long credit terms or if customers on their own extend agreed credit terms. If you make a decision to attract business by giving longer credit terms (say, six months) you should make absolutely sure that your customer pays in six months and does not take seven or eight months.

The best credit-control procedure (whether your system is computerized or manual) is to make sure that you know how old each of your debt is at each period-end. A useful method of analysing overall debtors is to calculate the number of days' sales outstanding at each month-end, as follows:

$$\frac{\text{Total trade debtors at period-end}}{\text{Total sales for year}} \times 365 = \frac{\text{Number of days'}}{\text{sales outstanding}}$$

For example, if trade debtors at the end of January are £30 000 and total sales for the year are £250 000 the number of day's sales outstanding is:

$$\frac{30\ 000}{250\ 000} \times 365 = \frac{\text{44 days' sales, which is approximately}}{\text{one and a half months}}$$

If trade debtors at the end of January are £75 000 then the number of days' sales outstanding would be 110 days, or three and a half months.

This would obviously be a danger sign if your credit terms were two months. If some of your debtors are actually paying within two months this means that others are taking, probably, more than four months.

Looking at the calculations from a different angle, if your terms are two months and your sales for the year are £250 000 then the maximum debtor at any time should be two/twelfths of £250 000, or £42 000 approximately. Any amount by which your debtors exceed £42 000 is the amount by which you are financing your customers' businesses and increasing your own overdraft. Additionally, you are paying overdraft interest on this amount, which at 15% on £33 000 (i.e. £75 000 less £42 000) for one month works out at approximately £400, and over a year could become quite substantial. It should be obvious from even these few figures that good credit control is fundamental to survival in business.

Credit control is necessary whenever you take on a new customer. The first thing you should do before selling him anything on credit is to check out his creditworthiness. This can be done by a credit-rating agency or through a banker's reference. Once his creditworthiness is established you should then agree with him, in writing, his credit limit and terms of payment.

You should also stipulate that if the customer defaults in any way he will not be supplied with any more goods or services until he has put matters right. As far as possible, your conditions should cover all customers, no matter their size or reputation. It is not unknown for larger companies to try to take advantage of their size and reputation to delay payment to smaller firms.

Having covered the administration of your trade debtors adequately you should look at the book-keeping aspect.

The sales ledger should be set up in such a way that it is an easy task to 'age' each debtor. This means that you can easily find out how old each balance on the sales ledger is. At each period-end the listing of the outstanding balances on the sales ledger should be done both in total and also on an aged basis. If credit terms were payment in two months then the listing would be compiled as follows:

SALES LEDGER BALANCES AT 31 JANUARY 1987

Customer name	Total balance £	Jan. and Dec. 1–2 mths £	Nov. 3 mths £	Oct. 4 mths £	Prior to Oct. over 4 mths £
AB Ltd	1000	1000			
CD Ltd	2000	1000	1000		
EF Ltd	3500		1000	1500	1000
GH Ltd	1500		1500		
IJ Ltd	750	400	350		

This listing should be prepared by the person in charge of the sales ledger as soon as possible after each period-end, and a copy given to you so that you can take steps to pursue any debtor balances that are seriously overdue. You may decide that all items of four months or over should be actively pursued. You may also decide to send a warning letter to all customers whose debts are three months old, reminding them what the agreed credit terms are. Stronger letters or telephone calls should be used with older debtors. It may be useful to set up a three-letter system as follows:

(1) *When account is over three months old.* Send a *first letter* pointing out

the terms of credit and that unless the debt is settled within these limits no further supplies will be delivered.

(2) *When account is over four months old and there is no response to first letter.* Send *second letter* referring to first letter and asking for an immediate response.

(3) *When no response to the second letter.* Send *third letter* stating that unless a reply is received within seven days the account will be passed to your lawyer for collection.

(4) *When no response to the third letter.* Pass the account with full details to your lawyer.

This last step is very important. Unless you carry through all your procedures your customer will soon realize that your letters are worthless and will ignore them completely.

Another item which can usefully be shown on your aged list of balances is the customer's credit limit. If the sales ledger card or sheet has a note of this limit on it, it will be obvious to the person who is compiling the list of balances whether a customer has exceeded his credit limit. If the customer is over his limit this fact should be noted on the list. This can easily be done by writing the credit limit in a different colour of ink alongside the total balance. When you examine the list of balances you will therefore see at a glance which customers are abusing this aspect of their credit terms. If the excess is material it should be pointed out to the customer in the same way as the overrun of time taken to pay by a three-letter system.

Another method of dealing with trade debtors is to pass them all to a debt-collecting agency or have them dealt with by a debt factor. Both of these methods can be expensive. To a certain extent they divorce you, the proprietor, from a material part of your given business. (Though debt factoring can play an invaluable role for rapidly expanding businesses whose invoiced business is accelerating more rapidly than cash receipts.) In general terms you or your salesmen will be the people who know your customers best. Therefore you are the best people to ensure that your customers pay on time and do not abuse their original credit agreement with you.

One other point to watch — a customer who is in financial difficulties may suggest that if he is supplied for another month or so he will turn the corner and will be buying even more goods from you then. Before you allow him extra credit you should investigate his situation thoroughly. You should make absolutely certain (if you can) that his statements are true and that all his other creditors will also allow him to continue.

The following is an example of the effects of good credit control which occurs in practice.

A firm whose general credit terms were six months due to its type of business never prepared an aged list of debtors. An aged list of trade debtors was then prepared, allocating debtors between six months old, one year old, eighteen months old and over eighteen months old. A major effort was mounted to get payment from all debtors whose debts were either eighteen months old or over eighteen months old. After this exercise was completed enough cash had been received to pay for a major new item of machinery. As the owner had originally contemplated approaching the bank for a loan to buy this machinery the result of this exercise was to save the interest on the loan and to leave open his credit lines in case other credit needs should arise.

Whilst we are not suggesting that your new business would ever let your trade debtors get so far behind in payment, this highlights the advantages of good credit control from day one.

COMPILATION

Before compiling the cash-flow forecast you must have estimated not only the costs and income taken into the profit and loss account but also the month in which each item is either receivable or payable. As will be seen, the timings of cash flow can make a significant difference to the amount of finance required. In a purely cash business, e.g. a window cleaner, it will be relatively easy to forecast the timing of your costs and income. It will also be easy to attempt to balance one against the other in order that little or no financing is required.

But in a manufacturing operation the cost of materials purchased, machinery and wages must be paid for when that cost is incurred. The income from items sold may be received three months or longer after the date of sale, and this time-lag will necessitate the introduction of an amount of money from one or more sources.

The compilation of the cash-flow forecast is therefore carried out mainly to calculate how much finance is required and how it fluctuates over the period. Once this is calculated a view can be taken on the type of finance which is best suited to support the business. Another point which is relevant and may be very important is whether your business can be grant-aided in any way. In some cases grants can be a major factor in the location of a business. Certain areas may get far greater grants than a neighbouring area, even though the distance between the two may be quite small. This subject of grants for new businesses is discussed in Part IV.

The cash-flow forecast includes the payment for both revenue items and capital items such as machinery, equipment, vehicles, the cost of the premises and all other items required to set up the business. An example of a simple cash flow is shown in Diagram 3. To construct a cash-flow projection you commence with the income side and allocate your sales between cash and credit sales. Items sold for cash are received in the

```
DIAGRAM ( 3 )
------------------
CASH FLOW FORECAST
------------------------
```

	MONTH		
	ONE	TWO	TOTAL

INFLOW

	ONE	TWO	TOTAL
Cash Sales	1000	1000	2000
Credit Sales	0	1000	1000
Total Income	1000	2000	3000

OUTFLOW

	ONE	TWO	TOTAL
Purchases Material	500	700	1200
Labour Costs	250	350	600
Factory Costs	450	50	500
Packaging Costs	150	200	350
Distribution Costs	1000	600	1600
Administration Costs	200	400	600
Finance Costs	0	109	109
Machinery Costs	3000	0	3000
Equipment	1500	0	1500
Motor Vehicles	7000	0	7000
Total Expenditure	14050	2409	16459
Bank Brought Forward	0	-13050	0
Bank Carried Forward	-13050	-13459	-13459

month sold, but you must estimate the length of time that customers allowed credit will take to pay. If you think they will take one month you show January's sales being received in February, February's sales in March and so on. This is an important part of the cash flow where sales are made on credit, and the time-lag should be estimated as accurately as possible to eliminate any material errors. Whilst you will agree credit terms with all your customers, it may be naive to hope that customers will always pay on time, and it is better to incorporate extra time in the cash-flow plan. You then include any other income receivable in the month, e.g. grants where applicable. If your business is entitled to a grant on purchase of machinery and equipment this is usually paid a certain number of months after the claim is submitted. Such grants usually require to be certified by an accountant and checked by a government department. It is always better to allow an extra month between the date of purchase of the equipment for which such grants are claimable and the date you estimate the grant will be received.

At the start of a new business there may be a considerable amount of

VAT being suffered on new equipment, stock, purchases, etc. This amount of VAT in the first VAT period may be in excess of the VAT received which is included in your sales. In this case the VAT return for your first period will show a figure of VAT reclaimable. If the business can manage to get the VAT return in quickly this amount recoverable will be received in the fourth month.

There may be other sundry items of income receivable and these should be included as and when they are estimated to be received. For example, under the Enterprise Allowance Scheme, which is organized by the Manpower Services Commission, an allowance is paid to the proprietor of the business fortnightly in arrears. In this case it would be necessary to estimate the date each payment would be received. If the cash flow was completed on a monthly basis then some months might show three amounts received and others might show two amounts received.

This covers all the cash receivable, and you should now move on to the cash payable. The most important figure in some businesses is the cost of materials used to produce the article(s) sold. This figure will not always relate directly to the items sold as there will be an element of stocking up during the first months, and this may well continue throughout the year.

You must estimate first, the numbers and values of purchases of materials and second, when payment for these materials must be made. The date of payment may be a trade-off between credit allowed from suppliers weighed against any cash discounts which can be obtained for prompt payment. Credit terms may, for example, be payment within two months subject to a 2.5% discount for cash. This cash discount must be set against the cost of obtaining it, i.e. the interest paid on an amount drawn from the bank two months early. In this example, if the overdraft interest rate was 15% there would be no financial advantage either way. The only advantage of paying after two months would be to keep your overdraft within a pre-arranged limit. If the overdraft interest was less than 15% the cash discount would be advantageous, and if the interest rate was more than 15% it would be better to take advantage of the two months' credit. To arrive at this decision you should pro-rate the discount rate for a year. In the example 2.5% for 2 months is equal to 1.25% for 1 month or 15% ($1\frac{1}{4} \times 12$) for a full year. (This ignores the effect of compound interest rate, but the point is valid for virtually all practical purposes.)

In your new business it may not be possible to obtain credit until you have become established in the eyes of your supplier. This may take six months or even a year, during which you will have to pay in cash for materials.

You should already have considered this problem and also whether the supplier offers large enough trade discounts to make it advantageous for you to buy items in larger quantities, bearing in mind the additional storage capacity you might require for large purchases and the larger initial payment you will have to make. (You will also require to estimate any wastage which may occur. This may be through deterioration of the material itself or by way of offcuts, etc. in a manufacturing process. You must make sure you are estimating the purchase of a sufficient quantity of materials to produce the number of items you will sell.) Having taken into account all these pros and cons you can arrive at figures to enter in your case flow for materials purchased.

You must then calculate the amount to be paid in each period for labour costs. When you compile the profit and loss account you must calculate the labour cost including any ancillary costs, e.g. National Insurance, pension scheme, luncheon vouchers, etc. You will be paying your net wages weekly or monthly in the period in which the work is done. The amounts payable for National Insurance (both deducted from the employee and payable by the employer) are due to be paid by the nineteenth day of the following month. The same is the case for Income Tax deducted from employees' wages under PAYE. In your forecast you must show National Insurance and PAYE taxation in the month following that in which it is incurred. On the other hand, luncheon vouchers are usually purchased in quantity and handed out to employees weekly. They will therefore be purchased in advance and you may, for instance, purchase three months' supply in month one. You must, of course, allow for this in your forecast of cash flow.

Although you normally think of labour costs as being payable on a cash basis the above-noted major items will be paid in either the next month or, in the case of luncheon vouchers and certain other items, in advance. With a fairly high combined rate of National Insurance (for employee and employer together) of up to 19.45% of gross wages and employers' pension contributions, where applicable, usually having a combined rate of over 10% of gross wages, it will be seen that these items can be very substantial. The fact that the majority of these costs are paid one month in arrears will have a beneficial effect on your cash flow, and this must be recognized in your forecasting.

The timing of other costs, such as factory, packaging and distribution costs, must also be estimated. It may be necessary, for example, to stock up with packaging materials. It could be financially advantageous to purchase a large quantity of cartons to obtain discounts or better service from suppliers. And if a large stock of packaging is available it is easier to fulfil a rush order without worrying about quickly obtaining additional packaging.

Distribution costs can cover the use of outside hauliers, the use of owned vehicles or a combination of both. If large quantities or numbers of items are being transported it may be possible to obtain special rates from hauliers and also special payment terms. You must take account of this when estimating the cost and timing of the payment of your distribution costs. You will have decided previously what your transport policy is to be, and you will have calculated your distribution costs for your profit and loss account using that policy. You must now carry that decision one stage further and incorporate into your cash-flow forecast the timing of payment of these costs.

Included in distribution costs may be wages of drivers and warehouse staff. As with other labour costs, it must be remembered that the ancillary costs of National Insurance, PAYE and pension-scheme contributions are paid later than the month when the net wages are actually paid.

The timing of vehicle-running costs must also be considered. For example, road tax and vehicle insurance will be paid in advance. This means that the road tax will be paid in the first month for a full year. It is possible to pay insurance over a number of months on an instalment basis, but it is usually less than twelve months, so at some stage during the year insurance will be paid in advance. It may also be that repairs to vehicles are to be carried out by a garage which will allow one month's credit. So even simple items like vehicle costs are not usually paid on a cash basis, and you must estimate carefully the timing of all such payments to arrive at a true forecast of cash flow.

You must also calculate your estimated timing of administration payments which have already been calculated for the profit and loss account. Some may be paid as the cost is incurred, and others paid either before or after the cost is incurred. For example, the cost of stationery may be paid in the first month, but that stationery will be used over a longer period. On the other hand, telephone bills other than initial installation costs will be paid every three months after the costs are incurred. Again, administration costs may include salary costs and, as noted before, the ancillary costs for these will be paid in the month after they are incurred.

Other outflows of cash must also be estimated. There may be purchases of machinery, equipment, motor vehicles and other fixed assets. If these are straight purchases the forecasting is fairly straightforward. If they are to be leased then the timing of payments will depend on when the agreements are made with the leasing company. Usually the leasing company demand three months' payment in the first month and from the second month you will commence paying the normal monthly charge. This will result in two 'free' months at the end of the leasing term. If you are buying under a hire-purchase agreement there is normally an initial deposit and then monthly or periodical payments. These payments are a repayment of both capital and interest, and in forecasting these you must estimate a reasonable interest rate. A finance house will usually be happy to quote you typical hire-purchase and leasing rates which can then be incorporated into your cash flow.

There will still be more cash expenditure. In the case of a sole trader or partnership the proprietor(s) will wish to draw money from the business, and you will need to estimate this, allowing for the cost of Class 2 National Insurance stamps. (In a company these costs will all already be incorporated as salaries, either as administration costs or under a separate heading of directors' remuneration.)

The last category you should forecast is finance costs. A decision will be required as to what type of finance you should secure. It is normally better to set up the cash-flow forecast to show the financing initially as an overdraft. This is done to calculate, first, what size of overdraft you will require and second, how much that overdraft will cost. You estimate an overdraft interest rate at, say, 10%, and each period-end calculate what your overdraft will be. You take your total income for the first month and deduct it from the total expenditure for that month. The resultant figure is your projected overdraft at the end of the first month. (This is shown in detail in Diagram 3.) You then calculate your overdraft interest for that first month on this figure. Taking a 10% rate for simplicity, you would multiply that overdraft figure by 10% and divide it by twelve to arrive at one month's overdraft interest. You would then enter this overdraft interest figure in your profit and loss forecast. You should then estimate how often overdraft interest is payable. It is better to be conservative here and assume that you must pay it every quarter (i.e. the interest for months one to three will be paid in month four).

This being the case, you can complete the first three months of your cash flow showing no finance costs but calculating the interest for each of these months and entering it on your profit and loss account forecast. The figure which you will enter for finance costs in the cash flow in month four will be the total of the finance costs shown in the profit and loss account for months one to three. (Month one will have no figure as it is the start-up month.) You will continue this system for the whole year, i.e. in month seven in the cash flow you will show the total of months four to six in the profit and loss account.

You should now have a total cash-flow projection for the year which will show how much your overdraft will be at each month-end, how it will change over the year and what the maximum will be during the year. You must now decide if such an overdraft is the best way to finance the business. You will also require to consider whether such an overdraft is obtainable. It may be better or easier to obtain both a fixed-rate bank loan and an overdraft. You may have spare capital which you wish to invest in the business and you can bring this into your cash flow projections on the dates and in the amounts you have available. This would obviously reduce your requirement for other cash. You may wish a return on this capital of a certain percentage, and this will be an additional finance cost. Additionally, in the case of a limited company there is the possibility of issuing either ordinary or preference shares, or loan stock (debentures). The capitalization of your business is really a specialist field on which you will require the advice of your lawyer or accountant, though some of the tax considerations are dealt with in Part III.

If a large sum of finance is required it may be necessary to approach other sources of finance, such as venture-capital funds looking for equity stakes in growth companies. All these avenues must be explored and a decision made as to the ideal and achievable finance package before you finalize your cash-flow projection. When you have made your final decision you can amend your preliminary cash flow to take account of any adjustments required due to differing methods of financing.

Lastly, when you are compiling your cash-flow forecast (and profit and loss forecast) you must carefully note all the assumptions you have made on costs, amounts payable and dates payable, of income, amounts receivable and dates receivable and of the financing method or methods used. When you write your business plan you should incorporate into it full details of these assumptions in order that your readers can measure the realism of the plan and, perhaps, offer constructive comments.

5.3   BALANCE SHEET

The balance sheet is nothing more than the listing of the remainder of the balances on your accounts and should be compiled for each period-end. These are the balances which are not included in the profit and loss account. They are usually subdivided into fixed assets, current assets and current liabilities on one side. On the other side you show how these amounts are financed. This will either be by share capital or proprietor's capital, revenue earned and long-term loans.

Fixed assets are shown at the cost to the business less any amounts written off for depreciation to date. This item will cover plant, equipment, vehicles, furniture and fittings, buildings, etc. You then show current assets which are stocks, debtors, pre-payments and the bank balance (if in credit). For your previous forecasting you will have estimated all these figures, and it should be merely a case of entering them here.

The same is true for current liabilities, which covers creditors, accruals and bank overdraft. VAT at each period-end may be an asset or a

```
                         DIAGRAM ( 4 )
                         -----------------

                        CAPITAL ACCOUNTS
                        -----------------------

                   (1) BALANCE SHEET of a SOLE TRADER
                   --------------------------------------

                                    MONTH
                                    --------------
                                    ONE      TWO
                                    -----------------

Balance Brought Forward              0      6000
Capital Introduced                10000       0
Add.Profit for period                0      2000
Less.Loss for period              3000         0
                                    -----    -----
                                    7000     8000
Drawings for period               1000      1000
                                    -----    -----
Total Capital at end of Period    6000      7000
                                    =====    =====

                   (2) BALANCE SHEET of a PARTNERSHIP
                   --------------------------------------

PARTNER A CAPITAL ACCOUNT
---------------------------

Balance Brought Forward              0      3000
Capital Introduced                5000         0
Add.Share of Profit for period       0      1000
Less.Share of Loss for period     1500         0
                                    -----    -----
                                    3500     4000
Drawings for period                500       500
                                    -----    -----
Balance at end of period          3000      3500
                                    -----    -----

PARTNER B CAPITAL ACCOUNT
---------------------------

Balance Brought Forward              0      2500
Capital Introduced                5000         0
Add.Share of Profit for period       0      1000
Less.Share of Loss for period     1500         0
                                    -----    -----
                                    3500     3500
Drawings for period               1000      1000
                                    -----    -----
Balance at end of period          2500      2500
                                    -----    -----
TOTAL CAPITAL AT END OF PERIOD    5500      6000
                                    =====    =====
```

The above assumes profit sharing of 50:50.

DIAGRAM (5)

BALANCE SHEET OF A LIMITED COMPANY

	MONTH	
	ONE	TWO
	----	----
FIXED ASSETS		

PLANT:COST	13000	15000
:DEPRECIATION	1000	1500
	-----	-----
:NET VALUE	12000	13500
	-----	-----
VEHICLE:COST	10000	10000
:DEPRECIATION	500	1000
	-----	-----
:NET VALUE	9500	9000
	-----	-----
TOTAL:NET VALUE	21500	22500
	-----	-----
CURRENT ASSETS		

STOCKS	10000	15000
DEBTORS	15000	16000
BANK	0	0
	-----	-----
	25000	31000
	-----	-----
CURRENT LIABILITIES		

CREDITORS	12500	18000
BANK OVERDRAFT	22000	21500
	-----	-----
	34500	39500
	-----	-----
NET CURRENT ASSETS/LIABILITIES	-9500	-8500
------------------------------------	-----	-----
NET WORTH	12000	14000
=========	=====	=====
REPRESENTED BY:		

SHARE CAPITAL	10000	10000
REVENUE RESERVES	-3000	-1000
	-----	-----
	7000	9000
LOAN	5000	5000
	-----	-----
	12000	14000
	=====	=====

liability. This depends on whether the amount at each period-end is due to the Customs and Excise or due by them. You will have already calculated these figures and they should be shown separately in the balance sheet.

The figures on the other side can now be entered. You will already have decided on what finance you think you will require, and you will have used that decision to calculate your profit and loss account and cash-flow forecasts. In the case of a limited company you will have decided what your share capital will be and when you will receive the cash for it. You will have entered it on these dates in your cash flow and you can now enter it similarly in your balance sheet.

Your revenue reserves at each period-end will be the cumulative profit earned to date. At the end of month one your figure of revenue reserves will be the net profit after taxation from the profit and loss account for month one. At the end of month two the figure will be the total net profit after taxation for month one and two added together. And so on for the whole year.

You will also have decided previously which loans you will require and when the money from these will be paid to you, so you can enter these figures cumulatively on your balance sheet. For example, if you are to receive a loan in instalments of £2000 per month, you show £2000 at end of month one, £4000 at end of month two and so on. Complications will arise if these loans are repayable during the year. As each amount of loan is repaid it will be deducted from the total loan outstanding. At each month-end you will show the net amount of loan due to be repaid.

In the case of a sole trader or a partnership there will be no share capital or revenue reserves. Their place is taken by the proprietors' capital accounts. The proprietor(s) will have decided how much money they will put into the business. This is shown as capital introduced. To this is added the profit earned in the month, or deducted the loss suffered in the month. You then deduct any drawings made by the proprietor(s) in that month. The resulting figure is the total of proprietor(s) capital at the end of the month, as shown in detail in Diagram 4. The figure is approximately equivalent to the figure shown as shareholders' funds in the balance sheet of a limited company. This is the major difference between the balance sheet of a limited company and that of a sole trader or partnership. An example of a limited company balance sheet is shown in Diagram 5.

The balance sheet is simply a schedule which sets out the financial position of the business at one particular date. From it you can see if your debtors (monies due to you) are too high or represent too many weeks' sales. You can also see if you are paying your creditors too late or too soon. You should see if your current-asset position is as anticipated by all your other projections. This figure shows your liquidity and if it is always negative (i.e. current liabilities are always higher than your current assets) then you should re-examine all your figures. You may be projecting too high a stock. You may be projecting too long a period for new debtors to pay you. Alternatively, you may be projecting too-quick payments to creditors.

The balance sheet can be a means of checking your forecasting and making sure that what you have estimated is reasonable. It will also provide valuable information to finance sources.

5.4   MONTHLY, QUARTERLY, YEARLY FORECASTING

In the first year of business it is usually better to compile the forecasts on a monthly basis. By doing so you can see at a glance the month or months when cash is required and when the pressure on your balance at the bank lessens. It is also useful, as will be seen later, to be able to check the actual results against your forecast on a monthly basis. You can then rectify any fall-off in sales or increase in costs more quickly (i.e. within one month of this happening).

It is very difficult when commencing a business to estimate accurately your sales and costs for a year ahead, but it is essential to make the attempt. Therefore year two should normally be forecast in quarterly periods. This will make the calculations easier and, perhaps, more accurate. Forecasting a third year may be thought to be completely impossible. You should nevertheless attempt this even if only on a total yearly basis. This will give you an idea of where the business will be during the first three years, and more importantly, you will know how much finance it will need throughout that period.

Forecasting is essential for all types and sizes of businesses. Even the very smallest proprietor will benefit from the discipline of preparing such forecasts, and he will be forced to examine his assumptions rigorously. It will show the cash-flow effects of leasing expensive plant instead of purchasing it as well as differences indicated by any other methods of spreading the payment of costs, such as giving discounts to customers who pay cash or taking discounts from suppliers because you yourself pay cash.

If you complete your schedules on a computer spreadsheet model it is fairly easy to change items of income or expenditure and see how these changes affect your final balance on the bank account or your liquidity position in the balance sheet.

Compiling the schedules manually will be more time-consuming and you will be less likely to experiment so much with differing figures to show differing results. Even when compiling these manually you should make sure your forecasts have covered all possibilities and that you have made all the decisions necessary before you end up with your final forecast. This final forecast will be the basis of your business plan and on it will depend the success of your business in attracting finance and trading as profitably as possible. Although your forecasting at this stage must rest largely on your own opinion of markets, costs, etc., you will now have a fixed idea of your business. In actually writing your business plan your main aim will be to explain your business to outside investors.

Chapter 6

Writing the Plan

6.1 DESCRIPTION OF BUSINESS

Your plan should start with a detailed explanation of what the business is going to do and why you think your business can do it better than others in the same market. You should also describe the market sector you are considering entering and its history, the reason why this market came into being and its future prospects. For example, if your business is installing aluminium double-glazing units you would describe the decline of timber-framed units and growth in other materials. Or if you will be involved in milk retailing and to be selling only plasticized cartons you would describe the advantages of this method of packaging over glass or plastic bottles, i.e. non-breakages, easier storage, less need for crates, etc.

You should then estimate the percentage of the market you hope to gain and whether or not this percentage can be increased. You should also explain future trends. Will the market grow or contract? Will you have the same percentage or a larger or smaller percentage of a changing market? Will the market survive into the future for many years? If it is to alter, what strategy can you adopt to change with it?

It is also important to describe your major customers and suppliers, and to estimate how much of the market they control. Will they always be customers and suppliers or do you see them eventually as competitors? Will you be a one-product business or will you market and/or produce a range of products? If you are a one-product business you must be very sure of that product's future saleability, and of any future changes which may happen to the product. Swiss watchmakers were very badly caught out by the development of the quartz watch, for instance. Could something like this happen to you? If you intend to sell a range of products, are they all profitable or are you selling certain items simply to complete the range and thus make all your products saleable?

In this part of the plan you must spell out what you are going to do and emphasize the positive effect each aspect of your policy will have on profits, cash flow and, last but not least, your 'market image'. You should already have decided what quality of product you will be selling, and this should be made clear in your plan. If you are selling a top-quality product and are attacking the top end of the market then you should charge a top-quality price. You may have decided to make your market début at a discount on your achievable price in order to obtain a larger slice of the market, but this should be shown as an initial marketing strategy in the plan. The expectation of your correct price and when it will be achieved should also be shown. You may have decided that you can make a product similar to one already on the market at a lower price, either because of lower overheads, lower materials costs or because of a different method of manufacture. All this must be stated in your plan.

The plan should be written as a factual document, but its tone should be persuasive enough to convince the source of finance that your business is a reasonable investment and that you have the type of business which it can safely support. The last paragraph of this section, the initial summary of the plan, should justify the investment required to finance your business. After this above summary you can then go into greater detail. First you should describe the individual products and attempt to forecast which of your products will be most saleable and most profitable. You should then point out which you intend to manufacture in the greatest numbers and why.

It may be that you will only manufacture one product, but you will make sure that, if necessary, you can manufacture other products. Or you may feel that you should start by making more of one product than another, but in time change your product mix. When this happens you will wish to have the manufacturing flexibility to change your production. You may also decide to buy some products where you have calculated that this is cheaper than manufacturing them. Other products you may make yourself.

A purely retail business faces different problems. You may wish to sell a full range, but to do so may involve buying from different producers at different locations with differing credit terms and delivery costs. Some of these suppliers' product ranges may overlap. In these cases there may be good business and/or financial reasons why you intend buying products A and B from X Ltd, although Y Ltd sells B at a cheaper price.

All this should have been researched and thought out, and by the time you write this section of the plan you will be able to state which items you will be buying and from whom. You will also be able to state the terms and the price. If you buy in larger quantities it is usually possible to obtain better terms, but again you must be sure that you can store the larger quantity, and, more important, that you can sell it.

This covers the details of products to be sold and your strategy of purchase and manufacture. You then move on to your detailed review of the market and your market strategy.

6.2   MARKET AT WHICH PRODUCT IS AIMED

You have already analysed the market and decided on your strategy for attacking it. In this section of the plan you should show the reader of your plan (who will usually be the finance source) that you have carried out your research and that your approach is sensible and will achieve its object. First of all you should state in more detail your intention of setting up business to manufacture or retail your product, describing your location and the geographical extent of the market you intend to serve. You can then describe the sources supplying the market at present (if any), giving details of names, areas, bases of operation and proportions of the market held. At this stage you are concentrating on the present market and its present size. You should not estimate any increase which will be attributable to your joining the market, nor any decrease in the market share of any competitors due to your entry into the market.

In detailing the types of firms in the market you can also note whether they are only operating in this market or if this market is only a small part of their total operation. In other words, you are estimating the size and efficiency of your competitors. If these firms are in a great number of markets you want to discover whether they are genuine competitors, whether they may drop out if competition gets too fierce, or whether they would be prepared to invest money to capture a larger share of the market. The sources who are supplying this market should also be described in as much detail as possible, with information on what percentage of the market they supply and whether their share of it is growing or not. This should give you a fair idea of the present total market into which you intend to enter and of the nature of the competition. You should highlight any competitor who has, at present, a large proportion of the market and whose share is increasing. You should also point out suppliers whose market share is falling and from whom you think you can acquire a part of the market. Also detail which of your competitors are manufacturers and which are only 'middlemen' (businesses buying in the product and then reselling it). In the latter case you may be able to find out what their profit margin is and from whom they are buying the product. In this way you can give a total view of the market, detailing all the weaknesses and strengths of your future competitors.

The existing sales outlets should be analysed, particularly the ones you intend to supply. You may already have approached, or been approached by, some major outlet and thus have a 'captive' purchaser. If this purchaser's business is growing it should help your business to grow as well. Against this you should balance the need to demonstrate your independence of any one outlet. Dependence can cause all manners of problems, even when you think everything is going smoothly. For example, other purchasers might suspect that they are being treated as second-rate customers and feel that their supplies do not rate the priority accorded to your major outlet. If anything goes wrong — for instance, if your outlet runs into financial difficulty — you could be left in a very vulnerable position. If your major outlet is taking a large percentage of your goods and is unable to pay the debt due for these goods at the expected time this could cripple you financially and even force your business to close down.

It is always better, if at all possible, to spread your sales outlets and not have too great a dependence on any one purchaser. It is obviously better from the point of view of someone giving finance to the firm on the basis of the business plan. One of the first things which most finance sources will look at in detail is whether the cash coming into the business for sales is mainly from one firm or not. They will be happier to put money into a business where the cash for sales is coming from a number of firms. It may be possible to sell your products or services to government departments, either nationally or locally. Again, it is better not to depend too heavily on this as changes in policies of these departments can make your market vanish almost overnight. Differing shades of political opinion in local or national government can cause swings in the purchasing strategies of these bodies. Some councils use their own employees to service the properties they own, while other councils use private firms. This can affect office-cleaning businesses dramatically if they have a large contract to clean offices under one administration which disappears when an opposing party controls the administration. Government and local authority contracts may seem gilt-edged, but they also can create major problems.

Your finance source will also want to know how much of the market you intend to capture, whether this share will increase over the foreseeable future and whether your expansion will coincide with the overall expansion of the market. If you will be completely new in the market then to obtain a share you will probably have to advertise in some way. The plan should explain how you intend to make your presence known, whether by advertising in newspapers, over the radio, by mailshots, by cold-calling or by word of mouth. In a large enough business commercial television may be considered. The best advertisement for a business or product is a satisfied customer, and no amount of money spent on advertising in any part of the media can be a substitute for that. But in a start-up situation it is necessary to make your firm or product (if the product is new) known to your prospective customers. The most effective way of doing this will have been considered by this stage and the costs estimated.

So you have described your market and the strategy by which you mean to acquire a share of that market and you have described how you hope the business will expand. You have also explained the relevant costs involved in entering the market initially and in expanding once you are established in that market. You can now go on to explain how you are going to organize the business and produce the goods or make the services available.

6.3 DESCRIPTION OF PREMISES, PLANT AND PERSONNEL

In this section you should describe in their order of importance the premises, personnel and plant of the business. The relative importance of each will depend on the type of business, and at this stage no-one can estimate their relative importance better than you.

PREMISES

The proposed location of your premises is a central feature of your business, and your choice of location must be fully explained. For example, there may be advantageous grants available in your chosen area, or a pool of suitable labour which can be trained for the type of work envisaged. The premises may be conveniently situated for either suppliers or customers, or where the proprietor lives or has worked and has built up a relationship with prospective customers.

The cost of the premises must be given along with a note of any alterations required to existing premises and the cost of these alterations, whether the premises are purchased or leased. There are schemes available where new businesses can obtain premises rent- and rates-free for a number of years. Sometimes in these cases the owners, who are usually local authorities or government-sponsored development organizations, can be persuaded to upgrade the facilities either free or for only a small contribution by occupiers towards the costs. Time spent researching this will be well spent.

By the time you are writing the plan you will have decided whether you are leasing or buying premises, and you should explain your thinking on this in the plan. You should also point out all the advantages of the particular premises you have chosen for your operation, and include the estimated costs of repairs on an on-going basis and the cost of rent and rates over the term of your plan.

In the case of rented premises one point which must be considered is the timing of rent reviews, and you should try to make sure that such reviews are as far in the future as possible. Many businesses starting up and paying a reasonable rent have suddenly found that at the time the rent is reviewed, possibly after only three years, it has increased enormously. In extreme cases the business may not be able to continue. If possible, when the lease is being drawn up you should insist on a lengthy time between rent reviews. It is also a great advantage if the increase in rent at such a time can be agreed at the outset of the lease to be no more than (say) the rate of inflation. If this is done you will then know when your rent will increase and the maximum amount by which it will increase.

Your initial premises may be only temporary, and you may contemplate using these for only the first year. When your business expands you may project moving to larger premises, or, alternatively, consider expanding your existing premises. Any financial implications of changing or altering your premises as you grow should be incorporated into the plan.

PLANT

Details of all the plant and machinery and other fixed assets which will be required over the period of the plan must be given. Again, by this stage you will have decided which items you are buying, which you are acquiring by hire-purchase and which you are leasing. Remember that although you know what each item of plant is and what it is used for, probably your reader will not. Make sure that technical terms used in the plan are also explained in layman's terms. You should also make sure that you have included a reasonable sum of money for loose tools and spares, even though when the business is operating these items will be charged to revenue costs and not plant costs, and will be purchased as and when needed. You should state in the plan the amount provided for such items, since at the start of the business you will require an adequate supply. You may also need items like benches, racking, etc. which are movable or removable when you vacate the premises. These items will always be your property and should be costed out as such and noted in your plan.

Do not omit the cost of office equipment, even though you are concentrating on listing production machinery. Although in a small business all the office work may be done by the proprietor in one room of his home using equipment already owned (second-hand typewriter, a desk and chair, for instance), if the business is larger and employs even one person to carry out the office work then that person will require some furniture and equipment. The larger the number of office staff, the more thought must be given to equipping the office and deciding on the standards to which the office must be decorated and furnished. Consider also the extent to which you can get away with second-hand plant and equipment, bearing in mind the extra running costs of used machines and vehicles and their effect on your image.

At this point you must consider another strategic aspect of your planning. Part of the salary structure for some of the employees may be the provision of a car which is paid for by the business. Usually, all the running costs except private petrol are also paid for by the business. As discussed in Part III, a car provided in this way is a particularly tax-effective benefit. You must therefore decide which employees, if any, you want to supply with cars. This decision will be reflected in the number and types of vehicles noted in your business plan.

Leading on from this you may require commercial vehicles. You will already have estimated their size, type and number and which tasks you require them for. You will also have decided whether it is better to use external hauliers for certain jobs, for example, where the alternative is to purchase larger, more expensive vehicles. You must also take into account the importance of the public-relations benefit of having at least one or two new vehicles on the roads displaying your business name, activity and telephone number. The value of this 'free' advertising must be set against the costs of running your own vehicles compared with hiring from hauliers. Once all these points have been decided you should note in the plan the vehicles you require, what they will be used for, whether they will be purchased or leased and the costs of each financing method.

A computer is one other expensive item which you may require, and by now you will have decided whether it will be cost-effective to use a computer or computers throughout the business and whether you should lease or purchase, or use the services of a bureau. If you use a bureau then you should note that fact in this section, though the running costs of operating in this way will be charged to revenue costs and not to plant. If you have decided to purchase or lease you should give details here and describe how cost-effective it is to use the computer(s), describing all the advantages you foresee arising from its use. For example:

(1) In a stock system you can obtain a note of your daily stock in hand which is automatically updated when items are received or dispatched.
(2) In an accounting system you can obtain monthly accounts within days of the end of the month concerned.

(3) You may save staff time and free them to do more productive and
    profitable work.

   In this section, as in all sections, you should be making clear to your
reader the advantages of the strategy you have chosen and pointing out
why you have dismissed other strategies. He may not agree with your
arguments, but at least he will be able to see that you have thought out all
the foreseeable problems and he will have an opportunity to make
constructive comments.

   Above all, let your reader know that your plan can be adapted in the
light of changing circumstances. What is the likelihood of the need to re-
equip to create larger capacity if you expand rapidly and what would this
cost? To what extent will you have to re-equip to vary your product range?
Try to anticipate the question that a hard-headed banker would ask.

PERSONNEL

First, you should give a summary statement of the number of people to be
employed. You should state how you will attract these people, whether
you will be recruiting from the unemployed, from those presently employed in other firms in the same industry or those from other industries.
It may be best to do this in the form of a table showing how many staff you
intend to employ at the beginning of the business, and how many at the
end of years one, two and three, if you think this is appropriate. The staff
should be allocated between production, selling, administration and
whatever other different parts of the business are thought relevant. The
type of work each person will be doing will be shown (e.g. salesman, stock
controller, machine operator, quality controller, director, etc.).

   The plan must include detailed descriptions of the most important
people. In this section you should state the persons' names, ages, their
qualifications and past experience. If you think it relevant you should also
state why the person wishes to join you and leave their present employer.
This section should also be split between management, administration,
production, sales and distribution staff.

   It is important not to gloss over any past failings or weaknesses of your
staff. There is nothing wrong with having made mistakes in the past, so
long as one learns from them. Nothing will alienate your potential
financial backer more quickly than being made to think that the wool is
being pulled over his eyes.

   The philosophy of the business can also be shown in this section. Will
the business be run by a board of people, all of whom have equal
authority, or by one person? Will the workforce have any influence on
decisions? How great an influence will this be and how will it be

organized? It may be organized through a workers' committee or by a representative of the workers being elected to the board or in any way which appears suitable in your type of business. There can be significant advantages in this approach, allowing your staff to feel they are part of the team and preventing the inevitable disputes from growing into something worse due to lack of communication. If continual talks are held, grievances can be ironed out as they occur. The commitment to good industrial relations is in itself a hopeful and constructive sign for a financier. Unless the business is a one-man affair then staff relations will be important. This should be detailed in full, together with your strategy to make sure that everyone is working together to make the business a success. Schemes to motivate staff can include various incentive schemes, from commissions to salesmen, productivity bonuses to machine operators (for a number of goods produced in a certain period), to profit-sharing schemes for management or even the whole workforce.

In limited companies a special share scheme for employees is an option. Certain of these schemes are approved under Inland Revenue rules and are quite tax-efficient from the employees' point of view. This is an excellent way to increase involvement of all employees, although diluting your equity holding is a fundamental business decision which should not be taken lightly.

Your plan should also include a comparison of the terms and conditions of employment given to staff who are with similar companies. This would cover salaries, holiday entitlement, overtime payments and conditions for personal leave of absence, etc. All the points which you feel make the firm more attractive than its competitors and which will increase its potential to retain its employees should be noted.

It may also be useful at this stage to state how much of your business will be computerized and how this will affect staff numbers and costs. No matter how efficient staff are, they will not be as efficient as a properly controlled computerized system. For example, you may wish to send out sales invoices daily, and this will be a simple task for a computer. If payments are on invoices then the earlier the invoice is sent out the sooner you will be paid. Even if credit terms are one month after invoice date, it is still advantageous to send out invoices as soon as possible. If your accounting system is completely computerized it should be possible to produce monthly (or other period) accounts very soon after the month-end using a minimum number of staff. These accounts will show you very quickly where and why anything is going wrong or where you are making more profit than expected. The sooner you have this information the sooner you can react to it. Only in one-man businesses can manual records be used to keep a proper control of the business, and then only if the turnover or sales is fairly low.

If you will carry an extensive range of valuable stock which is a large part of your total assets it could also be controlled by a computerized system. You would then know what stock of each item you held at any time, both in numbers and value. The system can also warn you when to re-order or when you have overstocked certain items. It will also tell you if all stock leaving your factory and/or warehouse is actually being invoiced. The protection of stock both from outside burglary and staff pilfering is very important. A tight control on stock quantities in your records helps to control and, hopefully, eliminate pilfering.

By going into as much detail as possible in all these practical matters you are showing your readers how much planning you have done before deciding to ask for outside finance. You are letting these readers see that you have a picture in your mind of the future profile of your firm and how you wish to organize it.

6.4   MAJOR SUPPLIERS

You must also give a detailed description of all your major suppliers. In a solely manufacturing business this will include all the suppliers of raw materials. In a retailing business it will cover all the firms who are to supply the goods you are selling. You should point out whether you will be dealing solely with one supplier for each product or with several competing suppliers, detailing the reasons for your choice of suppliers, such as better quality, cheaper price, better discounts or easier or quicker delivery to your premises.

Some suppliers will only deliver certain minimum quantities, or may only be prepared to deliver smaller quantities at a larger premium. Other suppliers will not deliver small quantities at all. Credit terms can also be an important point. If a supplier of a new item to retailers wishes to break into the market he may give very long credit terms to help the retailer buy a large stock. It is not unusual in such circumstances to obtain credit of up to six months, which can be useful in reducing the finance you require.

As in all sections of the plan, full details should be given. For example, the size of the supplier in terms of his employees and turnover is valuable information, with a note of the proportion of the market that each supplier supplies, how long he has supplied the market and how sound you think is his business.

The supply of packing materials must not be forgotten. A safe supply is essential, unless you intend to stock a large amount. Again, it may be better to have a few suppliers instead of only one, thus covering you in case anything goes wrong with a sole supplier.

It may also be relevant in this section to state why you are buying in some parts or products instead of making them yourself. It may be that it is more convenient for you to buy in. Another manufacturer may be able to produce the article more cheaply than you because he is producing a large number of these articles, which may be only a small part of your product range. As long as the cost of buying in does not exceed your estimate of costs for producing the same article, and you get reasonable credit terms from the supplier, then you should end up in the same financial position as if you made them yourself. You will also be concentrating on producing the articles you wish to produce and not the smaller integral parts.

Watch out for 'reservation of title' clauses in contracts. Following various legal cases culminating in what was known as the 'Romalpa case' this subject has become a confused area for both suppliers and purchasers. A 'Romalpa clause', in broad terms, will state that title to the goods does not actually pass to you until you have paid for them. This can affect your business in two ways. First, when buying you should check all the terms of purchase exhaustively. Second, when drawing up your own sales invoices you should get legal advice on the possible advantages of including a 'Romalpa clause' before you have them printed.

6.5   FINANCE REQUIREMENT

By this time you will have evaluated the business in full and will know how much money you require to set it up and keep it going. You will have considered how you wish to fund it and will have put together a finance package in your mind. The package will generally comprise short-term funds, long-term funds and your own funds. In the case of a small one-man business it may be that the owner has sufficient funds himself and does not require any further finance. Or he may simply need short-term finance to get the business going. He may envisage that after six months to a year the business will be self-financing. In this case he might consider asking for assistance from his own bank in the shape of overdraft facilities.

Most banks are loath to offer overdraft facilities without some sort of security or, at the very least, a personal guarantee. So very often the proprietor will have to try to get someone to stand guarantor to the extent of this overdraft facility. If he is not in a position to do this, the bank may then ask for security over personal property or investments. This should be resisted as far as possible. If anything were to go wrong with the business all the proprietor's personal assets would be forfeited to the bank to clear the overdraft. Of course, offering such security may be the only means of raising finance.

It may be possible to obtain loans or grants from the various enterprise trusts which are in operation throughout the country, or from various government agencies. Certain of these loans are also interest-free. This should be borne in mind if the proprietor is on the point of putting in all his capital. It is obviously better to obtain an interest-free loan if at all possible.

A larger business operated by a partnership or through a limited company will very often be funded in part by a director's loan or by a partner's contribution of capital. Your remaining funding may be an overdraft or loan. If you need more capital you may consider approaching a venture-capital company or a government-sponsored development organization, although these institutions will often want an equity stake in the business.

As far as most small businessmen are concerned the disadvantage of setting up a company is mainly in making sure that all the legalities are properly carried out. The directors and secretary of a limited company, no matter how small, have certain legal duties which must be carried out scrupulously. While these may not be very onerous they must be fulfilled to the letter of the law. There are various returns to be filled regularly, and meetings to be held and minuted at regular intervals. One way to deal with these duties is to appoint your lawyer or accountant as company secretary and instruct him to make sure that all these legal duties are notified to you and completed at the correct time. Another method is to appoint someone else as company secretary (e.g. your wife) and ask your lawyer or accountant to notify you when all the legal duties should be carried out. This second method is better as the company secretary cannot act as auditor.

Once you have decided on the finance package you require you should explain it in detail in your plan. Broadly, it will be allocated as follows:

(1) EQUITY OR PROPRIETORS' CAPITAL

Equity is the share capital of a limited company, and you should show how it is made up. It will consist of ordinary shares and, possibly, preference shares and debentures. You will show who will own how many shares of each type, and when you expect them to pay for the shares. The proprietors' capital is the capital paid in by a sole trader or by partners, and you should also show when it will be paid in.

(2) SHORT-TERM FUNDING

You should show how much short-term funding there will be, where you will obtain it, when you have to repay it and what interest rates you will be required to pay on it. You should also show if you intend obtaining any loans or grants from the bodies already mentioned, and the relevant terms of these loans and grants.

(3) FUTURE FUNDING

You should explain how you intend to finance the business in the foreseeable future. If you are intending to expand in the long term it is a good idea to have at least some picture of your financing requirements and your sources for that finance.

6.6   ASSUMPTIONS

Having put together all the information for the plan you can now add to it appendices which give details of all the assumptions you have made and why you have made them. Detailed tables showing these assumptions are given in this section. We have started with Table 1, which shows the fixed percentage rates used. This could cover VAT, bank interest, employers' National Insurance, depreciation (for all assets to be owned), discounts receivable and payable and any such interest or other percentage rates. We follow this with Table 2, which shows our calculations for VAT, on the assumption that the business will be registered and will make only taxable supplies. It gives gross sales, VAT on these sales and the net

ASSUMPTIONS

TABLE (1) FIXED PERCENTAGE RATES

	MONTH					
	ONE	TWO	THREE	FOUR	FIVE	SIX
V.A.T.	15	15	15	15	15	15
INTEREST :SHORT TERM	14	14	14	14	14	14
:TERM LOAN	13	13	13	13	13	13
:HIRE PURCHASE	12.5	12.5	12.5	12.5	12.5	12.5
LOAN PREMIUM	5	5	5	5	5	5
EMPLOYER'S NAT. INSURANCE	12	12	12	12	12	12
DEPRECIATION:VEHICLES	25	25	25	25	25	25
DEPRECIATION:PLANT	20	20	20	20	20	20
DEPRECIATION:FIXTURES	15	15	15	15	15	15
DISCOUNT PAYABLE	2.5	2.5	2.5	2.5	2.5	2.5
DISCOUNT RECEIVABLE	0	0	3.5	3.5	3.5	3.5

TABLE (2) VAT CALCULATIONS

	MONTH					
	ONE	TWO	THREE	FOUR	FIVE	SIX
OUTPUTS						
GROSS SALES	1000	1500	2000	2500	3000	3500
VAT ON SALES	130	196	261	326	391	457
NET SALES	870	1304	1739	2174	2609	3043
INPUTS						
PURCHASES	2000	1000	1500	1800	1800	3200
OVERHEADS						
PROPERTY MAINTENANCE	50	60	60	100	100	200
TELEPHONE			300			400
MOTOR EXPENSES	250	300	200	500	270	350
PLANT LEASING	200	200	200	300	300	300
ETC.						
ETC.						
CAPITAL EXPENDITURE						
PLANT and MACHINERY	20000	2000				
FIXTURES and FITTINGS	5000	200				
VEHICLES (VANS and LORRIES)	20000	1000				
TOTAL INPUTS	47500	4760	2280	2700	2470	4450
VAT ON INPUTS	7125	714	342	405	371	668
V.A.T.						
VAT ON OUTPUTS	130	196	261	326	391	457
VAT ON INPUTS	7125	714	342	405	371	668
NET VAT PYBLE/(REPYBLE)	-6995	-518	-81	-79	20	-211
CUMLTVE VAT PYBLE/(REPYBLE)	-6995	-7513	-7594	-79	-59	-270

figure for sales. This is what is known as output VAT. VAT incurred on costs is known as input VAT. On it you detail all the items on which you pay VAT; for example, motor expenses, property maintenance, telephone and purchases. Adding these together gives total inputs subject to VAT. (Incidentally, this includes all capital expenditure except for motor cars. Input VAT on motor cars cannot be recovered.) You multiply the total Vatable inputs by the VAT rate to obtain your total VAT input tax paid. You now have your total output tax and input tax. By deducting input VAT from output VAT you arrive at the figure of VAT payable or repayable for each month. If, as is normal, you are on a three-monthly VAT period you should then show the cumulative VAT payable or repayable on a three-monthly basis. Up to and including month three you

TABLE (3) SALARY and WAGES CALCULATIONS

	ONE	TWO	THREE	FOUR	FIVE	SIX

(A) SALES and ADMINISTRATION

NUMBERS

	ONE	TWO	THREE	FOUR	FIVE	SIX
Managing Director	1	1	1	1	1	1
Sales Director	0	0	1	1	1	1
Salesmen	0	0	1	1	2	2

RATES

	ONE	TWO	THREE	FOUR	FIVE	SIX
Managing Director	800	800	800	800	800	800
Sales Director	0	0	600	600	600	600
Salesmen	0	0	500	500	500	500

TOTAL SALES and ADMIN. SALARIES

	ONE	TWO	THREE	FOUR	FIVE	SIX
SALARIES	800	800	1900	1900	2400	2400
EMPLOYERS NATIONAL INSURANCE	96	96	228	228	288	288
GROSS SALES And ADMIN. SALARIES	896	896	2128	2128	2688	2688

PRODUCTION

NUMBERS

	ONE	TWO	THREE	FOUR	FIVE	SIX
Production Director	0	1	1	1	1	1
Production Manager	0	0	1	1	1	1
Operators	3	3	4	4	4	4

RATES

	ONE	TWO	THREE	FOUR	FIVE	SIX
Production Director	0	600	600	600	600	600
Production Manager	0	0	500	500	500	500
Operators	400	400	400	400	400	400

TOTAL PRODUCTION SALARIES

	ONE	TWO	THREE	FOUR	FIVE	SIX
SALARIES	1200	1800	2700	2700	2700	2700
EMPLOYERS NATIONAL INSURANCE	144	216	324	324	324	324
GROSS PRODUCTION SALARIES	1344	2016	3024	3024	3024	3024

add together the net VAT payable/repayable figures for each month to show how much VAT you are due to pay or have repaid to you at the end of each month. At month four you start again, assuming that in that month you will have either paid over or had repaid to you the amount shown at the end of month three. Every three months you should transfer this total to VAT repayable or payable in the cash-flow statement for the following month. This means, for example, that the total VAT payable or repayable for months one to three will be shown in the cash-flow projection for month four. If there are a great many Vatable inputs you

TABLE (4) PRODUCT CALCULATIONS

	MONTH					
	ONE	TWO	THREE	FOUR	FIVE	SIX

SALES

	ONE	TWO	THREE	FOUR	FIVE	SIX
PRODUCT A	300	400	500	600	700	800
PRODUCT B	570	600	800	900	1000	1100
PRODUCT C	0	305	440	675	910	1145
TOTAL ALL PRODUCTS	870	1305	1740	2175	2610	3045
Add.VAT	131	196	261	326	392	457
GROSS SALES	1001	1501	2001	2501	3002	3502

DEBTORS COLLECTION

	ONE	TWO	THREE	FOUR	FIVE	SIX
CASH (20%)	200	300	400	500	600	700
ONE MONTH (60%)	0	600	900	1201	1501	1801
TWO MONTH (20%)	0	0	200	300	400	500
TOTAL DEBTORS RECEIVABLE	200	900	1500	2001	2501	3002

COST of SALES(% of SALES PRICE)

	ONE	TWO	THREE	FOUR	FIVE	SIX
PRODUCT A (50%)	150	200	250	300	350	400
PRODUCT B (75%)	428	450	600	675	750	825
PRODUCT C (30%)	0	92	132	203	273	344
	578	742	982	1178	1373	1569

PURCHASES

	ONE	TWO	THREE	FOUR	FIVE	SIX
STOCK to COMMENCE	2000	0	0	0	0	0
PRODUCT A (One Month)	200	250	300	350	400	400
PRODUCT B (Two Months)	1050	675	750	825	900	1000
PRODUCT C (As Required)	0	92	132	203	273	344
	3250	1017	1182	1378	1573	1744
Add.VAT	488	153	177	207	236	262
	3738	1170	1359	1585	1809	2006

PAYMENT TERMS

	ONE	TWO	THREE	FOUR	FIVE	SIX
One Month	0	3738	1170	1359	1585	1809
Less.DISCOUNT RECEIVABLE	0	0	40	48	55	63
TOTAL PURCHASES PAYABLE	0	3738	1130	1311	1530	1746

can note these alongside the relevant figures, rather than showing all the figures again on a separate schedule.

In Table 3 we show in detail how wages and salaries are calculated. You should give numbers of persons employed in and the rate of pay for each post. At the end of each section in the projections you should show a figure for total salaries and add to this the appropriate percentage for employers' National Insurance to obtain the total wage or salary cost for that section.

You should also explain in your assumptions the method by which you arrived at your rates of salary. Are they typical rates for this industry, or are you proposing to offer a premium to attract the people you want?

Table 4 details how you have prepared your sales and debtors collections figures, and your cost of sales and total purchases payable per month. You commence by showing the sales amounts in the various categories, total these amounts and add to this total the relevant amount of VAT to give your gross sales. This latter figure is the total debtors cash receivable. You then detail the lag-time for debtors, that is, the length of time you estimate between completing the sale and receiving payment. You can then calculate the debtors receivable each month. If you have decided to give discount to customers you must deduct the estimated discount from these amounts.

You now go on to explain how you calculate the cost of sales figures. This will cover all the material costs required to produce the article to be sold. You take these figures to Table 4, showing the total cost of sales figure for each product. As in the debtors collection calculation, you must estimate when payment for these purchases will be received. You should also estimate how much stock you will require to commence business and how much stock you require to hold for each product. You total these amounts monthly and add the relevant amount of VAT to obtain a figure of your total purchases per month. By taking into account the credit terms you will receive and any discount receivable you can also calculate the amount payable for purchases each month.

These tables are the building blocks with which to compile the projections.

(1) THE PROFIT AND LOSS ACCOUNT

You now go through in detail each line on both the Income and Expenditure sides, referring to those which are worked out in Tables 1–4. For the other figures you must give complete details of how they are calculated or estimated.

(2) THE CASH FLOW

Again, you explain how you calculate each line, cross-referencing to previous schedules where this is relevant. You will detail the timing of the payment of the other expenses either in the assumptions or, if they are too numerous, on the actual cash-flow projection. It is usually better to note in these assumptions the timing of the payments for capital expenditure and in general terms the timing of repayments of any loans. The assumptions and the cash flow should show between them exactly how all the figures are calculated.

(3) THE BALANCE SHEET

Here you explain completely but as concisely as possible how you arrive at all the figures at each month-end. For example, fixed assets are shown as cumulative costs as per the cash flow less cumulative depreciation as per the profit and loss account. Debtors would be the total gross sales to date less the cash received to date. The bank figure will come straight from the cash-flow projection.

You then move on to the compilation of the forecasts. These projections can be produced, as already mentioned, either manually or by using a computer package. If you use a computer you can easily make changes to your assumptions and the resultant changes to all the figures are automatically carried out. Doing this manually can be extremely time-consuming. If the proprietor is able to produce all the assumptions and the narrative for this part of the plan he should normally use the services of an accountant to put together the actual projections on a computer.

In a preliminary meeting the accountant and the proprietor could go through all the information required to produce a business plan, and the proprietor could then obtain all such information. Before putting together a detailed plan the accountant could compile a simple projection to get an idea of how much finance the business might require and what type of finance this should be. It is then a fairly simple matter to compile the more detailed plan, adding as appendices the detailed forecasts. In these forecasts the type of finance required will have already been decided and the cost of the finance will be included. Once the plan is put together it will be scrutinized in detail by both the proprietor and the accountant, and amended until both are certain that it gives a reasonable idea of the prospects of the business.

Even where the proprietor is certain that he has sufficient personal finance to commence the business and can keep it going without any external help, it is still a valuable exercise to prepare a full business plan. It concentrates his mind on what the business will do and how profitable it should be. It is also useful to update the projections on a regular basis. This will give a true idea of how the business is doing and will give an early warning of any danger signs, such as a very low gross profit percentage, a very long lag-time for debtors or an unacceptably high build-up of stocks.

Chapter 8 gives more detail on the importance of continually monitoring your cash flow.

Chapter 7

Approaching the Finance Source

7.1 IDENTIFYING RELEVANT SOURCES

Your first tasks are to identify what type of finance you require and the relevant sources of such finance. By this stage you will have decided whether you need finance from outside the business. The first source may be a private individual or family member who is prepared to invest in your business, though this does not often occur. The second source will be your present bank manager. He should be able to supply you with two basic types of finance; a bank overdraft or a bank loan.

In broad terms, a simple overdraft is the most advantageous form of finance for you and the most difficult to obtain. If you obtain an overdraft you only pay for the facility that you are using each day, and you pay interest at the rate in force from day to day. This varies with interest rates generally and has been rather volatile in recent years. To obtain an overdraft you may need some form of security or someone to guarantee it for you. As already stressed, if you are a one-man business you should resist as far as possible the temptation to use your own house as security. It is usually better to agree to a higher interest rate on the overdraft to avoid this. Remember also that an overdraft facility should only be used for short-term (say, up to twelve months) finance, and as a general rule should be used to finance working capital not the purchase of capital assets. If a short-term overdraft is used to purchase fixed assets the bank will almost certainly require security for this.

In many businesses the overdraft may appear to be long-term finance, but in theory it is repayable whenever proper notice to repay it is given. It is therefore better to use it as short-term finance. If the business is thought to be self-financing then you may only require the overdraft for, say, six months. By this time cash received for your sales will have been used to reduce or wipe out the overdraft.

The bank will also be able to supply a loan which may be either short-term or medium-term. This can be more expensive than an overdraft as you will pay interest on the loan whether you require it or not. A loan is more suitable for financing the purchase of assets and will normally be secured on those assets. Repayment terms may be variable. Interest rates may be fixed at the commencement of the loan or can be variable in line with other interest rates.

There is an added advantage in using your present bank for finance. If you operate your account satisfactorily and build up a good business relationship with the manager he can be a source of useful information. He may even be able to introduce you to potential customers or suppliers.

The next source of finance is other banks. If your present bank manager is not prepared to give you a finance facility it may be worthwhile approaching other banks either locally or in the nearest large financial centre. Different banks have different methods of assessing whether they should lend to a new business or not, and it may be that another bank will support you while your own bank will not.

Other sources of finance include enterprise agencies, merchant banks and venture-capital companies, including Business Expansion Scheme funds. These are discussed in Part IV. Hire-purchase and leasing finance for equipment is discussed in Part III, section 4.10.

7.2   ARRANGING THE MEETING

Having identified all the sources and types of finance available for your business you must now decide which to approach first and how to approach it. Probably the best person to approach first is your present bank manager. He may be able to give you all the finance you need. If not, he may be able to arrange a meeting for you with another organization which may be able to help you.

The best way to arrange the meeting is to telephone your bank manager and briefly outline the nature of your project and the type of finance you require. At this stage you are only arranging a preliminary meeting, so you should not go into any great depth. You should, however, tell him that you have prepared a full business plan which is available for him to examine. He will almost certainly agree to study this in preparation for your meeting. This will give him time to check with specialists in your industry on any assumptions you have made which are crucial to your business, and could lead to his making very helpful and positive suggestions.

Before you arrange the meeting you should decide whether you wish to attend it alone or with your accountant. There are conflicting views on whether the accountant should attend this first meeting or not, and much will depend on your relationship with your accountant. The bank manager may wish to see you alone: on the other hand, if he would like further information about the project he may wish to question your accountant. Normally, the initial meeting will not tackle the assumptions used in the calculated figures.

Of course, if you are involved in a partnership all the working partners should go to the meeting. Similarly, for a limited company the directors who are to be involved in the day-to-day operations should be present at the meeting. But take care that you do not have too many people at the meeting. Too many people making their own views known will simply lead to confusion. Only the business's key decision-makers and, possibly, your accountant should attend.

7.3 PRESENTATION OF THE CASE

You have arranged your initial meeting with the bank manager. You have sent the bank manager a copy of your business plan and he is scrutinizing it. He will be noting all the questions he wants to ask you at your meeting. Although you do not know what these questions will be you should have a good idea of the key questions he will ask and have tried to formulate answers.

Whether you have prepared the plan yourself or not, you should now have a long and exhaustive meeting with your accountant which will make sure that you are able to explain the plan in detail to the banker. If you have written the plan well it should be self-explanatory, but there will always be questions the banker will wish to ask. If you are putting capital into the business, where is that capital coming from ? Will it definitely be available when you say it will, or could there be any delays? If you are not putting any capital in he will want to be completely sure that any finance he gives you is either secured or guaranteed. He will require either security over property or other assets which are worth at least the amount of the finance, or he will require someone to stand guarantor for the total amount at risk.

Be ready to back up and expand on all the assumptions you have made. He will be particularly interested in your sales figures and details of your projected customers. Can you be absolutely sure that you will sell as many articles or hours as you have projected? Will you be able to obtain the price quoted? Are you sure there is no alternative to your product which is cheaper or longer-lasting or more attractive to your customer? It is useful, sometimes, if the product is not too cumbersome to take a sample to your meeting with the bank manager.

He will also want to know if you are sure that your projected customers are financially sound and really interested in your product. Do you have any correspondence from them showing their interest? If so, take these letters with you to the meeting. But be careful not to take to the meeting too many papers, products or exhibits. You should decide what is really relevant and take only those items.

At the meeting you should try, where possible, to answer all the bank manager's questions. Where you are unable to do so you should inform him that you will get the answer to him as soon as possible.

You should never try to gloss over a question which may, to you, seem unimportant. The bank manager may think it very important. You should also make sure that all your answers agree with your plan. Most important, do *not* try to paper over any weaknesses in your project. An experienced bank manager will spot this straightaway and your credibility will go through the floor. Remember that it is in your own interest, as well as your bank manager's, that your project should not begin if it is fundamentally unsound.

The main reason why the bank manager wishes to meet you initially is not to have the figures explained to him or to have the assumptions backed up by your explanations. It is to meet the person to whom he is being asked to lend money. He wishes to know if the person who is to operate the business is competent to do so and whether he will be able to deal with all the problems which may arise in the day-to-day running of the business. If, for example, one of the customers of the business goes bankrupt will the proprietor be able to replace the sales made to the customers with sales to another customer? Will these other sales be paid for promptly, and will they be equally profitable? The bank manager, at this meeting, is appraising you to see if you can cope with the harder side of the business world, and his questions can often seem irrelevant. When you think about these questions later you will see that he was testing you and trying to assess your all-round business sense.

If he is interested in your project he will make an appointment for another meeting with you. At that second meeting he should be able to tell you whether the bank will lend you the money required or not. He will not normally give a positive answer at the first meeting. But if he feels unable to help and states this at the first meeting, you should then ask his advice on what further avenues are open to you. He may be able to arrange meetings with other finance sources. Even if he does not give any further advice you should thank him for his help and end the meeting on a friendly note. This can be very difficult when your comprehensively thought-out plan has been totally dismissed. However, no advantage can be gained from recriminations, and it is useful to be on good terms with all the banks in your locality.

If the bank manager feels he cannot help you at all you should then try other banks until you find one more helpful. Your presentation of your case at the meeting with that bank should be on lines similar to those noted above, the only difference being that you can learn from your experience in meeting the first bank manager. It may be that the finance you require will be more suited to a merchant bank or a venture-capital company. You will require an introduction to one of these, and this can usually be arranged by your accountant or other professional adviser. When you are eventually offered finance facilities by one or more sources — it may be a financial package of bank overdraft, bank loan and venture capital — negotiating the terms can begin.

7.4 NEGOTIATION OF TYPE OF FINANCE AND COST

Let us assume that you have a bank manager or other finance source, or a combination of both, interested in lending you finance and perhaps even anxious to do so. If so, you should be very careful to obtain the finance package that you want at the best rates available.

In your plan you will have shown what type of finance you envisage for your business. Unless the bank manager or other sources detail a more attractive package, you should attempt to obtain the finance originally envisaged. You may not be able to get exactly what you want, of course. For example, you may have to pay a slightly higher rate of interest or you may have to pay the loan back sooner than you forecast. You should, where possible, resist any changes which are more fundamental than these unless your finance source has sound reasons for varying the package.

Of course, you may have only one finance source willing to help you. In this case your bargaining power will be very limited. You can merely explain why you think your financing strategy is more advantageous for both the lender and yourselves than any other strategy.

If there are two or three sources interested in financing you then you should make sure that the final package agreed on meets your needs as well as theirs. If you have decided on, for example, overdraft finance and venture capital, you may wish to get as little venture capital and as large an overdraft as possible. In this way you will restrict any move to interfere in the operation of the business by the venture-capital company. In all these negotiation meetings with finance sources it will be to your advantage to have your accountant with you. The fee he will charge for attending such meetings can be paid for many times over if his help and advice obtain for you a good financial package. Having negotiated the actual finance you may be able to negotiate as a separate matter the cost of the finance.

Many businessmen automatically think that the rate to be paid on a bank overdraft or a bank loan is a fixed percentage figure. In fact this rate can usually be the subject of negotiation. When new banks move into a town or area there is usually an increase in competition between the banks servicing that area. This can result in reduced rates of interest or different periods of repayment. It can therefore be worthwhile investigating all the possibilities of differing terms with different banks before you consider accepting any finance offered.

7.5   ACCEPTANCE OF FINANCE

Accepting the finance may seem the easiest part of the whole procedure so far. To a certain extent it is, but it is not simply a case of shaking hands with the financier, thanking him and setting up in business. The offer of finance of whatever type will be made in writing and either posted or handed to you. You should take this offer-document to your accountant, and, with his assistance, you should scrutinize it in detail to make sure it has no hidden conditions that you do not want. You should also make sure that it offers the type of finance you discussed with the lender and the terms are exactly as you discussed. If you have agreed to supply regular reports on your business this should be included in the document. In general terms you should make sure that this offer-document covers every aspect of the financing agreed at your last meeting, and that everything in the document is exactly as you understood it at that meeting.

All this should be simple in the case of an overdraft. The major items are the amount of the overdraft, the method by which the interest rates will be calculated, when interest will be paid and what security the bank will hold to cover the overdraft. Ancillary clauses will cover the reports you have to give to the bank about your business and how regularly you have to supply them.

When a loan from a bank is involved there will be additional clauses relating to the repayment terms for the loan. It may be by equal monthly or quarterly instalments or there may be a first year free of repayments, with the loan repaid in equal instalments over its remaining term. The offer-document will be more complicated still if you are receiving finance from a merchant bank, venture-capital firm, government-sponsored agency or a combination of some or all of these. If the finance source is to be issued with shares in your company or is to participate in decision-making in some way — for instance, by a seat on the board or by a right to veto certain types of action — this should all be spelled out in the offer-document.

You have now reached the position you have been aiming at from the first moment when you thought about setting up your own business. You have obtained the finance required to get your business off the ground and, if your projections are correct, to keep it in existence in the future. To make sure of your business's survival in its vulnerable early stages you now should set up accounting systems which are as simple as possible. These systems will enable you to observe how your business is performing financially, and will allow a comparison with the projections in your plan. In this way you can make sure that you are achieving the targets laid down in that plan. Perhaps the most important comparison to undertake is the actual performance of your cash flow against the projected cash flow. This subject is looked at in detail in the next section.

Chapter 8

Monitoring the Cash Flow

If you set up a proper accounting system you should be able to extract the actual figures of cash coming into the business and cash going out. You should also be able to analyse these figures over the headings shown in Diagram 3 (p.41). As mentioned, if you have a large number of expenses included under one heading (e.g. administration costs) you can compile a subsidiary schedule showing these individual costs which are totalled to arrive at the global figure shown in the cash-flow statement.

As soon as possible after each month-end you should calculate your cash flow for that month. You can use the statement shown in Diagram 3 and expand it by adding a column for the actual figures for month one and a column for the difference between actual results and forecast results for month one. You should do the same for month two and for the total column to arrive at a schedule as shown in Diagram 6. At the end of month one you should enter your actual figures in the appropriate column for month one. By deducting the actual figures from these budget figures you arrive at the figure for the difference column.

You can now begin the task of monitoring your cash-flow forecast. You should decide beforehand how large a difference each month will be acceptable. This may be a percentage figure (say, 5%), and only figures which vary more than that percentage need be investigated. You have entered your figures on Diagram 6 and have calculated the differences for month one. The results should now be scrutinized in detail. Your cash sales have decreased by £150 or 15% on the forecasted figure. Why is this?

Is it due to a reduction in numbers sold, or the sale price of items sold or a combination of both? If numbers are down why have you not sold as many as you projected, and will you be able to make up this shortfall in

DIAGRAM (6)

COMPARISON OF ACTUAL RESULTS WITH CASH FLOW FORECAST

	MONTH								
	ONE			TWO			TOTAL		
	ACTUAL	BUDGET	DIFF.	ACTUAL	BUDGET	DIFF.	ACTUAL	BUDGET	DIFF.
INFLOW									
Cash Sales	850	1000	-150	1200	1000	200	2050	2000	50
Credit Sales	0	0	0	900	1000	-100	900	1000	-100
Total Income	850	1000	-150	2100	2000	100	2950	3000	-50
OUTFLOW									
Purchases Material	450	500	-50	850	700	150	1300	1200	100
Labour Costs	275	250	25	400	350	50	675	600	75
Factory Costs	490	450	40	60	50	10	550	500	50
Packaging Costs	140	150	-10	250	-200	50	390	350	40
Distribution Costs	950	1000	-50	700	600	100	1650	1600	50
Administration Costs	175	200	-25	300	400	-100	475	600	-125
Finance Costs	0	0	0	112	109	3	112	109	3
Machinery Costs	2850	3000	-150	100	0	100	2950	3000	-50
Equipment	1700	1500	200	0	0	0	1700	1500	200
Motor Vehicles	7250	7000	250	0	0	0	7250	7000	250
Total Expenditure	14280	14050	230	2772	2409	363	17052	16459	593
Bank Brought Forward	0	0	0	-13430	-13050	-380	0	0	0
Bank Carried Forward	-13430	-13050	-380	-14102	-13459	-643	-14102	-13459	-643

the following months? If the price is less was your original price too optimistic or is this lower price only due to start-up factors? If you have seriously overestimated your price and you think your sales will remain as originally forecast you may wish to rework your forecasts with this new price in order to satisfy yourself that your finance facility will be adequate. You need only do this if you find that any item of income or expenditure is substantially different from budget. It is better, where possible, to let the business run for two or three months before you recalculate your forecasts. This will give you a slightly longer time to observe how every item of income and expenditure is working out and how close your budget is to the actual position.

Credit sales will not affect your cash flow for month one but you will know from your credit sales records whether you have made enough sales to hope to receive the £1000 projected for month two. It is worth checking this at this time.

You now look at the cash outflow or expenditure. Looking first at purchases of materials, this has decreased by £50 or by 10% of your budget. This does not directly relate to the decrease in your cash sales figure but may relate to the decrease in total sales including credit sales. Other possible causes are that you may have used less materials per product than forecast or you may have paid a smaller price than you originally expected. You should find out exactly what happened and make sure it will not have a very material affect on your forecast for the whole year. Continue investigating every item of cash outflow which has changed by more than your predetermined limit and carefully note the reasons for these differences. For example, the cost of motor vehicles has increased by £250. This may have been a price increase or you may have failed to obtain a discount which you anticipated.

If you have compiled subsidiary schedules for any of the headings in the cash flow you should investigate the differences on the individual expense headings on the subsidiary schedules as well.

You should carry out this exercise every month. It is useful also to compile your schedule on a cumulative basis, as shown in Diagram 6. After you enter the figures for month two and calculate the differences for month two you should add together months one and two to show the actual figures for the two months, the budget figures for the two months and the difference figures for the two months. You should continue this procedure after you enter month three to obtain a cumulative figure for the first three months.

At this stage, the end of the quarter, it is useful to look over the whole situation. Ask yourself if certain figures are consistently different from your budgets and if these figures will continue to be different for the remainder of the year. Will the results in the following months cancel out these differences? If not, consider reworking your projections with the new figures to find out what effect this has on your bank balance.

As will be seen from Diagram 6, you are also calculating each month how different your bank balance is from that projected. Obviously, if this difference is material you may have to take drastic action to correct it. Your bank may have asked you, as part of the conditions of granting you the financing facility, to foward to them a monthly or quarterly cash-flow report or some other similar type of report. If you are carrying out the regular monitoring exercise described above it is an easy task to compile a similar type of report for the bank. You will also be aware why there are differences from your forecasted figures.

Naturally, you must fully investigate the underlying causes of the differences and you should therefore be in a position to supply the bank manager with detailed explanations of all the material differences each month. You may also be able to tell the bank manager how you are rectifying the situation, or how these differences will affect your cash flow for the year (by reworking the whole year using the new figures). On the other hand, the differences may be an improvement to your profit position and cash flow. In this situation you will be able to tell the bank manager how you are going to take advantage of these differences to improve your cash flow and profitability.

By monitoring your cash flow monthly you should always know the position your business is in and you can take action quickly either to rectify shortcomings or concentrate your effort on items which are more profitable than forecast. You should therefore make a constant attempt to keep your records up to date monthly and to monitor your forecasts monthly.

Chapter 9

Case Studies

The following simplified case studies are designed to illustrate the points made in the preceding chapters. They are, of course, entirely fictional, and do not reflect in any way on the business sectors discussed in the case studies.

A. SIMPLE BUSINESS PLAN OF A SOLE TRADER

PETER WINTER TRADING AS DARKVIEW CLOTHING

1. Synopsis

Peter Winter will be a sole trader operating a retail shop selling clothes mainly to people in the age bracket from fifteen to twenty-five. He will also design clothes for manufacturers. He intends commencing business on 1 July 1986.

2. Product Details

The clothes for sale will be well designed and reasonably priced. They will range through jumpers, tops and dresses to trousers and coats. The clothes will be made from natural products, wool, cotton and leather. The clothes to be designed will be similar to this and he will sell some of his personally designed clothes in his shop. The remainder of his sales will be designed by people known to him whom he considers relate best to his project market.

3. Market Review and Stretegy

Mr Winter has reviewed the market for his product in Leeds through his experience as a sales manager in several shops of a similar kind in the area. He considers that no one shop concentrates on the range of clothes nor the age bracket to which he proposes to sell. The people of this age are becoming more conscious of fashion and style. He feels that the fact that the clothes are manufactured in Leeds and designed in Leeds will be a good selling factor and that the young people will support him. He knows a large number of them personally. He has constantly heard complaints of lack of innovation in clothing which is manufactured in Leeds.

The advertising of the shop will be mainly through local press advertising and through word of mouth by his friends. He already has contracts to design clothes with local manufacturers, and this will continue.

He will buy his clothes from these manufacturers and will sell both those designed by him and those designed by other similar designers. He will therefore largely be able to control the design of the clothes he intends selling.

4. Premises, Fittings and Employees

The shop is situated in a shopping arcade. It is well situated for passing trade and has a large display window. Previously it was used as a camera shop. It therefore requires complete refurbishment as far as display fittings are concerned. Mr Winter intends to do this before he opens and this will require to be paid for in the first month. Mr Winter estimates the cost of this at £1350. He will also require a till and has been quoted a price of £200 with one month's credit. He will therefore pay for it in August. Initially he will be the only person employed in the shop, but his wife will be able to take over from him when necessary.

He has been involved in similar types of shop for the past ten years. He is largely self-taught but his designs have been repeatedly asked for by various manufacturers throughout the North of England.

He hopes, once the shop is established, to employ his wife full-time. He will then use the back shop to carry out more design work and thus increase his income. He already had, as noted before, contracts with major manufacturers. He has agreed to carry out a number of commissions for them.

5. Funding

Mr Winter will fund the business mainly from his own resources. He will pay into the business in July 1986 the sum of two thousand pounds (£2000) from his building society savings. He will require overdraft finance to assist in paying for the shop fittings, the shop stock and the first quarter's rent. The business should become self-financing very quickly. Mr Winter has been unemployed for the past four months and has applied for assistance under the Government Enterprise Allowance Scheme. He has been accepted on to the scheme and will receive the standard allowance of £40 per week.

6. Assumptions to the Financial Projections

(a) Sales

The figures shown in the parameters for projected sales are estimated by Mr Winter on the basis of his experience in a similar shop.

(b) Stock
Mr Winter considers that he will require to maintain a stock level of £300, at cost price, of goods to sell to maintain his above-noted sales. This will be required for most of the year but can be reduced to £200 between November and February.

(c) Cost of Sales

This has been estimated at 50% of sales. The minimum mark-up in this type of enterprise is 100%.

(d) Bank Interest Rate

This is the overdraft interest rate quoted by various banks in Leeds for the amount and type of finance required.

(e) Commisions

As already noted, Mr Winter has orders on hand for commissions and the actual figures for those are included in the forecast from July to December. From January to June 1987 Mr Winter has estimated the commissions he will carry out. These are paid for in cash in the month carried out.

(f) Enterprise Allowance Scheme

As noted before, Mr Winter has been accepted on to the Scheme and will receive £40 per week.

PETER WINTER Trading as DARKVIEW CLOTHES

CASH FLOW AND PROFIT FORECAST   YEAR TO 30/6/87

PARAMETERS	JULY	AUG.	SEPT.	OCT.	NOV.	DEC.	JAN.	FEB.	MCH.	APRIL	MAY	JUNE	TOTAL
NO.OF WEEKS	4	4	5	4	4	5	4	4	5	4	4	5	52
SALES	1000	1000	1000	850	900	850	750	700	850	750	860	980	10490
COST of SALES													
OPENING STOCK	0	300	300	300	300	200	200	200	200	300	300	300	
PURCHASES	800	500	500	425	350	425	375	350	525	375	430	490	3924
CLOSING STOCK	300	300	300	300	200	200	200	200	300	300	300	300	2080
COST of SALES	500	500	500	425	450	425	375	350	425	375	430	490	
ACCRUALS/PREPAYMENTS	-639	-330	-44	-567	-281	25	-664	-358	-73	-592	-308	0	
INTEREST RATE BANK	15	15	15	15	15	15	15	15	15	15	15	15	
PROFIT AND LOSS ACCOUNT													
SALES	1000	1000	1000	850	900	850	750	700	850	750	860	980	10490
COMMISSIONS	324	300	450	450	500	500	200	200	250	250	250	250	3924
ENTERPRISE ALLOWANCE	160	160	200	160	160	200	160	160	200	160	160	200	2080
TOTAL INCOME	1484	1460	1650	1460	1560	1550	1110	1060	1300	1160	1270	1430	16494
OVERHEADS													
COST of SALES	500	500	500	425	450	425	375	350	425	375	430	490	5245
RENT AND RATES	275	275	275	275	275	275	275	275	275	275	275	275	3300
INSURANCE	55	55	55	55	55	55	55	55	55	55	55	55	660
PRINTING AND ADVERTISING	100	40	40	40	40	40	40	40	40	40	40	40	540
HEATING AND LIGHTING	30	30	30	30	50	50	50	50	30	30	30	30	440
DECORATION/PRESENTATION	100	30	30	30	30	30	30	30	30	30	30	30	430
PACKAGING	10	10	10	10	10	10	10	10	10	10	10	10	120
POSTAGES AND STATIONERY	10	10	10	10	10	10	10	10	10	10	10	10	120
PROFESSIONAL FEES	21	21	21	21	21	21	21	21	21	21	21	21	250
BANK INTEREST	0	3	0	0	0	0	0	0	0	0	0	0	3
TOTAL OVERHEADS	1101	974	971	856	941	916	866	841	896	846	901	961	11108
NET PROFIT													

CASH FLOW

INCOME													TOTAL
SALES	1000	1000	1000	850	900	850	750	700	850	750	860	580	10490
COMMISSIONS	324	300	450	450	500	500	200	200	250	250	250	250	3924
CAPITAL PAID IN	2000												2000
ENTERPRISE ALLOWANCE	160	160	200	160	160	200	160	160	200	160	160	200	2080
TOTAL INCOME	3484	1460	1650	1460	1560	1550	1110	1060	1300	1160	1270	1430	18494

EXPENDITURE													TOTAL
PURCHASES	800	500	500	425	350	425	375	350	525	375	430	490	5545
RENT AND RATES	825	0	0	825	0	0	825	0	0	825	0	0	3300
INSURANCE	55	55	55	55	55	55	55	55	55	55	55	55	660
PRINTING AND ADVERTISING	100	40	40	40	40	40	40	40	40	40	40	40	540
HEATING AND LIGHTING	30	30	30	30	50	50	50	50	30	30	30	30	440
DECORATION/PRESENTATION	100	30	30	30	30	30	30	30	30	30	30	30	430
PACKAGING	20	0	20	10	20	10	20	10	10	10	20	10	120
POSTAGES AND STATIONERY	10	10	10	10	10	10	10	10	10	10	10	10	120
PROFESSIONAL FEES	100	0	0	0	0	0	150	0	0	0	0	0	250
DRAWINGS	320	320	400	320	320	400	320	320	400	320	320	400	4160
N.I.	18	18	23	19	18	23	18	18	23	18	18	27	239
EQUIPMENT	1350	200	0										1550
BANK INTEREST				3									3
TOTAL EXPENDITURE.	3728	1203	1108	1756	893	1033	1893	873	1133	1703	953	1078	17357
BANK B.F.	0	-244	12	554	258	924	1441	658	845	1012	468	785	
BANK C.F.	-244	12	554	258	924	1441	658	845	1012	468	785	1137	

BALANCE SHEET
=============

CURRENT ASSETS												
STOCK	300	300	300	300	200	200	200	200	300	300	300	300
PREPAYMENTS	639	330	44	567	281	0	664	358	73	592	306	0
BANK	0	12	554	258	924	1441	658	845	1012	468	785	1137
	939	642	899	1124	1405	1641	1522	1403	1384	1360	1391	1437
CURRENT LIABILITIES												
ACCRUALS	0	0	0	0	0	25	0	0	0	0	0	0
BANK	244	0	0	0	0	0	0	0	0	0	0	0
	244	0	0	0	0	25	0	0	0	0	0	0
N.C.A.	695	642	899	1124	1405	1616	1522	1403	1384	1360	1391	1437
FIXED ASSETS	1350	1550	1550	1550	1550	1550	1550	1550	1550	1550	1550	1550
	2045	2192	2449	2674	2955	3166	3072	2953	2934	2910	2941	2987
CAPITAL ACCOUNT												
BALANCE BROUGHT FWD.	0	2045	2192	2449	2674	2955	3166	3072	2953	2934	2910	2941
CAPITAL PAID IN	2000											
PROFIT/LOSS	383	486	679	564	619	634	244	219	404	314	369	469
DRAWINGS	338	338	423	338	338	423	338	338	423	338	338	423
	2045	2192	2449	2674	2955	3166	3072	2953	2934	2910	2941	2987

PETER WINTER Trading as DARKVIEW CLOTHES
==
CASH FLOW AND PROFIT FORECAST   YEAR TO 30/6/88 and YEAR TO 30/6/89

PARAMETERS	3 MONTHS TO SEPT.	3 MONTHS TO DEC.	3 MONTHS TO MCH.	3 MONTHS TO JUNE	TOTAL	YEAR TO 30/6/89
NO.OF WEEKS	13	13	13	13	52	52
SALES	4500	3500	3000	4000	15000	17000
COST of SALES						
OPENING STOCK	300	500	400	500		600
PURCHASES	2450	1650	1600	2100		8600
CLOSING STOCK	500	400	500	600		700
COST of SALES	2250	1750	1500	2000		8500
ACCRUALS/PREPAYMENTS	40	0	40	0		100
INTEREST RATE BANK	15	15	15	15		15

PROFIT AND LOSS ACCOUNT
============================

SALES	4500	3500	3000	4000	15000	17000
COMMISSIONS	1000	1500	1500	1000	5000	6000
TOTAL INCOME	5500	5000	4500	5000	20000	23000

OVERHEADS
=========

COST of SALES	2250	1750	1500	2000	7500	8500
RENT AND RATES	900	900	900	900	3600	3800
INSURANCE	180	180	180	180	720	750
PRINTING AND ADVERTISING	150	150	150	150	600	650
HEATING AND LIGHTING	100	100	100	100	400	450
DECORATION/PRESENTATION	100	100	100	100	400	450
PACKAGING	40	40	40	40	160	180
POSTAGES AND STATIONERY	40	40	40	40	160	170
PROFESSIONAL FEES	60	60	60	50	240	250
BANK INTEREST	0	0	0	0	0	0
TOTAL OVERHEADS	3820	3320	3070	3570	13780	15200
NET PROFIT	1680	1680	1430	1430	6220	7800

(g) Rent and Rates

The rent and rates for the property will be paid quarterly in advance to the owner of the property. The figure has been agreed at £825 per quarter.

(h) Insurance

A quote has been received from an insurance broker for a fully comprehensive policy for the shop covering contents, public liability, loss of profits, etc. The premium payable will be £660 in twelve monthly instalments of £55 each.

(i) Printing and Advertising

The initial supply of leaflets and printed matter will cost £100. Mr Winter estimates that the normal monthly cost will be £40.

(j) Heating and Lighting

The shop will be heated by gas. The gas account will be paid by direct debit in equal instalments. It is estimated that the cost of this and electricity for lighting the shop will be £30 per month except for November–February, when it will be £50 per month.

(k) Decoration/Presentation

There will be an initial expenditure on shop displays of £70 and the monthly cost will be £30.

(l) Packaging

Mr Winter estimates that he will require to buy packaging materials costing £20 every two months. This will consist of wrapping paper and plastic carrier bags with the shop name printed on them.

(m) Postages and Stationery

On the basis of past experience this is estimated at £10 per month.

(n) Professional Fees

The lawyer who has negotiated the lease of the shop has stated that his fee will be £100. Mr Winter estimates that his first accounting fee will be £150 and be payable in January.

(o) Drawings

Mr Winter estimates that he will require to draw £80 from the business each week for his own living expenses.

(p) NI

This is the cost of the self-employed National Insurance contribution, which is estimated at £4.60 per week.

(q) Depreciation

No depreciation has been provided on the fittings and equipment as such depreciation is considered immaterial.

(r) General

Inflationary increases have been included for 1988 and 1989.

B. DETAILED BUSINESS PLAN OF A SMALL LIMITED COMPANY

AGRILIFT LIMITED

Business Plan Contents

1. Synopsis of Business Plan
2. Market Review
3. Directors/Management
4. Premises
5. Financial Control
6. Assumptions on Financial Projections
7. Financial Promections

1. Synopsis of Business Plan

Agrilift Limited has been incorporated to continue the manufacture and sale of a range of products already proven and accepted in the market place. The business was operated previously by two of the directors of Agrilift Limited at premises in Perthshire.

In 1980 a range of handling equipment was designed and developed for use along with the type of fork-lifts which are used in agriculture. The demand for these fork-lifts first arose when suppliers commenced delivering fertilizer in palletized loads. In order that these fork-lifts could be used for twelve months of the year various additional attachments were developed for handling grain, potatoes, silage, etc. Over the past few years the market has increased to include larger and heavier fork-lifts. These can be used in a way similar to those in industrial enterprises.

To expand their market share the directors have decided to open a further factory in North Yorkshire and will possibly expand further south in the ensuing years.

Both premises are capable of being extended and the directors intend to do so as soon as their market share improves enough to justify this. This will create security for their employees, both present and future.

This expansion will be a gradual process over a long term while the company attains a secure financial basis.

2. Market Review

The directors feel that by opening a second factory in Yorkshire this will significantly expand their share of the market.

The equipment they already manufacture has been approved by the two major manufacturers of rough-country fork-lifts. This approval has allowed them access to all the dealers in the UK for these two companies. The equipment is also available for use with other machines manufactured by the dominant names in agricultural machinery.

Orders from dealers are at present in line with the expectations and assumptions used in this plan.

Although other manufacturers exist in this market it would appear from the feedback from the various agricultural shows and handling exhibitions that dealers and farmers are not completely satisfied with the service provided by these firms, and do not think very highly of the quality of their products.

From this information it would appear that the time is ripe for Agrilift Limited to expand and obtain a larger share of the market with their already acknowledged top-quality products.

3. Directors/Management

Two of the directors of Agrilift Limited have been engaged in this market for the past ten years. As noted before, they were in partnership in the business for five years before incorporating Agrilift and transferring the trade to it.

Brief details of the directors are as follows:

David Syme — Senior partner in the previous business. He had a long record of senior management positions in manufacturing companies before deciding to set up in partnership five years ago. His responsibility will be the overall management of the company.

Henry Duncan — A qualified mechanical engineer with a great deal of experience in the agricultural equipment world. He was previously in partnership with Mr Syme. Prior to the partnership he held both technical and design management positions in manufacturing companies in the mechanized handling business. He will be the technical director of the company.

Brian Turnbull — A fully qualified electrician who moved into sales and marketing fifteen years ago. Ten years ago he joined a company specializing in the sale of agricultural handling machinery and attachments. He will be the sales director of the company.

It is envisaged that the directors will hold, between them, all the ordinary share capital of the company as follows:

David Syme	8 000
Henry Duncan	8 000
Brian Turnbull	4 000
	———
Total issued ordinary shares	20 000 of £1 each

4. Premises

The premises presently used in Perthshire are under-utilized by approximately 50%. It is felt that this will be used up by the expansion of the business due to the company's increasing share of the market.

The company is at present negotiating the lease of a similarly sized factory in North Yorkshire. This factory already includes all the facilities which the company will require. The rental proposed is extremely favourable in comparison with even a subsidized new unit. It is hoped to conclude negotiations on the lease shortly.

5. Financial Control

It is recognized by the directors that a business of this kind which is expanding considerably from the smaller business of the partnership will require positive financial control from day one. The directors have decided, because of this, to ask a firm of CAs which is experienced in handling start-ups to assist in the production of the firm's projections. They have also been asked to assist in setting up a system of management reporting which will monitor the performance of the company. This monitoring will have two aspects:

(1) Comparing important figures (e.g. sales, gross profit, debtors, creditors, bank, stock, etc.) on a monthly basis.
(2) Comparing actual quarterly accounts with budgeted accounts. With the above information the directors will be able to rectify any major shortfalls from the budget very quickly.

6. Assumptions on Financial Projections: Forecast for the years to 30 September 1986 and 1987

Parameters

Sales   Based on directors' experience and market review. At harvest time and at agricultural show dates there are peaks in activity. Overall, an upward trend has been projected.

Debtors collection   Based on past experience it is thought that a conservative estimate of payment by debtors is two months. The directors feel this should be achieved.

Cost of sales materials   These are calculated at prices quoted for all parts required to be purchased. The cost of these parts is approximately 53% of sales values.

Stock taken over   This is the value of finished stock purchased from the previous partnership at cost of production.

Materials purchased payment terms   It is estimated that, as with the previous partnership, the company will be allowed one month's credit from the suppliers of materials.

Remuneration and staffing assemblers   The directors have calculated the most efficient staff level. They have used currently paid salary levels.

Directors   All management functions will be fulfilled by the directors. Remuneration has been agreed by the directors.

Administration staff   The present book-keeper will take care of all accounting functions and her salary is shown at the current level.

Employer's National Insurance   This is calculated at the current level.

Overdraft interest rate It is assumed that the company will be funded by a bank overdraft. The rate charged presently has been used throughout the two years' projections.

Depreciation As is normal in this industry, this had been provided, as shown, on a straight-line basis on all assets at 25%.

VAT It is assumed that all Vatable items will be invoiced monthly. The current rate of 15% has been used for both years.

General In the year to 30 September 1987 remuneration levels are increased by 7%. Any increase in the cost of materials will be reflected in increased sales prices.

Profit and loss account

Sales As computed in parameters net of VAT.

Cost of sales materials As computed in parameters.

Plant hire Present cost of hiring a fork-lift truck.

Assembly As computed in parameters.

Consumables Amount estimated to cover consumable materials used during assembly. This approximates to 1% of sales.

Overheads: (a) Premises

Rent and rates Based on current amount payable and on figures being negotiated for new premises.

Insurance Estimated cost of all insurance.

Repairs An estimate for the upkeep of both premises.

Heat and light Estimates to cover the costs involved for both production and the building.

(b) Administration and sales

Telephone Based on normal business usage expected. Rising in first year due to new sales contacts and levelling out in second year as the business is consolidated.

Stationery and postages   This covers all the stationery required based on past experience. Postages are also included for all purposes including initial advertising brochures.

Sales expenses   This covers all allowances for lunches, hotel bills etc. at a constant level.

Advertising   This is the cost of all advertising in magazines, etc. and the cost of the initial brochures.

Professional fees   This is an estimate for the cost of all legal and accountancy fees for the year, including the preparation of the business plan.

Miscellaneous expenses   This covers all sundry expenses including exhibiting at trade shows, etc.

Vehicle expenses

Leasing   This is the agreed cost of leasing two Vauxhall Cavalier 1600GL hatchback saloon cars for the first year and an additional one for the second year. The cost includes road tax, insurance and Automobile Association membership.

Fuel and services   The estimated running costs of the above cars.

Repairs and maintenance   Estimated cost of the upkeep of the plant and machinery.

Salaries   All as calculated in the parameters.

Depreciation   As calculated in the parameters.

Overdraft interest   Calculated at the parameter rate on the previous month-end balance.

Taxation   Calculated at 30% on pre-tax profit.

General   An inflationary increase has been incorporated on the relevant overheads for the second year.

Cash flow: income

Debtors   As calculated in parameters.

Capital   Included at date of estimated receipt.

Trade creditors, sundry creditors and cash expenses
As shown in calculations on cash flow.

Salaries   As calculated in parameters.

Heat and light   Paid every two months.

Telephone, professional fees and bank interest   Paid quarterly.

Fittings and plant   Cost of items taken over from the previous partnership paid for in the first month.

VAT   As shown in calculations on cash flow (payable/recoverable
quarterly).

Stock   Cost of stock taken over from the previous partnership and paid
in the first month.

Balance sheet

Fixed assets   Cost of plant and fittings as purchased in cash flow net of
VAT.

Depreciation   Cumulative total of profit and loss account charges.

Stock   As calculated in parameters.

Debtors   As calculated in parameters.

Bank/bank overdraft   Balance per cash flow.

Creditors   As per calculations in cash flow.

Taxation   Cumulative total of profit and loss account charges.

VAT   Cumulative figure in calculations in cash flow.

Share capital   Initial amount paid in.

Reserves   Cumulative total of profit and loss account results to date.

```
CASH FLOW
=========
INCOME
---------

SALES                        4500    3500    3000    4000   15000   17000
COMMISSIONS                  1000    1500    1500    1000    5000    6000
CAPITAL PAID IN                                                 0       0
                             ---     ---     ---     ---    ----    ----
TOTAL INCOME                 5500    5000    4500    5000   20000   23000
                             ---     ---     ---     ---    ----    ----
EXPENDITURE
--------------

PURCHASES                    2450    1650    1600    2100    7800    8600
RENT AND RATES                900     900     900     900    3600    3800
INSURANCE                     180     180     180     180     720     750
PRINTING AND ADVERTISING      150     150     150     150     600     650
HEATING AND LIGHTING          100     100     100     100     400     450
DECORATION/PRESENTATION       100     100     100     100     400     450
PACKAGING                      60      20      60      20     160     180
POSTAGES AND STATIONERY        40      40      40      40     160     170
PROFESSIONAL FEES                     120             120     240     150
DRAWINGS                     1300    1300    1300    1300    5200    6240
N.I.                           65      65      65      65     260     260
EQUIPMENT                     250                             250
BANK INTEREST                   0       0       0       0       0       0
                             ---     ---     ---     ---    ----    ----
TOTAL EXPENDITURE.           5595    4625    4495    5075   19790   21700
                             ---     ---     ---     ---    ----    ----
BANK B.F.                    1137    1042    1417    1422            1347
BANK C.F.                    1042    1417    1422    1347            2647


BALANCE SHEET
==============
CURRENT ASSETS
---------------

STOCK                         500     400     500     600             700
PREPAYMENTS                     0       0       0       0               0
BANK                         1042    1417    1422    1347            2647
                             ----    ----    ----    ----            ----
                             1542    1817    1922    1947            3347
                             ----    ----    ----    ----            ----
CURRENT LIABILITIES
--------------------

ACCRUALS                       40       0      40       0             100
BANK                            0       0       0       0               0
                             ----    ----    ----    ----            ----
                               40       0      40       0             100
                             ----    ----    ----    ----            ----
N.C.A.                       1502    1817    1882    1947            3247
FIXED ASSETS                 1800    1800    1800    1800            1800
                             ----    ----    ----    ----            ----
                             3302    3617    3682    3747            5047
                             ====    ====    ====    ====            ====
CAPITAL ACCOUNT
----------------

BALANCE BROUGHT FWD.         2987    3302    3617    3682            3747
CAPITAL PAID IN                 0                                       0
PROFIT/LOSS                  1680    1680    1430    1430            7800
DRAWINGS                     1365    1365    1365    1365            6500
                             ----    ----    ----    ----            ----
                             3302    3617    3682    3747            5047
                             ====    ====    ====    ====            ====
```

AGRILIFT LIMITED   FORECAST FOR THE YEAR ENDING 30TH SEPTEMBER 1986

OPERATING PARAMETERS	OCT.	NOV.	DEC.	JAN.	FEB.	MCH.	APRIL	MAY	JUNE	JULY	AUG.	SEPT.	TOTAL
SALES	15000	18000	20000	20000	24000	24000	24000	20000	20000	27000	27000 ·	27000	
VAT at 15%	2250	2700	3000	3000	3600	3600	3600	3000	3000	4050	4050	4050	
	17250	20700	23000	23000	27600	27600	27600	23000	23000	31050	31050	31050	
DEBTORS COLLECTION (MONTHS)	2	2	2	2	2	2	2	2	2	2	2	2	
DEBTORS COLLECTED	0	0	17250	20700	23000	23000	27600	27600	27600	23000	23000	31050	
COST of SALES													
OPENING STOCK	0	10250	12910	13210	13510	13790	13570	13850	14250	14650	14340	14030	
MATERIALS PURCHASED	10200	12200	10900	10900	13000	12500	13000	11000	11000	14000	14000	14500	
STOCK TAKEN OVER	8000	0	0	0	0	0	0	0	0	0	0	0	
CLOSING STOCK	10250	12910	13210	13510	13790	13570	13850	14250	14650	14340	14030	14220	
COST of SALES	7950	9540	10600	10600	12720	12720	12720	10600	10600	14310	14310	14310	
MATERIALS PURCHASED	10200	12200	10900	10900	13000	12500	13000	11000	11000	14000	14000	14500	
VAT at 15%	1530	1830	1635	1635	1950	1875	1950	1650	1650	2100	2100	2175	
	11730	14030	12535	12535	14950	14375	14950	12650	12650	16100	16100	16675	
MATERIALS PAYMENT TERMS (MONTHS)	1	1	1	1	1	1	1	1	1	1	1	1	
REMUNERATION													
ASSEMBLERS NUMBER	2	2	2	2	2	2	2	2	2	2	2	2	
MONTHLY SALARY	600	600	600	600	600	600	600	600	600	600	600	600	
SALES DIRECTOR NUMBER	1	1	1	1	1	1	1	1	1	1	1	1	
MONTHLY SALARY	750	750	750	750	750	750	750	750	750	750	750	750	
TECHNICAL DIRECTOR NUMBER	1	1	1	1	1	1	1	1	1	1	1	1	
MONTHLY SALARY	875	875	875	875	875	875	875	875	875	875	875	875	
ADMIN.DIRECTOR NUMBER	1	1	1	1	1	1	1	1	1	1	1	1	
MONTHLY SALARY	1000	1000	1000	1000	1000	1000	1000	1000	1000	1000	1000	1000	
ADMIN. STAFF NUMBER	1	1	1	1	1	1	1	1	1	1	1	1	
MONTHLY SALARY	375	375	375	375	375	375	375	375	375	375	375	375	
EMPLOYERS NAT.INSURANCE %	10.5	10.5	10.5	10.5	10.5	10.5	10.5	10.5	10.5	10.5	10.5	10.5	
ASSEMBLY COST	1326	1326	1326	1326	1326	1326	1326	1326	1326	1326	1326	1326	
SALES COST	829	829	829	829	829	829	829	829	829	829	829	829	
TECHNICAL COST	967	967	967	967	967	967	967	967	967	967	967	967	
ADMIN.COST	414	1519	1519	1519	1519	1519	1519	1519	1519	1519	1519	1519	
TOTAL SALARIES	3536	4641	4641	4641	4641	4641	4641	4641	4641	4641	4641	4641	
V.A.T.													
OUTPUT (SALES) V.A.T.	2250	2700	3000	3000	3600	3600	3600	3000	3000	4050	4050	4050	
INPUT V.A.T.													
TRADE CREDITORS	1530	1830	1635	1635	1950	1875	1950	1650	1650	2100	2100	2175	
SUNDRY CREDITORS	62	66	69	69	75	75	75	69	69	80	80	80	
CASH EXPENSES	124	124	124	124	124	124	124	124	124	124	124	124	
TELEPHONE	0	0	0	45	0	0	60	0	0	68	0	0	
PROFESSIONAL FEES	0	0	0	68	0	0	68	0	0	68	0	0	
FITTINGS	75	0	0	0	0	0	0	0	0	0	0	0	
PLANT	225	0	0	0	75	0	0	75	0	0	0	75	
	2015	2020	1828	1940	2224	2074	2276	1918	1843	2438	2303	2453	
V.A.T.PAYABLE/RECEIVABLE	235	680	1172	1060	1376	1526	1324	1082	1157	1612	1747	1597	
CUMULATIVE V.A.T.PYBLE/RCVBLE	235	915	2087	1060	2436	3962	1324	2406	3563	1612	3359	4955	
OVERDRAFT INTEREST RATE %	14	14	14	14	14	14	14	14	14	14	14	14	
DEPRECIATION STRAIGHT LINE %	25	25	25	25	25	25	25	25	25	25	25	25	

AGRILIFT LIMITED   FORECAST FOR THE YEAR ENDING 30TH SEPTEMBER 1986

PROFIT AND LOSS ACCOUNT

	OCT.	NOV.	DEC.	JAN.	FEB.	MCH.	APRIL	MAY	JUNE	JULY	AUG.	SEPT.	TOTAL
SALES	15000	18000	20000	20000	24000	24000	24000	20000	20000	27000	27000	27000	266000
COST of SALES													
MATERIALS	7950	9540	10600	10600	12720	12720	12720	10600	10600	14310	14310	14310	140980
PLANT HIRE	160	160	160	160	160	160	160	160	160	160	160	160	1920
ASSEMBLY	1326	1326	1326	1326	1326	1326	1326	1326	1326	1326	1326	1326	15912
CONSUMABLES	150	180	200	200	240	240	240	200	200	270	270	270	2660
TOTAL COST of SALES	9586	11206	12286	12286	14446	14446	14446	12286	12286	16066	16066	16066	161472
GROSS PROFIT	5414	6794	7714	7714	9554	9554	9554	7714	7714	10934	10934	10934	104528
GROSS PROFIT %	36	38	39	39	40	40	40	39	39	40	40	40	39
OVERHEADS													
PREMISES-RENT	400	400	400	400	400	400	400	400	400	400	400	400	4800
RATES	300	300	300	300	300	300	300	300	300	300	300	300	3600
INSURANCE	120	120	120	120	120	120	120	120	120	120	120	120	1440
REPAIRS	50	50	50	50	50	50	50	50	50	50	50	50	600
HEAT AND LIGHT	130	130	130	130	130	130	130	130	130	130	130	130	1560
	1000	1000	1000	1000	1000	1000	1000	1000	1000	1000	1000	1000	12000
ADMIN.& SALES													
TELEPHONE	100	100	100	100	150	150	150	150	150	150	150	150	1600
STATIONERY AND POSTAGES	125	125	125	125	125	125	125	125	125	125	125	125	1500
SALES EXPENSES	145	145	145	145	145	145	145	145	145	145	145	145	1740
ADVERTISING	500	300	500	300	600	400	600	400	500	500	500	500	5600
PROFESSIONAL FEES	150	150	150	150	150	150	150	150	150	150	150	150	1800
MISCELLANEOUS EXPENSES	180	180	180	180	180	180	180	180	180	180	180	180	2160
	1200	1000	1200	1000	1350	1150	1350	1150	1250	1250	1250	1250	14400
VEHICLE EXPENSES													
LEASING	300	300	300	300	300	300	300	300	300	300	300	300	3600
FUEL & SERVICES	150	150	150	150	150	150	150	150	150	150	150	150	1800
	450	450	450	450	450	450	450	450	450	450	450	450	5400
REPAIRS AND MAINTENANCE	100	100	100	100	100	100	100	100	100	100	100	100	1200
SALARIES													
SALES	829	829	829	829	829	829	829	829	829	829	829	829	9945
TECHNICAL	967	967	967	967	967	967	967	967	967	967	967	967	11603
ADMINISTRATION	414	1519	1519	1519	1519	1519	1519	1519	1519	1519	1519	1519	17128
	2210	3315	3315	3315	3315	3315	3315	3315	3315	3315	3315	3315	38675
DEPRECIATION	42	42	42	42	52	52	52	63	63	63	63	73	646
TOTAL OVERHEADS	5002	5907	6107	5907	6267	6067	6267	6078	6178	6178	6178	6188	72321
TRADING PROFIT	412	887	1607	1807	3287	3487	3287	1637	1537	4757	4757	4746	32207
FINANCE COSTS													
OVERDRAFT INTEREST	0	0	165	216	245	219	215	217	166	82	110	122	1757
PROFIT BEFORE TAXATION	412	887	1442	1591	3041	3268	3072	1420	1370	4675	4647	4624	30450
CORPORATION TAX	124	266	433	477	912	980	922	426	411	1402	1394	1387	9135
PROFIT AFTER TAXATION	289	621	1010	1114	2129	2288	2150	994	959	3272	3253	3237	21315

AGRILIFT LIMITED   FORECAST FOR THE YEAR ENDING 30TH SEPTEMBER 1987
----

                              and THE YEAR ENDING 30TH SEPTEMBER 1988

		QUARTER TO				YEAR TO
CASH FLOW		DEC.	MCH.	JUNE	SEPT.	TOTAL	SEPT. 1988
----------		---	---	---	---	---	--------
CALCULATIONS							

TRADE CREDITORS							

MATERIALS PAYMENTS		47342	47533	46767	50600	192242	217925
SUNDRY CREDITORS							

PLANT HIRE	'v'	525	525	525	525	2100	2300
CONSUMABLES	'v'	700	800	750	850	3100	3500
PREMISES-RENT		1200	1200	1200	1200	4800	4800
RATES		1000	1000	1000	1000	4000	4250
INSURANCE		400	400	400	400	1600	1750
ADVERTISING		1200	1200	1200	1200	4800	5000
REPAIRS AND MAINTENANCE	'v'	400	400	400	400	1600	1750
		-----	-----	-----	-----	-----	-------
		5425	5525	5475	5575	22000	23350
V.A.T. at 15%(items marked 'v')		244	259	251	266	1020	1133
		-----	-----	-----	-----	-----	-------
		5669	5784	5726	5841	23020	24483
		-----	-----	-----	-----	-----	-------
CASH EXPENSES							

STATIONERY AND POSTAGES		400	400	400	400	1600	1750
SALES EXPENSES	'v'	500	500	500	500	2000	2200
PREMISES-REPAIRS	'v'	200	200	200	200	800	1000
MISCELLANEOUS EXPENSES	'v'	600	600	600	600	2400	2500
VEHICLE EXPENSES							
LEASING	'v'	1500	1500	1500	1500	6000	6300
FUEL & SERVICES	'v'	750	750	750	750	3000	3200
		-----	-----	-----	-----	-----	-------
		3950	3950	3950	3950	15800	16950
V.A.T. at 15%(items marked 'v')		533	533	533	533	2130	2280
		-----	-----	-----	-----	-----	-------
		4483	4483	4483	4483	17930	19230
		-----	-----	-----	-----	-----	-------
INCOME							

DEBTORS CASH		88933	84333	90083	90083	353433	400583
		-----	-----	-----	-----	------	-------
EXPENDITURE							

TRADE CREDITORS		47342	47533	46767	50600	192242	217925
SUNDRY CREDITORS		5709	5745	5745	5803	23003	24389
CASH EXPENSES		4483	4483	4483	4483	17930	19230
SALARIES		15788	15788	15788	15788	63154	70200
HEAT & LIGHT		410	450	450	450	1760	1883
TELEPHONE		518	575	575	575	2243	2516
PROFESSIONAL FEES		518	575	575	575	2243	2516
BANK INTEREST		313	43	0	0	356	0
FITTINGS		0	0	0	0	0	0
PLANT		0	0	0	0	0	0
CORPORATION TAX		0	0	9135	0	9135	11409
VAT		4955	3589	4759	4316	17619	19850
		-----	-----	-----	-----	------	-------
		80035	78781	88277	82590	329683	369917
		-----	-----	-----	-----	------	-------
BANK BALANCE BRT.FWD.		-3691	5208	10759	12566		20059
BANK BALANCE CRD.FWD.		5208	10759	12566	20059		50726

AGRILIFT LIMITED   FORECAST FOR THE YEAR ENDING 30TH SEPTEMBER 1986

BALANCE SHEET

	OCT.	NOV.	DEC.	JAN.	FEB.	MCH.	APRIL	MAY	JUNE	JULY	AUG.	SEPT.	TOTAL
FIXED ASSETS													
PLANT & EQUIPMENT	1500	1500	1500	1500	2000	2000	2000	2500	2500	2500	2500	3000	
FIXTURES & FITTINGS	500	500	500	500	500	500	500	500	500	500	500	500	
	2000	2000	2000	2000	2500	2500	2500	3000	3000	3000	3000	3500	
AGGREGATE DEPN.	42	83	125	167	219	271	323	385	448	510	573	646	
NET BOOK VALUE	1958	1917	1875	1833	2281	2229	2177	2615	2552	2490	2427	2854	
CURRENT ASSETS													
STOCK & WORK IN PROGRESS	10250	12910	13210	13510	13790	13570	13850	14250	14650	14340	14030	14220	
DEBTORS	17250	37950	43700	46000	50600	55200	55200	50600	46000	54050	62100	62100	
BANK	5090	0	0	0	0	0	0	0	0	0	0	0	
	32590	50860	56910	59510	64390	68770	69050	64850	60650	68390	76130	76320	
CURRENT LIABILITIES													
CREDITORS	11730	14030	12535	12535	14950	14375	14950	12650	12650	16100	16100	16675	
SUNDRY CREDITORS	1792	1626	1849	1649	1995	1795	1995	1749	1849	1930	1930	1930	
ACCRUALS	380	760	1045	726	1142	1791	645	1292	1628	642	922	1473	
CORPORATION TAX	124	390	823	1300	2212	3193	4114	4540	4951	6354	7748	9135	
V.A.T.	235	915	2087	1060	2436	3962	1324	2406	3563	1612	3359	4955	
BANK OVERDRAFT	0	14146	18527	21040	19774	18434	18599	14234	7007	9418	10422	3691	
	14260	31867	36866	38310	41509	43549	41627	36871	31649	36054	40479	37859	
NET CURRENT ASSETS	18330	18993	20044	21200	22881	25221	27423	27979	29001	32336	35651	38461	
	20289	20910	21919	23033	25162	27450	29600	30594	31553	34825	38078	41315	
REPRESENTED BY:													
SHARE CAPITAL/LOAN	20000	20000	20000	20000	20000	20000	20000	20000	20000	20000	20000	20000	
RESERVES	289	910	1919	3033	5162	7450	9600	10594	11553	14825	18078	21315	
	20289	20910	21919	23033	25162	27450	29600	30594	31553	34825	38078	41315	

AGRILIFT LIMITED   FORECAST FOR THE YEAR ENDING 30TH SEPTEMBER 1987
----
                      and THE YEAR ENDING 30TH SEPTEMBER 1988

			QUARTER TO			YEAR TO
OPERATING PARAMETERS	DEC.	MCH.	JUNE	SEPT.	TOTAL	SEPT.1988
SALES	70000	80000	75000	85000		350000
VAT at 15%	10500	12000	11250	12750		52500
	80500	92000	86250	97750		402500
DEBTORS COLLECTION (MONTHS)	2	2	2	2		2
DEBTORS COLLECTED	88933	84333	90083	90083		400583
COST of SALES						
OPENING STOCK	14220	17120	16720	16970		17920
MATERIALS PURCHASED	40000	42000	40000	46000		190000
CLOSING STOCK	17120	16720	16970	17920		22420
COST of SALES	37100	42400	39750	45050		185500
MATERIALS PURCHASED	40000	42000	40000	46000		190000
VAT at 15%	6000	6300	6000	6900		28500
	46000	48300	46000	52900		218500
MATERIALS PAYMENT TERMS (MONTHS)	1	1	1	1		1
REMUNERATION						
ASSEMBLERS NUMBER	2	2	2	2		2
QUARTERLY SALARY	1980	1980	1980	1980		2200
SALES DIRECTOR NUMBER	1	1	1	1		1
QUARTERLY SALARY	2550	2550	2550	2550		2800
TECHNICAL DIRECTOR NUMBER	1	1	1	1		1
QUARTERLY SALARY	3000	3000	3000	3000		3300
ADMIN.DIRECTOR NUMBER	1	1	1	1		1
QUARTERLY SALARY	3300	3300	3300	3300		3600
ADMIN. STAFF NUMBER	1	1	1	1		1
QUARTERLY SALARY	1350	1350	1350	1350		1500
EMPLOYERS NAT.INSURANCE	11.5	11.5	11.5	11.5		12.5
ASSEMBLY COST	4415	4415	4415	4415		19800
SALES COST	2843	2843	2843	2843		12600
TECHNICAL COST	3345	3345	3345	3345		14850
ADMIN.COST	5185	5185	5185	5185		22950
TOTAL SALARIES	15788	15788	15788	15788		70200
V.A.T.						
OUTPUT (SALES) V.A.T.	10500	12000	11250	12750		52500
INPUT V.A.T.						
TRADE CREDITORS	6000	6300	6000	6900		28500
SUNDRY CREDITORS	244	259	251	266		1133
CASH EXPENSES	533	533	533	533		2280
TELEPHONE	68	75	75	75		328
PROFESSIONAL FEES	68	75	75	75		328
FITTINGS	0	0	0	0		0
PLANT	0	0	0	0		0
	6911	7241	6934	7849		32569
V.A.T.PAYABLE/RECEIVABLE	3589	4759	4316	4901		19931
CUMULATIVE V.A.T.PYBLE/RCVBLE	3589	4759	4316	4901		19931
OVERDRAFT INTEREST RATE %	14	14	14	14		14
DEPRECIATION STRAIGHT LINE %	25	25	25	25		25

AGRILIFT LIMITED   FORECAST FOR THE YEAR ENDING 30TH SEPTEMBER 1987
----
                       and THE YEAR ENDING 30TH SEPTEMBER 1988

PROFIT AND LOSS ACCOUNT	QUARTER TO					YEAR TO
	DEC.	MCH.	JUNE	SEPT.	TOTAL	SEPT.1988
SALES	70000	80000	75000	85000	310000	350000
COST of SALES						
MATERIALS	37100	42400	39750	45050	164300	185500
PLANT HIRE	525	525	525	525	2100	2300
ASSEMBLY	4415	4415	4415	4415	17662	19800
CONSUMABLES	700	800	750	850	3100	3500
TOTAL COST of SALES	42740	48140	45440	50840	187162	211100
GROSS PROFIT	27260	31860	29560	34160	122838	138900
GROSS PROFIT %	39	40	39	40	40	40
OVERHEADS						
PREMISES-RENT	1200	1200	1200	1200	4800	4800
RATES	1000	1000	1000	1000	4000	4250
INSURANCE	400	400	400	400	1600	1750
REPAIRS	200	200	200	200	800	1000
HEAT AND LIGHT	450	450	450	450	1800	1900
	3250	3250	3250	3250	13000	13700
ADMIN.& SALES						
TELEPHONE	500	500	500	500	2000	2250
STATIONERY AND POSTAGES	400	400	400	400	1600	1750
SALES EXPENSES	500	500	500	500	2000	2200
ADVERTISING	1200	1200	1200	1200	4800	5000
PROFESSIONAL FEES	500	500	500	500	2000	2250
MISCELLANEOUS EXPENSES	600	600	600	600	2400	2500
	3700	3700	3700	3700	14800	15950
VEHICLE EXPENSES						
LEASING	1500	1500	1500	1500	6000	6300
FUEL & SERVICES	750	750	750	750	3000	3200
	2250	2250	2250	2250	9000	9500
REPAIRS AND MAINTENANCE	400	400	400	400	1600	1750
SALARIES						
SALES	2843	2843	2843	2843	11373	12600
TECHNICAL	3345	3345	3345	3345	13380	14850
ADMINISTRATION	5185	5185	5185	5185	20739	22950
	11373	11373	11373	11373	45492	50400
DEPRECIATION	219	219	219	219	875	875
TOTAL OVERHEADS	21192	21192	21192	21192	84767	92175
TRADING PROFIT	6068	10668	8368	12968	38071	46725
FINANCE COSTS						
OVERDRAFT INTEREST	43	0	0	0	43	0
PROFIT BEFORE TAXATION	6025	10668	8368	12968	38028	46725
CORPORATION .TAX	1807	3200	2510	3890	11409	14018
PROFIT AFTER TAXATION	4217	7467	5857	9077	26620	32708

AGRILIFT LIMITED   FORECAST FOR THE YEAR ENDING 30TH SEPTEMBER 1986

CASH FLOW	OCT.	NOV.	DEC.	JAN.	FEB.	MCH.	APRIL	MAY	JUNE	JULY	AUG.	SEPT.	TOTAL
----------	---	---	---	---	---	---	---	---	---	---	---	---	---
CALCULATIONS													

TRADE CREDITORS													

MATERIALS PAYMENTS	0	11730	14030	12535	12535	14950	14375	14950	12650	12650	16100	16100	
SUNDRY CREDITORS													

PLANT HIRE 'v'	160	160	160	160	160	160	160	160	160	160	160	160	1920
CONSUMABLES 'v'	150	180	200	200	240	240	240	200	200	270	270	270	2660
PREMISES-RENT	400	400	400	400	400	400	400	400	400	400	400	400	4800
RATES	300	300	300	300	300	300	300	300	300	300	300	300	3600
INSURANCE	120	120	120	120	120	120	120	120	120	120	120	120	1440
ADVERTISING	500	300	500	300	600	400	600	400	500	500	500	500	5600
REPAIRS AND MAINTENANCE 'v'	100	100	100	100	100	100	100	100	100	100	100	100	1200
	-----	-----	-----	-----	-----	-----	-----	-----	-----	-----	-----	-----	-----
	1730	1560	1780	1580	1920	1720	1920	1680	1780	1850	1850	1850	21220
V.A.T. at 15%(items marked 'v')	62	66	69	69	75	75	75	69	69	80	80	80	867
	-----	-----	-----	-----	-----	-----	-----	-----	-----	-----	-----	-----	-----
	1792	1626	1849	1649	1995	1795	1995	1749	1849	1930	1930	1930	22087
	-----	-----	-----	-----	-----	-----	-----	-----	-----	-----	-----	-----	-----
CASH EXPENSES													

STATIONERY AND POSTAGES	125	125	125	125	125	125	125	125	125	125	125	125	1500
SALES EXPENSES 'v'	145	145	145	145	145	145	145	145	145	145	145	145	1740
PREMISES-REPAIRS 'v'	50	50	50	50	50	50	50	50	50	50	50	50	600
MISCELLANEOUS EXPENSES 'v'	180	180	180	180	180	180	180	180	180	180	180	180	2160
VEHICLE EXPENSES													
LEASING 'v'	300	300	300	300	300	300	300	300	300	300	300	300	3600
FUEL & SERVICES 'v'	150	150	150	150	150	150	150	150	150	150	150	150	1800
	-----	-----	-----	-----	-----	-----	-----	-----	-----	-----	-----	-----	-----
	950	950	950	950	950	950	950	950	950	950	950	950	11400
V.A.T. at 15%(items marked 'v')	124	124	124	124	124	124	124	124	124	124	124	124	1485
	-----	-----	-----	-----	-----	-----	-----	-----	-----	-----	-----	-----	-----
	1074	1074	1074	1074	1074	1074	1074	1074	1074	1074	1074	1074	12885
	-----	-----	-----	-----	-----	-----	-----	-----	-----	-----	-----	-----	-----
INCOME													

DEBTORS CASH	0	0	17250	20700	23000	23000	27600	27600	27600	23000	23000	31050	243800
CAPITAL	20000												20000
	-----	-----	-----	-----	-----	-----	-----	-----	-----	-----	-----	-----	------
	20000	0	17250	20700	23000	23000	27600	27600	27600	23000	23000	31050	263800
	-----	-----	-----	-----	-----	-----	-----	-----	-----	-----	-----	-----	------
EXPENDITURE													0
------------													0
TRADE CREDITORS	0	11730	14030	12535	12535	14950	14375	14950	12650	12650	16100	16100	152605
SUNDRY CREDITORS	0	1792	1626	1849	1649	1995	1795	1995	1749	1849	1930	1930	20158
CASH EXPENSES	1074	1074	1074	1074	1074	1074	1074	1074	1074	1074	1074	1074	12885
SALARIES	3536	4641	4641	4641	4641	4641	4641	4641	4641	4641	4641	4641	54587
HEAT & LIGHT	0	0	260	0	260	0	260	0	260	0	260	0	1300
TELEPHONE	0	0	0	345	0	0	460	0	0	518	0	0	1323
PROFESSIONAL FEES	0	0	0	518	0	0	518	0	0	518	0	0	1553
BANK INTEREST	0	0	0	165	0	0	681	0	0	598	0	0	1444
FITTINGS	575												575
PLANT	1725				575			575				575	3450
V.A.T.	0	0	0	2087	0	0	3962	0	0	3563	0	0	9613
STOCK TAKEN OVER	8000												8000
	-----	-----	-----	-----	-----	-----	-----	-----	-----	-----	-----	-----	------
	14910	19236	21631	23214	20734	22660	27765	23235	20374	25410	24004	24319	267491
	-----	-----	-----	-----	-----	-----	-----	-----	-----	-----	-----	-----	------
BANK BALANCE BRT.FWD.	0	5090	-14146	-18527	-21040	-18774	-18434	-18599	-14234	-7007	-9418	-10422	
BANK BALANCE CRD.FWD.	5090	-14146	-18527	-21040	-18774	-18434	-18599	-14234	-7007	-9418	-10422	-3691	

AGRILIFT LIMITED   FORECAST FOR THE YEAR ENDING 30TH SEPTEMBER 1986
----
                              and THE YEAR ENDING 30TH SEPTEMBER 1988

BALANCE SHEET	QUARTER TO					YEAR TO
	DEC.	MCH.	JUNE	SEPT.	TOTAL	SEPT.1988
	---	---	---	---	---	--------
FIXED ASSETS						
PLANT & EQUIPMENT	3000	3000	3000	3000		3000
FIXTURES & FITTINGS	500	500	500	500		500
	----	----	----	----		-------
	3500	3500	3500	3500		3500
AGGREGATE DEPN.	865	1084	1302	1521		2396
	----	----	----	----		-------
NET BOOK VALUE	2635	2417	2198	1979		1104
	----	----	----	----		-------
CURRENT ASSETS						
STOCK & WORK IN PROGRESS	17120	16720	16970	17920		22420
DEBTORS	53667	61333	57500	65167		67083
BANK	5208	10759	12566	20059		50726
	----	----	----	----		-------
	75994	88813	87036	103146		140229
	----	----	----	----		-------
CURRENT LIABILITIES						
CREDITORS	15333	16100	15333	17633		18208
SUNDRY CREDITORS	1890	1928	1909	1947		2040
ACCRUALS	1343	1300	1300	1300		1442
CORPORATION TAX	10942	14143	7518	11409		14018
V.A.T.	3589	4759	4316	4901		4983
BANK OVERDRAFT	0	0	0	0		0
	----	----	----	----		-------
	33097	38229	30376	37190		40691
	----	----	----	----		-------
NET CURRENT ASSETS	42897	50583	56660	65956		99538
	----	----	----	----		-------
	45532	53000	58857	67935		100642
	====	====	====	====		======
REPRESENTED BY:						
SHARE CAPITAL/LOAN	20000	20000	20000	20000		20000
RESERVES	25532	33000	38857	47935		80642
	----	----	----	----		-------
	45532	53000	58857	67935		100642
	====	====	====	====		======

III Tax Planning

Chapter 1

Value Added Tax

1.1   INTRODUCTION

One of the first discoveries you are likely to make when starting in business is that you have just volunteered to join the massive army of unwilling, unpaid tax collectors which the VAT and Taxes Acts conscript for the state. Not only will you have to calculate and account for PAYE and NI contributions on employees' salaries, you may also have to devote a great deal of time to calculating and accounting for VAT to Customs and Excise. Do not assume that because you are not actually paying the tax, but are simply collecting other peoples' tax, that if you mistakenly collect too little tax you will be all right. The legislation is framed to put *you* on the spot, and it will not be long before the Revenue, the DHSS and Customs are hammering on your door for unpaid taxes.

That is the system, and the best approach from the very beginning is to understand your legal responsibilities and to comply with them to the letter. There will, of course, be a cost in carrying out your role of unpaid tax collector, quite apart from the cost of stamps, stationery and telephone calls. Much of the time you spend in tax collection and administration could have been spent in promoting your business. Sole traders might easily spend three or four hours a week in tax collecting, which amounts to a substantial drain on time available for earning a living.

It is naive to think that starting in business will make you independent. Instead of having to account to your employer for your activities, you suddenly have to account to the Revenue, Customs, the DHSS, the Department of Trade and Industry, your employees and, last but not least, your customer.

That is one of the drawbacks of being in business, and it is something

'Starting in business? You have just volunteered to join the massive army of unwilling, unpaid tax collectors which the VAT and Taxes Acts conscripts for the state.'

that you must accept and make the best of all your responsibilities. It is perhaps most important to get your VAT compliance right. If you fail to collect and pay over the correct amount of VAT, Customs will raise a VAT assessment which could be ruinous. More positively, getting it right can help your cash flow by ensuring that the VAT you suffer on supplies made to you is recovered as fully and as efficiently as possible.

1.2   SOURCES OF INFORMATION

Your best source of information on VAT is an accountant experienced in advising new businesses. But with a little effort there is a great deal you can find out for yourself. Probably the best sources of readily understandable information are the Customs' own leaflets and guidance notes issued free of charge by all VAT offices. (You can find your local VAT office by looking up Customs and Excise in the telephone directory.) With a subject as complicated as VAT, it naturally takes a great deal of literature to cover it in full, and Customs and Excise has leaflets on the application of VAT to many specific business activities. But what the starting-out businessman needs is a copy of *General Guide (Public Notice 700)*. A copy of *Should I be Registered for VAT* 700/1/85 is also essential reading. Thereafter, you should ask your accountant or Customs itself what specific leaflets there are, if any, which cover your particular activity.

It is worth remembering that, as a general rule, Customs notices, excellent though they may be, are merely interpretations of the law and do not in themselves have the force of law (apart from certain leaflets such as those on special schemes for retailers). However, at least you have the comfort of knowing that if you stick within the guidelines offered in its publications you should stay on the right side of Customs. Apart from specialist journals and books, there is very little worth reading on VAT for the layman. For guidance on problems that may arise, or whenever you have a dispute with your local VAT officers for any reason, your accountant is the best person to call on. VAT disputes can be very technical and, as a general rule, it is not advisable for you to argue with Customs without professional help.

1.3   WHAT IS VAT?

VAT is a tax on business turnover, unlike Income Tax or Corporation Tax, which are taxes on profits. It arises whenever a 'taxable person' makes a 'supply of goods or services' in the UK in the course or furtherance of his business. The theory is that the burden of VAT is carried by the end-consumer, not by the business, which is merely collecting the VAT on behalf of Customs. But the reality is not quite so simple.

Where a VAT-registered business makes a taxable supply, it has to charge 'output VAT' on that supply at the appropriate rate. Some outputs are positive-rated and VAT has to be charged on these outputs at the rate of 15%. If, for instance, you are an office-cleaning contractor, and you invoice your clients monthly, you have to add 15% VAT to your invoice, assuming that you are VAT-registered. You then have to account for that VAT on your next VAT return. (Public Notice 700 gives useful guidance on the completion of VAT returns.) Remember that you have to hand the VAT over to Customs whether or not your customer has handed it over to you — one good reason for keeping on top of your debtors.

Some outputs, such as newspapers and magazines, are 'zero-rated'. They are still taxable, but they attract VAT at the zero rate. Other outputs are 'exempt' from VAT. No VAT is charged on an exempt supply, so what is the difference between an exempt output and a zero-rated output? The important point is that input VAT — the VAT that your business pays over on supplies made to it — can be recovered only insofar as your business is VAT-registered and makes taxable outputs. It does not matter whether the taxable outputs are positive-rated or zero-rated. So long as your business is VAT-registered and makes only taxable outputs it can recover its input VAT in full. (Certain input VAT cannot be recovered however, i.e. VAT on motor cars or on entertaining UK customers.) When it starts to make exempt outputs a problem arises, since input VAT cannot be recovered insofar as it relates to exempt outputs. Calculating how much VAT can be recovered in these circumstances is a technical matter on which you should certainly take advice. The point to note here is that taxable outputs are good news — they let you recover your input VAT. Exempt outputs, or 'dirty outputs', as they are sometimes known, are bad news — they may prevent you from recovering your input VAT. In this case VAT becomes more than just an administrative pest, and starts to be a financial drain on your business.

To complicate matters, some activities are outside the scope of VAT altogether and are really 'non-supplies'. Before a supply can be exempt, positive-rated or zero-rated it has to be within the scope of VAT in the first place. If it is 'outside the scope' you ignore it altogether for VAT purposes. You do not have to charge output VAT on the supply, nor does it lead to any restriction of input VAT recovery. Before a supply comes within the scope of VAT the following ingredients must all be present.

- It has to be a supply of goods or services.
- The supply has to be made in the United Kingdom.
- The supply has to be made by a 'taxable person'; that is, by a VAT-registered person, or by someone who *should* be VAT-registered but is not.
- The supply must be in the course or furtherance of a business.

Unless all of these ingredients are present, it is a 'non-supply' with no VAT implications. If, for example, a VAT-registered architect keeps bees as a hobby and sells his honey crop, the sale will be a 'non-supply', as it is not made in the course of furtherance of a business. If, on the other hand, he is a serious bee-keeper who systematically manages his bees with a view to realizing a profit, his bee-keeping could amount to a business, which would bring his honey sales within the scope of VAT. Fortunately, the supplies would be zero-rated as supplies of food used for human consumption, so he would not have to account for output VAT. He would, however, have the pleasure of reclaiming the input VAT on all his business costs.

1.4   REGISTRATION

Will you have to register for VAT? The answer depends largely on what taxable outputs you expect to make when you start trading, and perhaps also on the outputs you do actually make once you are trading. Only 'taxable persons' are required to register, and you can become a 'taxable person' in several ways.

First, if you are commencing in business you must register if there is a reasonable expectation that your taxable turnover will exceed £19 500 in the year then beginning. If you are already in business but are not yet registered, you must register as soon as there is a reasonable prospect of your taxable turnover exceeding £19 500 in the year then beginning. Remember that 'taxable turnover' means your outputs of both zero-rated and positive-rated supplies. Supplies that are exempt or are outside the scope of VAT altogether should be ignored. If you are liable to be registered under this provision, you should notify Customs at the beginning of the period.

Second, if your taxable turnover for any quarter exceeds £6500 you are liable to be registered, and must notify Customs of this within 10 days of the end of the quarter in question, and Customs will register your business within 21 days of the start of the following quarter. (For the purposes of registration a 'quarter' is a calendar quarter; i.e. a period of three months ending at the end of March, June, September or December.) However, you are not liable to be registered under this provision if you can satisfy Customs that your turnover for both the quarter just ended and the three coming quarters will be below £19 500.

Third, if at the end of any period of four quarters your taxable turnover has exceeded £19 500, you are liable to be registered and must notify Customs within 10 days of the end of the quarter. Customs will register you with effect from 21 days following the end of the quarter.

It is vital that you comply strictly with these provisions, and keep a close watch on your turnover each quarter. If, through ignorance or negligence, you fail to register in time, Customs is entitled to treat you as VAT-registered from the date on which you should actually have been registered, with the result that Customs can collect output tax on your turnover from that date. Almost certainly penalties would also be levied. You would, of course, also be able to reclaim input tax on supplies to your business from that date, but unless you could go back and collect the output tax from your customers, your profit margin would be slashed — the last thing a young business needs.

1.5   VOLUNTARY REGISTRATION

The thresholds described above are the turnover thresholds for compulsory VAT-registration: if you pass any of them you must register for VAT, whether you want to or not. There are circumstances in which you can register for VAT voluntarily, though Customs is becoming noticeably more reluctant to allow voluntary registrations.

If you make taxable supplies (or intend to) but you are not liable to be registered under the turnover thresholds, Customs may, at its discretion, register you anyway. To persuade Customs to register you, it is necessary to demonstrate that there is a genuine and continuing need for your business to be registered; in other words, that there will be a significant loss of input VAT which could make the business non-viable. Furthermore, you will need to persuade Customs that the income which is derived from the business is your only or principal means of livelihood. Hobby income is not good enough. Because Customs is reluctant to allow voluntary registration it is important that your application gives full information, and it is probably wise to use your accountant or other advisers for this.

Given that the annual threshold of £19 500 is quite low, even for sole traders, few businesses will require voluntary registration. Most new businesses will expect £19 500 turnover in the first twelve months, and should encounter no difficulties in registering for VAT. Problems can arise where businesses make largely exempt outputs, and only a small part of turnover is derived from taxable outputs, though even here there is scope for persuading Customs to register the business voluntarily.

1.6   INTENDING TRADER-REGISTRATION

Tax legislation is designed, on the whole, not to penalize new businesses, and Customs is usually happy to act in this spirit. Whilst the legislation defines taxable persons as being persons who make taxable supplies, special provision is made for *intending traders* — persons who are planning to make taxable supplies but have not yet done so. Knowing these rules can save a new business a great deal of lost input VAT.

There is very often a delay between planning a new business, buying materials, fitting-out premises, incurring input VAT on these costs and actually starting to make taxable outputs. Fortunately, where you intend to make taxable supplies from a specified date and will be liable to be registered when you do so, Customs will usually agree to register you from a date prior to when you first start making taxable supplies. The effect is that it will be possible to reclaim input VAT on pre-trading expenditure, which can substantially improve cash flow. Provisions also exist for recovery of input VAT incurred on pre-trading expenditure where the trade is to be carried on by a company which has not yet been incorporated.

Intending-trader registration is so important that, as a general rule, it is wise to work through your accountant when lodging the application. Customs will invariably attach conditions to an intending-trader's registration, but the conditions are not harsh. In particular, Customs may require you to sign an undertaking that you will in fact make a taxable supply by a certain date, and that if you fail to meet this condition then all the input VAT which you have provisionally reclaimed will be forfeited. If you should find yourself approaching that deadline without having made a taxable supply, it is imperative that you do make a taxable supply in time, or else ask Customs to extend the deadline. It will usually do so if there is a genuine reason for the delay.

> Fred is the manager of the service department of a main motor dealership, and is planning to set up in business as a self-employed mechanic by 1 January 1986. From July 1985 he begins to build up his stock of power tools and equipment, and fits out a small industrial unit which he has rented with a power ramp and lifting equipment. He also builds up a stock of spare parts, and by the time he hands in his resignation in December 1985 he has spent £4600 on tools and parts. Fred anticipates that his first year's turnover for labour and parts will exceed £20 000, and on this basis Fred's accountant lodges a request for intending-trader registration from 1 July 1985, when Fred incurred his first input VAT. As a result, Fred can recover £600 of input VAT when he lodges his first VAT return, which cheers his bank manager up no end.

1.7   CREDIT FOR PRE-REGISTRATION INPUT VAT

Although any VAT that is incurred before the date of registration is not technically allowable input VAT, there is a provision which allows you to claim a credit for such VAT when submitting your first VAT return. The provision is designed for traders who have been in business for a period, and then have become liable to register, probably because of crossing the registration thresholds for the first time. From the date of registration Customs will want output VAT on sales of stock and other business assets, so it would be unfair to deny a recovery of input VAT already incurred on the assets of the business at the date of registration.

In outline, a taxable person (i.e. a person who is registered or should be registered for VAT) can treat as input VAT the VAT incurred on the supply of goods to him which was made before the date from which he was required to register. Needless to say, there are certain stringent conditions to be met.

- The goods must have been acquired for the purposes of a business which either was being carried on, or was going to be carried on, at the time of the supply of the goods.
- The goods must not have been supplied onwards by you before the date from which you were required to register.
- The goods must not have been consumed by you before the date from which you were required to register.
- The input VAT must be available for credit under the normal rules (i.e. it does not relate to motor cars, entertainment, etc.).
- A stock account must be compiled and preserved for a period specified by Customs, which shows separately the quantities purchased, the quantities used in the making of other goods, the date of purchase and the date and manner of subsequent disposal of these items.

It is also possible to reclaim input VAT on services which were supplied to you before the date on which you were required to be registered, though again there are strict tests to pass. There is a technical definition of goods and services for VAT purposes, and you may therefore have to take advice on whether you have been supplied with goods or services. In very broad terms, a supply of goods takes place when you acquire the whole property in the goods. Any supply which is not a supply of goods is a supply of services. For example, if you buy a car you have received a supply of goods; if you lease a car, you do not own the car and you are therefore receiving a supply of services. To secure input VAT recovery on services supplied before VAT registration the following tests must be satisfied.

- The services must not relate to goods which have been supplied onwards by you, or which have been consumed by you, prior to registration. (So if you sell a machine prior to registration, you cannot recover the input VAT in relation to the machine itself, nor can you recover the input VAT on any services supplied in relation to that machine, such as repairs or maintenance. But if you sell the machine after registration, you can recover the input VAT incurred on both the goods and the services.)
- The services must have been supplied not more than six months before the date of registration.

- The input VAT must be available for credit under the normal rules.
- You must supply a list describing the services, and specifying the date of purchase and subsequent sale (if any), and the list must be preserved for a period specified by Customs.

Lastly, special rules are required for persons who trade through limited companies, as the company itself might not have existed when the pre-registration input VAT was incurred. This applies to any 'body corporate', which can include certain charities, clubs and associations.

- The person to whom the supply was made must become an employee, member or officer of the body corporate, and must be reimbursed by the body for the full price paid for the pre-incorporation goods and services.
- Further, that person must not himself have been a taxable person at the time of the supply, and the goods or services must have been supplied to him for the purposes of a business to be carried on by the body corporate. It is also required that he does not actually use the goods or services for any other purpose.
- The goods must not have been supplied by or consumed by the person who acquired them before the date on which the body was required to be registered.
- Services must have been supplied within the six months prior to registration, and must not relate to goods which have been supplied by or consumed by the person who acquired them.
- The input VAT must be available for credit under the normal rules.
- Full records must be maintained in respect of the goods and services, as in other cases of credit for pre-registration input VAT.

All this may sound complicated and off-putting, but in practice the rules are straightforward and your accountant and local Customs officer will be pleased to help. Understanding the rules will help you make a maximum input VAT recovery, and could provide your business with a useful cash injection at a vital point in its development.

1.8   SHOULD YOU REGISTER?

Things are fairly straightforward when you know that you must register for VAT because your turnover of taxable supplies is above the registration threshold. But what if you have the choice of registration? If you are below the turnover thresholds, for instance, you must decide whether it would be worthwhile for you to pursue registration by increasing your turnover or by requesting voluntary registration. Alternatively, if you are just below the thresholds for compulsory registration, should you make sure that you continue to stay just below them so that you do not trigger a requirement to register? Or if your turnover is approaching the registration thresholds could you hive off part of the trade to your wife perhaps, or to a partnership of yourself and your wife, so that your own taxable turnover sticks below the registration thresholds?

Where you can exercise some choice over whether or not to register, as a general rule you will be better off by registering if your customers are largely registered traders themselves. If, for instance, you supply to shopkeepers and you become VAT-registered, your customers are unlikely to mind an additional 15% VAT on top of your prices; they know that they can reclaim that amount in their next VAT return. You will have to pay over this VAT to Customs as your output VAT, but you will be able to reclaim the input VAT which you have suffered. At the end of the day you will be better off by registering, since your input VAT will be recoverable.

Things become less clearcut when you supply to individuals and non-registered persons who cannot reclaim any output VAT which you charge. If you think your customers will bear a 15% price increase and remain loyal should you register for VAT, then you can still benefit by registration. Again, Customs will take the additional output VAT which you charge, and you will be able to reclaim the input VAT which you suffer. You will be better off by the amount of input VAT which you recover.

But if you cannot risk a price increase you have a problem. The output tax will have to come out of your existing turnover, and cannot be passed on to your customer. True, you will be able to recover your input VAT once you are registered. But will the recovery of input VAT match or exceed the loss of profit in the form of output tax? The answer depends very much on your specific circumstances, and there is no substitute for working out the arithmetic for a trial period to see what would happen to your net profit. You could take a period of, say, the last three or four quarters, and work out what would have happened if you had been VAT-registered over that period. It may be that you think your customers could bear a 15% price rise should you become registered. Or it may be that only half your customers are VAT-registered and can therefore stand a 15% increase for VAT. There is no difficulty with working these assumptions into your calculation to see what would happen at the end of the day. The important point is to base your decision on whether or not to register on a proper understanding of what registration will do to your business. If registration will be beneficial, you should take what steps you can to register. If it will be harmful, obviously, you should try to keep out

Joanna runs a very small riding school and derives roughly £19 000 fees anually for riding lessons. She has some spare stabling, and a local brewery asks if she will look after their dray horses, as they are closing down their own stables. The fee will be £1000 annually, which will take Joanna over the registration limits if she accepts the brewery's request. Joanna calculates that her annual input VAT on saddlery, veterinary bills, car expenses, etc. amounts to £600 on costs of £4000. Feed for the horses costs £2000, so total costs inclusive of VAT are £6600. (Animal feedstuffs are zero-rated, so there is no input VAT incurred on the cost of feeding the horses.) Joanna knows that there is no problem with the brewery accepting a 15% uplift on the £1000 fee; it will simply recover it as input VAT. However, she knows that there would be much resistance to a fee increase among her pupils, since she lost several pupils when her fees last went up. The VAT would therefore have to come out of her £19 000 fee income. Her accountant explains that Customs would want 15/115ths of £19 000 as output VAT.

This gives the VAT element of her turnover as follows:

	£
£19 000 $\times$ 15/115	2 478
Exclusive of VAT turnover: £19 000 − £2 478	16 522
VAT at 15% on £16 522	2 478
Gross of VAT turnover	19 000

Armed with these facts Joanna compares her projected pre-registration and post-registration profits.

	Before registration		After registration (net of VAT)	
	£		£	
Fees (Pupils)	19 000		16 522	(Net of output VAT)
Brewery	NIL		1 000	(Net of output VAT)
	19 000		17 522	
Less Costs:	6 600	(including input VAT)	6 000	(excluding input VAT)
Profit	12 400		11 522	

Joanna will actually be worse off by registering for VAT. Reluctantly, she has to turn down the brewery's request. The problem is that since her customers will be unable to meet the additional burden of output VAT, she must in effect fund it out of her own pocket.

of the position where you will be required by law to register.

Deciding whether or not to register can, however, be more than a matter of arithmetic. Registration can be useful to some traders, particularly new businesses, who feel that VAT-registration will give their image some substance. The lack of a VAT-registration number can be an indication of the size of a business, which might put off certain customers. Seeing that your business is young and small, they might wonder whether you can deliver the goods and services which you offer, so making your selling job that much more difficult.

The administrative nuisance of complying with the VAT requirements is no small consideration. You will have to lodge VAT returns at regular intervals — most probably each quarter, though you can usually have a monthly return period if you will consistently claim repayments in your VAT returns. On the other hand, you may pay your accountant to do this if you cannot cope yourself or if your time is too valuable. You will also have to put up with Customs officers examining your records from time to time. They will be as quick and as courteous as possible, but sitting through a Customs control visit is never a pleasant experience. Last but not least, you will have to keep up with constantly changing VAT legislation to make sure you are not falling foul of the law. Registering for VAT is not a step to be taken lightly.

1.9   WHO IS REGISTERED FOR VAT?

A vital point to bear in mind, and a point which is often misunderstood, is *that it is persons that are registered for VAT, not businesses.* If you are a shopkeeper and you have just become VAT registered, it is *you* that is VAT-registered, not your shop. It follows that if you start to make other taxable supplies once you are registered, you will have to account for output VAT on those supplies. Take the case of a VAT-registered grocer, who operates bed and breakfast as a sideline. The bed and breakfast receipts are entirely separate from the grocery trade, but it is the trader who is VAT-registered, not the grocery business. He must therefore account for output VAT on the bed and breakfast receipts, and so lose 15/115ths of his bed and breakfast turnover. True, he can recover input VAT on the costs relating to the bed and breakfast trade, but this will not amount to much. Food is zero-rated; heat and light is zero-rated. The only significant sums of input VAT will be on items such as blankets, crockery, furniture, etc., which are really start-up costs and will not be recurring items. Simply to ignore the requirement to account for output VAT on the bed and breakfast receipts would be to court disaster, and in any case would be illegal. Customs officers are well aware of what goes on in their areas, and would soon pick up the fact that VAT was being lost. The result could be a ruinous VAT assessment with penalties, collecting output VAT on bed and breakfast receipts for several years.

What might someone in this position do? It could be possible to improve on the situation by organizing things properly from the start. For example, he could run the grocer's shop and his wife could run the bed and breakfast business. His wife is a separate person for VAT purposes, so she would not have to register for VAT as the bed and breakfast receipts would probably be below the registration thresholds. Alternatively, he could run the grocer's shop as a sole trader, whilst he and his wife in partnership operate the bed and breakfast business. Again, the partnership is a different entity from himself for VAT purposes, and so is treated as a 'person' in its own right for VAT registration.

A word of warning is in order here. Such a scheme will not work unless it is borne out by the actual facts of the situation, and is properly documented. The advice of your accountant or lawyer will be indispensible if this strategy is to have a chance of success. To back up the argument that separate persons are carrying on separate businesses, the following steps should be taken.

(1) Where there is a husband and wife partnership, the partnership should be evidenced by a partnership agreement, and partnership accounts should be produced showing the names of each partner and their respective profit shares.
(2) Separate bank accounts should be operated for each business.
(3) Separate accounts should be prepared for each business.
(4) Sales invoices and letterheads should be distinct for each business.

These points will be taken as an indication of who runs which business for VAT purposes, though it is worth stressing that at the end of the day it is the underlying facts that matter, not the outward appearance.

1.10   DE-REGISTRATION

The only circumstances in which you *must* de-register is when you cease altogether to make taxable supplies. If you stop trading altogether you will obviously stop making taxable supplies, but you could also be required to de-register if you continue in business but make only exempt supplies. After 1 June 1984, for instance, sales of certain reconstructed buildings by developers became exempt outputs, whereas before that date they had been zero-rated outputs. As a result, many developers ceased making taxable outputs from 1 June 1984, and were obliged to de-register from that date.

It is possible to de-register voluntarily if you meet certain requirements. You can apply for voluntary de-registration if, after the end of the
VAT quarter (or VAT month if you have a monthly VAT accounting
period);

- You have been registered for the preceding two years, *and*
- The value of your taxable supplies in each of these years is £19 500 or
  less, *and*
- There are no reasonable grounds for believing that the value of your
  taxable turnover in the 12 months then beginning will exceed £19 500.

There is another, simpler, test under which you can voluntarily de-
register. Your VAT officer will accept a de-registration application if you
can show him that the value of your taxable supplies in the coming twelve
months will be £18 500 or less. Remember, that these thresholds tend to
increase with each year's Finance Act, so if you are not currently able to
de-register, you might become able if the de-registration thresholds are
raised above your taxable turnover. It is also worth bearing in mind that
Customs are prepared to ignore the value of sales of capital items from
your business (fixed assets such as vans and equipment) in looking at your
taxable turnover for the purposes of de-registration.

In working out whether you should voluntarily de-register there is no
substitute for actually doing the arithmetic for a trial period, and seeing
whether you would be better off by de-registering. However, you must
also be aware of a twist in the VAT legislation in deciding whether or not
to de-register. When you de-register you are treated as making a supply
of all your business assets immediately prior to de-registration. So you
could end up by creating a charge to output VAT simply by cancelling
your registration.

This rule is intended to stop you from acquiring goods for personal use
free of VAT. For instance, if you traded as a television retailer and ceased
trading, you could acquire a television set from your stock on cessation
even though you had already recovered input VAT on that item. The
effect would be that you acquire a set without a VAT cost — not what the
legislation intended. That is why the legislation requires you to account
for output VAT on business assets on de-registration. Fortunately, there
are several exceptions to this rule, and for many businesses the charge to
output VAT on de-registration will not be a problem. For example, there
will be no charge to output VAT if you did not actually recover the input
VAT in the first place. Nor will there be a charge to output VAT if the
VAT on the notional supply on de-registration would be £250 or less.
However, good planning is essential here, and you should certainly seek
the advice of your accountant before de-registering.

1.11   BUYING A BUSINESS AS A GOING CONCERN

Special VAT problems arise if you are buying a business as a going concern, though, fortunately for start-up businessmen, the problems apply more to the seller of the going concern than to the buyer. The disposal of business assets is a disposal for VAT purposes like any other, and the seller must account for VAT on the assets sold. The buyer, on the other hand, will incur input VAT on the acquisition of the business assets, and should make sure that this input VAT is recovered. If he is already VAT-registered there is no problem; but if he is not registered he should take steps to become registered as quickly as possible so that the input VAT can be recovered.

In certain cases a special provision applies to the sale of a business as a going concern which will allow the seller not to charge VAT on the sale proceeds. This will probably be beneficial to the buyer as well, since he will not have the cash flow disadvantage of incurring input VAT on the assets of the business and waiting for over three months before the input VAT can be recovered.

To qualify under this provision the assets must be used by you for the purposes of the same kind of business as was carried on by the seller. You must already be a taxable person at the time of the transfer, or become a taxable person as a result of the transfer. In other words, if you buy a business with a taxable turnover of £40 000 per annum, and you intend to operate the business in the same way as it has been operated in the past, then you will obviously become a taxable person as soon as you buy the business. In these circumstances it will be possible for the seller to treat the supply of the business as a going concern, as being outside the scope of VAT. He might well require an indemnity from you to the effect that you will make good any loss to him if it should turn out that you are not a taxable person and do not become one as a result of the transfer of the business. Needless to say, any indemnities should not be given lightly, and certainly not without taking the advice of your accountant or lawyer. (VAT is not a problem if you buy the shares of a company instead of the actual assets, as no VAT is charged on sales of shares.)

Alarm bells should ring if you are buying a business as a going concern and the vendor tries to charge output VAT. If this is indeed the transfer of a business as a going concern, then the tax charged by the vendor will not be reclaimable by you as input VAT. Only VAT which is properly *chargeable* in the first place can be recovered as input VAT.

Once you are VAT-registered it is vital that you keep a proper record of all your transactions and, in particular, full records of your input and output VAT. Your accountant will be able to guide you on record-keeping systems, and you can also find useful comments in the *General Guide* (Notice 700). You will save yourself much time, bother and money by keeping proper records from the start.

1.12   VAT RETURNS AND RECORDS

In brief, you are required to keep records and accounts of all the taxable outputs you make, which includes your zero-rated outputs, together with details of exempt outputs. They must be up-to-date and sufficiently detailed to allow you to calculate your output and input VAT. Whilst Customs does not require you to keep your records in any particular way, there is a general requirement that your records must be kept in such a form that Customs officers will be able to check your VAT returns. Remember that you will at some time receive a control visit from Customs, probably in your first year of registration, and if your records do not square with your VAT returns you will have some explaining to do. You might even lose some of the input VAT you have already reclaimed. If it turns out that you have failed to charge VAT on some items, even if you innocently thought they were zero-rated or exempt, you will be issued with an assessment for unpaid output VAT and perhaps also interest and penalties.

You are also required to preserve your records and accounts and all related documents for at least three years, unless Customs specifically allows you a shorter period, and you must make your records available for inspection as required from time to time by Customs officers. (At the time of writing it is anticipated that in the near future this period will be increased to six years.)

So long as your records are properly kept, and so long as you follow the directions on completing VAT returns given in the Customs' *General Guide*, completing your VAT returns is straightforward. Normally, a trader is given a three-month VAT accounting period, and that is the period for which you should make up your VAT return. However, it is possible to have a monthly VAT period, so long as you are not voluntarily registered. If you are likely to make a net recovery of VAT for each period you should consider requesting a monthly rather than a quarterly VAT period. You will get your input VAT back more quickly, and so improve your cash flow. Persons who make mostly zero-rated outputs such as builders of new houses or food retailers will be 'repayment traders', and should probably have a monthly VAT accounting period. Whether you have a monthly or quarterly VAT accounting period, you should make sure that it coincides with your annual accounting date. You will make life easier for your accountant if you do.

You are required to have paid your VAT on or before the date by which your VAT return is due. This is the last day of the month following the end of the prescribed accounting period in question. So if your VAT quarter ends on 31 March, you must have submitted your VAT return along with any payment that is due by 30 April at the latest. Failure to make a return is actually a criminal offence at the time of writing, though in practice Customs will issue an estimated assessment for output VAT which should force you to bring your VAT affairs up-to-date. The 1985 Finance Act contains provisions which will 'de-criminalize' many VAT offences, but which will allow Customs to impose an interest charge on VAT paid late, and in addition to impose a 'default surcharge' on persistent late payers. A penalty for 'serious misdeclaration' of VAT can also be imposed in certain circumstances. The best policy is to make prompt and accurate returns.

1.13   ACCOUNTING FOR OUTPUT VAT

On each VAT return you are required to enter your total output VAT for the period. In straightforward cases, this is simply the VAT that you have charged to your customers, and can easily be extracted from your records of invoices issued. If you deal in certain second-hand goods such as cars, caravans, motor cycles, etc. you are subject to special rules, and you should ask Customs for information on the VAT scheme that relates to your particular activity.

If you do not issue tax invoices, but merely keep a record of all your receipts, your total receipts will be treated as your *tax-inclusive* output. In other words, if your month's takings are £1150, all of which relates to outputs which are taxable at the positive rate, Customs will want £150 output VAT for that period. To extract the VAT element from a VAT-inclusive sum you multiply that sum 15/115ths (£1150 × 15/115 = £150). This will leave you with a VAT-exclusive element, on which VAT at 15% is charged (£1000 at 15% = £150).

RETAIL SCHEMES

Special problems arise for retailers who make a variety of outputs, some of which are positive-rated and some of which are zero-rated. A few retailers will make exempt outputs as well. It is often not practical to operate separate tills for different types of output, and even if you operate one till on which you identify positive-rated and zero-rated outputs, mistakes will always occur. Imagine a harrassed shop assistant in a mini-supermarket trying to remember which items of food and drink are positive-rated and which are zero-rated!

To get round these problems a variety of 'retail schemes' exist, full details of which can be had from Customs' guidance notes (*Retail Schemes*, Notice 727). It would be possible to write a chapter on the retail schemes themselves, but the main point to bear in mind is that if you are a retailer who makes multi-rate outputs you should give a great deal of thought to the problem of which scheme to choose for your business. You should certainly *not* accept the scheme that your Customs officer suggests without satisfying yourself that it is the best available scheme for your particular business.

For the purposes of the retail schemes a retailer is a person (who may or may not be a shopkeeper) who deals largely with the public, and, because of the nature of his business, does not issue tax invoices. There are no fewer than nine basic schemes, ranging from the simple to the extremely complex. Moreover, it is possible to negotiate a special scheme with Customs which is unique to your business if you cannot find an existing scheme which gives a satisfactory result.

Whatever scheme you settle on, bear in mind that having chosen a scheme you must operate it for at least one year, and any change in schemes must take place at the anniversary of the start of the scheme. Customs has discretion to vary these dates, but you should not enter into a particular scheme thinking that you can always change it if you do not like the way it works in practice.

Choosing a scheme can require a great deal of arithmetic to work out which will give you the best result. But if your VAT affairs are at all complicated (for instance, if you have several outlets all making a variety of positive-rated, zero-rated and exempt outputs) then selecting the correct scheme is well worth the trouble. It can in fact make a significant difference to your retained profits at the end of the day. To find the correct scheme you should first study Customs' explanations of the schemes and decide which of them *can* apply to your business. You should then calculate the output VAT that you would have had to pay under each of the available schemes for a control period of, say, 12 months. Assuming that your trading pattern is likely to remain constant, the scheme that results in the least output VAT for the trial period is the one that you want.

1.14   HIDDEN SUPPLIES

In calculating your output VAT you must remember that VAT law often treats you as having made a supply on which output VAT should be charged, even though you have received no money for the supply. Barter is a typical example. A mechanic who agrees to service his accountant's car in return for a reduced accountancy fee is making a taxable output equivalent in value to what he would have received had he charged for his services in money. He will have to enter the output VAT on that value on his tax return.

Harsh as it may seem, where you give goods freely, perhaps to relatives or friends, you are also required to account for output VAT on the market value of these supplies. On the other hand, if you make supplies to a connected person for a consideration in money which is less than market value you are not actually required automatically to substitute market value on the supply. Customs can *direct* you to apply VAT on the market value, but there is no obligation on you to do so unless and until you receive such a direction. In very broad terms, a 'connected person' is your spouse, a relative or a relative of your spouse.

Where you supply goods, the general rule is that when goods which have formed part of your business assets are disposed of so that the goods no longer form part of your business assets then you have made a supply of goods whether or not you receive any consideration. So a publican who regularly supplies himself with a pint of beer has made a supply of goods, on which he will have to account for output VAT. There are some minor exceptions to this rule. First, a gift which costs £10 or less will be outside the scope of VAT so long as it is made in the course or furtherance of the business, and so long as it is not a part of a series of gifts to the same person. (Our publican would fail on both counts!) Second, gifts of industrial samples which are in a form not usually available to the general public are outside the scope of VAT.

Free supplies of services do not carry VAT under present rules, except where business assets are put to private use, or where they are made available to any person for any purpose other than a purpose of the business.

1.15   INPUT VAT

Calculating your recoverable input VAT can be every bit as complicated as calculating your output VAT. Again, it is in your interest to get it right, first, to make sure that you are recovering all the input VAT you are entitled to recover, and second to make sure that you are not building up a hidden liability which could lead to a ruinous VAT assessment following a control visit by Customs officers.

In order to be entitled to reclaim input VAT there must be a supply of goods or services to a taxable business, and the supplies must be made for business purposes. It follows that there can be no input VAT recovery for goods and services that are:

- Supplied for private use,
- Supplied for another person's business,
- Supplied for another person, even though the taxable person pays for them,
- Supplied to a business but used in connection with a non-business activity.

Obviously, these rules prevent you from buying assets through your business, and appropriating them for private use without any VAT cost. But what happens where you buy an asset which will be used partly for business and partly for private purposes? The rule is that you can only recover the input VAT which is attributable to business usage. So if you are a computer retailer who uses a computer partly for business demonstrations and partly for personal pleasure, in theory you can only recover a portion of the input VAT. It will be up to you to negotiate a reasonable portion with Customs, though in practice your Customs Officer will not quibble so long as you suggest a fair apportionment. Items commonly requiring an apportionment are telephone bills and repair and maintenance expenditure when a business is conducted from home.

You must also disclaim input VAT credit for petrol which your business has bought and which you put to private or non-business use. Unfortunately, 'private use' includes travel from your home to your normal place of work, and the disallowance of input VAT on petrol in a year can therefore mount up to a significant sum. It is up to you to negotiate a fair percentage with Customs, and you will need to retain your petrol invoices and keep a record of business and non-business travel, as you may well have to justify your claim for input VAT credit.

Where you have employees for whom you supply a car, or for whom you pay for private mileage, the same broad principles apply, and Customs will not allow you to recover input VAT on any portion of petrol. At the time of writing Customs is also investigating the possibility of disallowing a portion of repair and maintenance and leasing costs. With employees the position can be rather more complicated, depending on how you meet motoring costs (i.e. do you pay a mileage allowance, do you reimburse employees for amounts they have paid, or do you pay for all the petrol yourself?). If you are in this category, you should read the Customs' guidance notes carefully (*General Guide*, Notice 700), and apply the rules as closely as you can.

Remember also that input VAT on certain items cannot be recovered, even though they are used wholly for business purposes. In broad terms these include;

- Motor cars (apart from commercial vehicles),

- Accessories installed in motor cars (except when the accessories are not supplied at the same time as the motor car is supplied),
- Business entertainment (apart from entertainment of overseas customers),
- Goods which you have purchased under one of the second-hand schemes,
- For builders, certain materials and articles that are installed in dwellings,
- Certain imported goods.

You can generally reclaim your input VAT on subsistence expenses (meals, accommodation, etc.) which you and your employees have incurred whilst away on business, but again you should read the Customs' *General Guide*, to make sure that you meet the requirements for input tax credit on this item.

1.16   PARTIAL EXEMPTION

Exempt outputs cause headaches since, as a general principle, it is not permitted to reclaim any input VAT which relates to exempt outputs. Any business that makes exempt outputs has a potential, or actual, VAT problem, since the input VAT which cannot be recovered is a true cost to the business. Typically, this affects certain financial service businesses (for example, insurance brokers) and land and property businesses that sell land or reconstructed buildings. But many small traders also make exempt outputs. Rents, for instance, are generally exempt outputs; so if you own a grocer's store and rent out the flat above, you could lose a portion of your total input VAT.

Partial exemption is one of the most complicated areas of VAT practice, and you should certainly seek your accountant's advice if you are making both taxable and exempt outputs. If, for instance, your rents represented a quarter of your total outputs, you could lose a quarter of your input VAT.

Partially exempt traders have no problem so long as their exempt outputs are below any of the following limits;

- Less than £200 per month on average,
- Less than £8000 per month on average and less than 50% of all supplies,
- Less than £16 000 per month on average and less than 25% of all supplies,
- Less than 1% of all supplies.

So long as your exempt outputs are below any of these thresholds you will be treated as fully taxable and entitled to recover all your input VAT. If they are above all these thresholds you have a VAT problem. Given sufficient warning of this situation, your accountant might well be able to help you plan your affairs to minimize the loss of input VAT. There is a great deal more to the partial exemption rules than can be explained here, and, needless to say, the planning points that can help you minimize any loss of input VAT are not discussed in Customs notice on partial exemption (Notice 706).

1.17   CASH FLOW

For fully taxable businesses VAT is not a cost but is merely an accounting headache. Whatever you collect in output tax must be handed over to Customs; whatever you pay in input tax can be recovered from Customs (apart from the input VAT on motor cars and certain other items). But careful timing of supplies can improve cash flow, and cash flow is a vital consideration for new businesses.

VAT returns must be lodged and payments of output VAT made to Customs within one month of the end of your VAT quarter. It follows that if you render an invoice on the first day of your VAT quarter, you will not actually have to pay over the output VAT on that invoice until four months later. Hopefully, you will have received payment within one month of rendering the invoice, so that the collection of output VAT will actually contribute positively to your cash flow. On the other hand, if you render an invoice on the last day of your VAT quarter you will have to pay over the output VAT after one month. If you have not received payment from your customer by that time, you will have to fund the adverse cash flow from your own resources.

Exactly the opposite considerations apply to input VAT. If you are invoiced on the last day of your VAT quarter you need only wait thirty days for credit for the input VAT from Customs. If you are invoiced on the first day of your VAT quarter, you will have to wait four months for credit for input VAT.

Normally, commercial considerations will override the comparatively minor cash-flow advantages that can be derived from timing of inputs and outputs. But where a cash-flow advantage can be gained at no commercial cost, it should obviously be taken. It is important to note, however, that the 'tax point' (broadly, the time at which the supply takes place for VAT purposes) is not necessarily the invoice date. For a supply of goods, the general rule is that the tax points occurs at the earlier of:

- The time of the removal of the goods,
- If the goods are not to be removed, then the time at which they are made available to a customer,
- When payment is received,
- When an invoice is issued.

However, if an invoice is issued within 14 days of any other event that creates a tax point, then, unless you notify Customs in writing that you do not wish this rule to apply, the tax point will be the date of the invoice.

For supplies of services, the general rule is that the supply takes place at the earlier of:

- When the services are performed (i.e. when all the work except invoicing has been completed),
- Payment is received,
- An invoice is issued.

Special rules exist for continuous supplies of services, such as lease rentals, over and above these requirements.

Chapter 2

Pay-As-You-Earn and National Insurance Contributions

2.1 INTRODUCTION

Whether you trade as a sole proprietor, in partnership or as a limited company, if you employ people you have certain financial responsibilities which you must meet. In particular, you will have to deduct tax under the PAYE system from your employees' salaries and account for it to the Collector of Taxes. You must also deduct employees' Class I National Insurance (NI) contributions, and account for these to the Collector. And lastly, you must pay, as employer, your own employer's Class I contributions. (For NI rates see Appendix A.) Directors of companies are employees in tax law, so even if your company employs only you, the company must still comply with its PAYE and NI responsibilities.

All this is a heavy burden in terms of time and effort, but it is vital to get it right. If you fail to collect the full amount of PAYE and NI that is due, the Revenue and DHSS may come to you for the outstanding amount, and not necessarily your employee. The Revenue now conducts PAYE audits, and you will be wise if you make sure that you have applied the PAYE and NI rules to the letter. Fortunately, many accountants can now offer a computerized payroll service, and if you have several employees and no computer facilities, this is probably the easiest and cheapest way of handling the problem, leaving you free to manage your business or to get out and sell.

If you are going to manage your own payroll the first thing to do is get all the relevant literature and study it carefully. This includes the Re-

'The Revenue now conducts PAYE audits, and you will be wise if you make sure that you have applied the PAYE and NI rules to the letter.'

venue's *Employer's Package* and the *Employer's Guide to PAYE*, which are available from any PAYE office. You should also get the DHSS guide to employer's National Insurance contributions, and, if you are trading through a limited company, the DHSS guide to National Insurance contributions for directors. These will explain the procedures for calculating and accounting for PAYE and NI contributions. The following sections therefore deal with the planning points that may save you time and money in meeting your responsibilities as employer.

2.2   WHEN PAYE AND NIC APPLY

There are certain circumstances when you are not required to apply PAYE. Most important, PAYE need not be applied if the rate of pay is less than either £42.40 weekly, or £183.75 monthly, although there is an exception to this rule when new employees come to you without a P45 from their last employer.

Second, there is no need to pay employee's and employer's NI contributions when the pay is less than £35.50 per week, or less than £153.83 per month. The simple planning point which emerges from these rules is that if you would like to employ people, but do not want the administrative problems of PAYE and NI compliance, and particularly do not want the added burden of employer's NI, then you could achieve this by employing part-time staff, all of whose wages are below the PAYE and NI thresholds. As the employer's NI contributions reaches 10.45% (except for those who have contracted out of the state pension scheme), this can be a material consideration. Further planning points emerge from a study of the NI charging structure detailed at Appendix A. Employers' and employees' liabilities from 6 October 1985 start at a flat rate of 5% on earnings over £35.49 and below £55 per week. Thereafter the charge increases by a sliding scale to 9% employees' NI on earnings of over £89.99 and below £265. The employers' charge is 10.45% on earnings over £129.99, but there is no Upper Earnings Limit of £265; the 10.45% charge applies to total earnings in excess of £129.99, no matter how large.

The major planning point is that care should be taken, where possible, not to trigger a higher employees' and employers' NI charge by crossing one of the thresholds in the sliding scale. Even 1p over the threshold could result in a significant additional charge. Better still, in labour-intensive industries, such as retailing or catering, it may be possible to use part-time staff at pay levels below the weekly Lower Earnings Limit.

NI SAVINGS ON PART-TIME STAFF

Bill and Joe are brothers who each operate fast-food franchises. Both franchises are open six evenings each week. For his evening staff, Bill employs three ladies who all work six evenings a week for him. Joe employs six ladies, each of whom works for three evenings a week. Both Bill and Joe pay £10 for an evening's work, and both have three staff on duty each evening. But at the end of the day Joe is better of than Bill.

Bill

Annual wages for evening staff:	£
3 (staff) × 6 (evenings) × 52 (weeks) × £10	9 360
Employer's NIC	
£9360 × 7% (each employee earning £60 p.w.)	655
Total Cost	10 015

Joe

Annual wages for evening staff:

6 (staff × 3 (evenings) × 52 (weeks) × £10	9 360
Employer's NIC (each employee earns £30 p.w.)	NIL
Total Cost	9 360

Joe's staff are paid at a rate below the NI threshold of £35.50 weekly, so he avoids an annual cost of £655 in Employer's NI. In addition, he saves himself the time, worry and costs in operating full PAYE and NI collection procedures. If Joe managed to operate his morning and afternoon trade with part-time staff all paid at a rate below the PAYE and NI thresholds, the annual saving in Employer's NI could amount to several thousand pounds.

Another planning point relates to your spouse. Many self-employed businessmen and company directors pay their wives a salary for assistance in running the business. (Of course, wives can also pay husbands a salary, where it is the wife who runs the business.) This is almost always an allowable tax deduction for the business. It is not difficult to justify a salary of, say, £2000 for answering the telephone, making appointments, helping with administration, etc. Imagine how much you would have to pay a secretary to be always available to answer the telephone. Unless your wife has other earned income of her own, the salary you pay her will be covered by the Wife's Earned Income Relief (currently £2205), and will therefore escape tax altogether. However, it is important to keep this below the PAYE and NI thresholds. First, if you cross the PAYE threshold you will immediately become bogged down in unwanted paperwork imposed by the PAYE rules. More important, as soon as you cross the NI threshold you will trigger a charge to both employees' and employers' NIC, which could make the whole exercise an expensive waste of time. Class I employers' and employees' NI contributions are not charged on the excess of earnings over the NI threshold. They are charged on the *whole* earnings for the earnings period as soon as the earnings exceed the threshold. Watch out for this if you want to avoid making an irritating mistake.

PAYING YOUR SPOUSE

John and Jack both pay their wives for secretarial help in running their businesses. John thinks he will save most tax by paying his wife up to the full amount of the Wife's Earned Income Relief (£2205), so he pays her

£42.40 per week. Jack pays his wife £35 per week.

	John £	Jack £
Tax saved by paying salary to wife		
John: £2205 at 30%	661	
Jack: £1820 at 30%		546
Employee's NIC		
John's Wife: £2205 at 5%	(110)	
Jack's Wife: below threshold		NIL
Employer's NIC		
John: £2205 at 5%	(110)	
Jack: below threshold		NIL
Total Saving	441	546

At the end of the day, Jack has saved £546 by employing his wife, whereas John has only saved £441. John is worse off than Jack by £105 because he failed to bear in mind the NI penalty of paying employees more than the current NI threshold.

2.3   MINIMIZING NATIONAL INSURANCE CONTRIBUTIONS

What other methods can be used to minimize payment of employers' Class I contributions? First, it is noteworthy that 'pay' for NI purposes does not include benefits-in-kind. If, for instance, Jack and John were to pay superannuation contributions on behalf of their wives into a pension scheme they would still get tax relief for the superannuation contributions, and there would be no tax or NI payable in respect of these payments. (Superannuation contributions paid by an employer are not a taxable benefit on the employee.) How much Jack and John could pay in this way would depend on their respective wives' ages, their salaries and the length of time they had each worked for their husbands. Any insurance company or pensions broker would quickly be able to supply illustrative figures. The premium can be a surprisingly high figure in relation to the employee's salary, and in Jack's and John's case could be £100 or more annually. In short, Jack and John could purchase pension provision for their wives, and each save tax on a further £100 of income each year, without incurring any further liability to employers' or employees' Class I contributions. This arrangement has a further attraction. Even when their wives do eventually draw their pensions, they are likely to escape an income tax charge. Their Wife's Earned Income Relief will be available to set against the pension, and should shelter it in full from tax.

There are other methods for minimizing Class I contributions but they are not usually worth the trouble involved, particularly for small businesses. However, the circumstances of some businesses lend themselves to NI planning. National Insurance Class I contributions are calculated according to the employees earnings for an 'earnings period'. In broad terms, an 'earnings period' means the interval for which remuneration is calculated and paid. Thus an employee who is paid weekly has a weekly earnings period, and an employee who is paid monthly has a monthly earnings period. Class I contributions are levied on earnings when they exceed the Lower Earnings Limit for the earnings period. But once earnings exceed the Upper Earnings Limit for the earnings period, Class I contributions are not charged on the excess of earnings over the Upper Earnings Limit. From 6 October 1985, however, there will be no Upper Earnings Limit for employers' Class 1 contributions, and this will create a heavy additional cost for companies with highly paid directors and employees.

The current Class I thresholds are:

Earnings Period	Lower Earnings Limit £	Upper Earnings Limit £
Weekly	35.50	265.00
Monthly	153.83	1 148.33
Annual	1 845.96	13 779.96

It can be possible to structure remuneration so that some of the earnings exceed the Upper Earnings Limit for the earnings period, though after 6 October 1985, when the Upper Earnings Limit for employers' contributions is removed, this will be less effective.

Before leaving the subject of NI earnings periods, some further points are worth emphasizing. The DHSS can in certain circumstances apply a longer earnings period where it thinks that the rules are being manipulated to reduce the NI charge, although it is not able to apply such a direction retrospectively. First, where an employee has two or more pay intervals, the DHSS can direct that the earnings period should be the period relating to the *longest* pay interval, providing that most of an employee's remuneration is paid at the longer pay intervals. Second, if NI is being reduced by 'abnormal' pay practices the DHSS can rule that the employer should calculate NI as though he had followed a pay practice

Using Earnings Periods

John operates a retail motor dealership and he appoints Jim as his service manager at a monthly salary of £666, and an annual bonus, payable in March, of £4000. Jim has a monthly earnings period, so the relevant Upper Earnings Limit is £1148.33.

	£
NI for 11 months from April to February	
Employers' NI: 11 × £666 × 10.45%	765
Employees' NI: 11 × £666 × 9%	659
NI for March	
Employers' NI: 1 × £1 148.33 × 10.45%	120
Employees' NI: 1 × £1 148.33 × 9%	103
Total Employers' and Employees' NIC	1647

If Jim had been remunerated at the rate of £1000 per month his total annual salary would still be £12 000, but the DHSS's share would be much larger:

	£
Employers' NI: 12 × £1000 × 10.45%	1254
Employees' NI: 12 × £1000 × 9%	1080
Total Employers' and Employees' NI	2334

Joe and Jim between them have saved £687 (i.e. £2334 − £1647) by structuring the remuneration package carefully.

which was normal for that particular employment. Third, if the employee has irregular or unequal payments the DHSS can also direct that NI should be calculated as though that practice were not being followed. It is understood that the DHSS is unlikely to make such a direction unless contributions are being avoided on at least 25% of earnings, though this cannot be regarded as a hard and fast rule.

It is important to note that it is not usually possible to use the rules of earnings periods in relation to directors' remuneration, even though a company director will very often be remunerated by a monthly salary and an annual bonus. The DHSS's view is that directors have an annual earnings period, regardless of the intervals at which they draw their remuneration. Directors' remuneration is agreed at the company's annual general meeting, argues the DHSS, so they must have an annual earnings period. However, there is a view that if a director has a contract of employment with his company which determines the amount of payments and their frequency, then the normal rules on earnings periods will apply.

2.4   PAY DIVIDENDS INSTEAD OF SALARY

One method of reducing employers' and employees' Class I NI which can be very effective in certain circumstances is for directors to restrict their salaries below the NI Upper Earnings Limit and to vote themselves a dividend instead of remuneration. A dividend is not remuneration for NI purposes, and although Advance Corporation Tax (ACT) at 3/7ths of the dividend must be paid to the Collector of Taxes shortly after payment of the dividend this does not amount to a tax charge in itself, but is merely an advance payment of Corporation Tax. So long as there is a liability to Mainstream Corporation Tax, against which Advance Corporation Tax can be set, the payment of a dividend will not lead to an additional tax cost. The recipient of a dividend is treated as receiving net income, with an accompanying tax credit of 3/7ths of the net income. In other words, the basic rate tax charge at 30% on the gross dividend will have been met, and no other Income Tax charge will arise unless the recipient is a higher-rate taxpayer.

ACT ON DIVIDENDS

Prosper Ltd has taxable profits of £30 000 in an accounting period during which a dividend of £7000 is paid. On payment of the dividend, ACT of £3000 must be accounted for to the Collector of Taxes. However, Prosper Ltd's MCT liability of £9000 (£30 000 at 30%) is reduced by the £3000 ACT already paid.

ACT up to a maximum of 30% of taxable profits can be set against MCT, but any surplus ACT can be carried back and set against MCT arising in any of the preceding six years. If there is still surplus ACT it can be carried forward and used to reduce MCT of subsequent accounting periods.

Until the 1984 Finance Act the strategy of paying dividends instead of remuneration was less useful. Dividends are investment income, and for 1983/4 and earlier tax years investment income in excess of certain thresholds attracted an additional tax charge at 15% known as 'Investment Income Surcharge'. The rates of Corporation Tax were also higher, and in many cases it was better to draw profits as remuneration in order to reduce profits for Corporation Tax purposes, since the Income Tax charge on the remuneration could be less than the equivalent Corporation Tax charge on profits. With the fall in the rates of Corporation Tax this will now only be true in exceptional circumstances.

Given that there is no tax cost in paying a dividend instead of a salary, the following example shows the possible NI savings.

Paying Dividends Instead of Remuneration
Flourish Ltd and Flounder Ltd are both run by husband-and-wife teams, and in both cases husband and wife each own half the shares. Fourish Ltd pays each director an annual salary of £6000 and a dividend of £7000 (i.e. equivalent to gross investment income of £10 000 each, being net income of £7000 with an accompanying tax credit of £3000). Flounder Ltd pays its directors an annual salary of £13 000 each. The respective NI charges are:

		Flourish Ltd £	Flounder Ltd £
Husband's Salary			
Employers' NI:	£ 6 000 at 10.45%	627	–
	£13 000 at 10.45%	–	1358
Employees' NI:	£ 6 000 at 9%	540	–
	£13 000 at 9%	–	1170
Wife's Salaries			
Employers' NI:	£ 6 000 at 10.45%	627	–
	£13 000 at 10.45%	–	1358
Employees' NI:	£ 6 000 at 9%	540	–
	£13 000 at 9%	–	1170
Total Class I NIC		2334	5056

Flourish Ltd saves Class I contributions of £2722 annually (£5056 less £2334) by paying a dividend instead of paying a salary.

This technique is usually not quite as straightforward as it looks in the above example, and directors wishing to use it should certainly talk to their accountants first. You have to be sure, first, that the ACT on the dividends can be readily set against MCT. You also need to know that the charge to Corporation Tax on profits is not more than any Income Tax and National Insurance charge on director's remuneration. If it is, it will obviously be better to receive a bonus rather than a dividend, since the Income Tax charge on the bonus will be more than offset by the fall in Corporation Tax as a result of paying the bonus.

There is also a Capital Transfer Tax implication which needs to be considered. Capital Transfer Tax, very broadly, is levied on transfers of value by individuals, where the transfers are in excess of certain limits. Gifts of shares are transfers of value which might well attract Capital Transfer Tax, so anything which affects the value of an individual's shares must be considered in the context of his overall Capital Transfer Tax position. Valuing shares of unquoted companies for the purposes of Capital Transfer Tax can be very complicated, and will usually involve lengthy negotiations with the Capital Taxes Office. One measure of value is the dividend yield of private company shares. Obviously, the Capital Taxes Office will look at a company's dividend record, and if there is a consistent record of large dividend payments the value of the shares is very likely to be increased for Capital Transfer Tax purposes.

This will only be a problem for a few family companies, particularly where the shareholders are wealthy individuals in their own right. Even then it will not usually be insurmountable. Nevertheless Capital Transfer Tax aspects certainly need to be considered before embarking on such an exercise.

2.5   SELF-EMPLOYED LABOUR

There is one other method for minimizing NI costs which is so important that it merits a section of its own — using self-employed labour. When you employ someone, you have a responsibility to deduct employees' Class I contributions from earnings and account for them to the DHSS. You also must pay over your own employers' Class I contributions. Quite apart from the administrative burdens you have acquired by becoming an employer, you have also incurred an additional cost in the form of employers' Class I contributions. Worse still, you have also taken on the responsibility of calculating and collecting PAYE from his salary, accounting for it to the Collector of Taxes and submitting year-end PAYE returns.

The simple way round this is not to employ anyone but to contract out work to self-employed labour. Self-employed persons are, in general, responsible for their own tax and NI affairs. They must lodge their own returns of profits on which Income Tax and Class 4 NI are calculated. They are responsible for buying their own Class 2 NI stamps. If they fail to meet their responsibilities that is their problem, not yours. (But note that special rules apply to building industry subcontractors and to certain workers supplied by agencies.)

Unfortunately, this technique can only apply in certain limited circumstances. It is not enough for you and your subcontractor to tell the Revenue that there is no employer/employee relationship. The Inspector will want to be satisfied that in hard fact the contract between you does not amount to a contract of employment. Not surprisingly, Inspectors are becoming harder to persuade on this point, as so much tax and NI is at stake. Not only will the DHSS lose employers' Class I contributions if self-employment is established; the Revenue is also likely to lose significant amounts of Income Tax.

The reason lies in the different tax rules that apply to income from employment, known as Schedule E earnings, and self-employed earnings, taxed under the rules of Schedule D Case I. The Taxes Acts are much more restrictive in the allowable deductions from earnings from employment than they are for deductions from self-employed earnings. The broad rule is that expenses which are incurred 'wholly and exclusively' for the purposes of a trade or profession can be deducted in arriving at the taxable profits of that trade or profession. For income from employment the rule is much harsher; the expenses have to be incurred 'wholly, exclusively *and necessarily*' for the purposes of fulfilling the contract of employment before they can be relieved for tax. Needless to say, there has been a great deal of case law on what expenses can be relieved under these rules, and the courts have tended to pursue a strict line in relation to allowable Schedule E expenses.

The essential difference between allowable expenses for trading profits and allowable expenses for earnings from employment is that expenses incurred in the course of one's employment can only be allowable if they necessarily result from the conduct of that employment. The Inspector will want to be satisfied that *anyone* fulfilling the duties of that particular employment would necessarily incur those expenses before he will be prepared to allow them. For expenses incurred in the course of trading it is only necessary to demonstrate that they have been incurred wholly and exclusively for the purposes of that trade. The fact that a different person operating that trade might have chosen not to incur the particular expenses in question is immaterial. The following example is a broad illustration of how much tax and NI can be at stake in any argument over employed/self-employed status.

EMPLOYMENT VERSUS SELF-EMPLOYMENT

Fred is a freelance engineer who works from home, and has agreed to a one year's contract with an oil company to oversee and quality test work on a construction site. He spends approximately seven hours each day on-site and one to two hours at home each evening on paperwork. His rumuneration is £1400 per month. (See opposite page.)

There is an overall annual saving of Income Tax and NI of £2622 if self-employed status for John can be achieved. (John's employer would probably receive tax relief for the employer's Class I contributions, which would reduce their cost by perhaps 40%. Taking account of this, the overall tax and NI saving would be £1920 — still well worth having.)

2.6   HALLMARKS OF SELF-EMPLOYMENT

Not surprisingly, tax inspectors will fight very hard nowadays to establish

	Schedule E (Employed) £	Schedule D (Self-employed) £
Total remuneration for 12 months	16 800	16 800
Less: Subscription to Professional Association	(80)	(80)
Stationery, postage, etc.	—	(140)
Telephone	—	(140)
Car Expenses	—	(400)
Capital allowances on car	—	(400)
Taxable Income	16 720	15 640
Less: Personal Allowance	3 455	3 455
	13 265	12 185
Tax at 30%	3 979	3 655
NI		
Employers' Class I NI £16 800 at 10.45%	1 756	—
Employees' Class I NI £13 780 at 9%	1 240	—
Self-employed Class II NI £3.50 × 52	—	182
Self-employed Class IV NI (£13 780–£4150) at 6.3%		607
Income Tax Relief on 50% of Class 4 (50% × £607) × 30%	—	(91)
Total Tax and NIC	6 975	4 353

that there is a contract of service which amounts to a contract of employment, rather than a contract for the services of a self-employed person. This argument has gone before the courts on many occasions, and several hallmarks of self-employment have emerged. There are still many marginal cases, however, and businesses should take advice as to what measures would help to create self-employed status for their subcontractors. Where doubt still exists, it could be a good idea to seek a ruling from your tax inspector. A recent Inland Revenue pamphlet (IR56) is available to help differentiate between employment and self-employment. If, in reality, there is a contract of employment it is better to know about it sooner rather than later, before a large liability to PAYE and Class I NI has built up. Self-employed contractors should also do what they can to preserve their self-employed status, otherwise many of their business expenses could be disallowed in calculating their Income Tax liabilities.

In strict law, there are actually two classes of employed persons: first, a person who is treated as an employed earner for the purposes of paying Class I NI, and second, an employee who, for Income Tax purposes, is subject to the rules of Schedule E. Fortunately, in practice, a ruling on a person's status for Income Tax purposes will almost always settle the question of his status for NI purposes. The following points have been derived from case law.

- Employees are under a contract *of* service; self-employed persons are subject to a contract *for* services. It does not matter if the contract is written or oral, and it is the true substance of the contract which matters. Thus a written contract *for* services would not be conclusive evidence of self-employment if the underlying facts and relationships demonstrated that a contract *of* service existed. As one judge said: 'If the true relationship of the parties is that of master and servant under a contract of service the parties cannot alter the truth of that relationship by putting a different label on it.'

  A written agreement can still be of value, however, particularly if the facts are ambiguous and do not point to an obvious conclusion.
- A contract of service will exist where the 'employee' agrees that in return for a wage or other remuneration he will provide his own work and skill in the performance of a service. At the same time he agrees, either expressly or by implication, that in performing that service he will be subject to supervision and control, or at least that there will be a *right* of supervision and control.
- There is unlikely to be a contract of service where the services of a subcontractor are called upon only from time to time and there is no obligation on anyone's part to provide him with work, and at the same time there is no obligation on his part to accept work which is offered to him. (In one case, casual waitresses who assisted occasionally at banquets were held to be self-employed because on each occasion they were free to decline the work, and in between engagements the caterer had no obligation to provide them with work. On each engagement there was a separate contract for services.)
- As a general rule, when a person can be told what to do, when to do it, where to do it and how to do it, he will be an employee subject to a contract of service. However, if a person cannot be directed in this way, that does not necessarily demonstrate that he is self-employed. A

surgeon, for example, could be employed by a health board, but the board would never attempt to tell him when or how to operate.

- If the services which the person is performing are an integral part of the services which the business itself is set up to perform, he is more likely to be employed. A cook who works for a restaurateur is likely to be employed, but a caterer who provides services, say to an assembly plant is more likely to be self-employed.
- Someone who provides his own equipment and hires his own helpers is more likely to be self-employed.
- Someone who takes a financial risk, and who can improve the profitability of his services by his own skill, effort and sound management, is more likely to be self-employed.
- Someone who is not committed to working fixed hours is more likely to be self-employed.
- Someone who is not paid during illness or holidays is more likely to be self-employed.
- Someone who is not required to give *personal* service but can delegate his duties to others or supply a substitute is more likely to be self-employed.

It must be stressed that these are broad indications of self-employment, and, taken by themselves, are not necessarily conclusive. It is, of course, very important that your contractor understands and accepts that he is self-employed. Problems often arise where someone is dismissed, and subsequently claims that he is an employee who has been unfairly dismissed. Occasionally, a person who has been treated as self-employed runs into financial problems through illness, and complains to the DHSS that he has not received Statutory Sick Pay as an employee. More often, an Inland revenue PAYE audit raises the problem. In all these situations a written contract for services which bears some or all of the hallmarks of self-employment will be a valuable defence, though, at the end of the day, it is the underlying facts which matter.

2.7   CASUAL EMPLOYEES AND PAYE

One quick way to fall foul of the PAYE system is to employ casual workers for short periods, and, because their wages are below the PAYE and NI thresholds, to pay them gross of tax and NI. Whenever you take on casual workers it is vital to your own interests that you apply proper PAYE procedure, as laid down in Inland revenue pamphlet P7 (*The Employer's Guide to PAYE*), otherwise you could end up paying someone else's tax and NI.

'One quick way to fall foul of the PAYE system is to emply casual workers for short periods and . . . pay them gross of tax and NI.'

When a new employee is taken on, for whatever length of time, you must ask for his P45. If he can produce this, you will know what PAYE code to apply, and it is a simple matter to follow the instructions on Part 2 of the P45 itself. However, very often a casual worker will not be able to produce a P45. If the employment is for one week or less and the total pay in the week is more than the PAYE threshold, you must apply PAYE using the emergency code. If you know that the employee has other employment, you are required to deduct tax at the basic rate (30%) from the entire pay — whether your employee likes it or not! Should the pay be less than the PAYE threshold you must keep a record of the employee's name, address and amount of pay, but you are not required to apply PAYE.

A separate procedure must be followed where form P45 is not produced, and the period of employment is for more than one week and either the pay is more than the PAYE threshold or the employee had other employment. In this case you must:

● Complete form P46 and send it to the tax office immediately.

- Issue a coding claim form P15 to the employee.
- Apply PAYE to wages in accordance with para. 98 of *The Employer's Guide to PAYE*.

Where the pay is less than the PAYE threshold, and the employee certifies that this is his only or main employment, you must retain the certified form P46, and keep a record of the employee's name, address and amount of pay. Lastly, remember that in all cases where the pay is above the NI threshold but below the PAYE threshold you must still account for employers' and employees' Class I contributions, even though there may be no requirement to apply PAYE.

Where the casual employee is a student employed during the vacation it may not be necessary to deduct PAYE. Provided the student signs a form P38(S) at the commencement of the employment then the employer need only prepare a Deductions Working Sheet for recording Class I contributions if the lower threshold is exceeded. The completed forms P38(S) are forwarded with the other end of year returns to the tax office.

Employers can be sorely tempted to ignore these compliance requirements where casual labour is concerned, partly because of the administrative burden, and often partly because of resistance from the workers themselves. But it is much better in the long term to apply the system as rigorously as possible. The alternative could be to build up a hidden tax and NI liability which could crystallize at a crucial stage in the business's development.

Chapter 3

The First Year: Income Tax Planning for the First Year of Self-Employment

3.1 BASIS OF ASSESSMENT

Nowhere do the cracks and strains in the UK's ramshackle tax system show through more clearly than in the taxation of new businesses. The rules are excessively complicated, but, on the whole, they are designed to encourage rather than discourage new businesses, and it is possible with planning and foresight to produce useful tax savings at critical times in the development of a business. It can even be possible to contribute positively to business cash flow by skillful use of certain tax reliefs. Taxation can, in fact, be a help rather than a hindrance to enterprise. Before discussing the tax planning aspects of the first year of self-employment it is necessary to leave the real world for a short time and enter the Byzantine world of tax rules on trading profits of unincorporated businesses.

To begin with, the general rule is that trading profits which are earned in a tax year are treated as taxable income of the following tax year. In practice, this means that the profits for an accounting year which ends in a given tax year form the basis of the tax assessment for the following tax year. The tax year is the year to 5 April. The year from 6 April 1985 to 5th April 1986 is the tax year 1985/6, and so on. It follows that profits for the accounting year to, say, 30 June 1985 will be taxed as income of 1986/7. (Though special rules apply on commencement or cessation of a trade, or when there is a change of accounting date.)

One useful planning point follows from this 'preceding-year' basis of assessment. Other things being equal, it is better to have an annual accounting date which is just after 5 April rather than just before 5 April. (But as we will see, in the first year of trading there can be a benefit in choosing an accounting date before 5 April.) From a purely practical point of view both you and your accountant will be under far less time-pressure to produce accounts for a business with a 30 April year-end than for a business with a 31 March year-end. Accounts for the year to 30 April 1985 will form the basis of the 1986/7 Income Tax assessment. If the accounting year-end was 31 March, on the other hand, the 1986/7 assessment would be based on the profit for the year to 31 March 1986. In other words, a 30 April year-end gives almost a full year's additional time to prepare accounts and agree taxable profits with the Inspector. This can actually save you money. With a 31 March year-end your accountant, with the best will in the world, may not be able to agree your tax liabilities before the Inspector starts to issue estimated tax assessments. Estimated assessments will have to be appealed and often postponements of tax must be requested. All this takes time and trouble, and could well add to your accountancy fee.

More important, a 30 April year-end gives you advance warning of your tax position for a year of assessment. If you have very low taxable profits for a tax year, or even a tax loss, you will have time to plan your financial affairs to maximum advantage. You might wish to restructure investments to create more income, for example. On the other hand, if you have unexpectedly high profits which you know will attract higher rates of tax you will have time to take steps to minimize investment income, or to invest in tax shelters such as the Business Expansion Scheme.

The due dates for payment of Income Tax also encourage the adoption of a post–5 April accounting date. Regardless of your accounting date, Income Tax and Class 4 NI are paid in two equal instalments; the first on 1 January in the tax year for which the profits are assessed and the second on 1 July following the end of the tax year for which the profits are assessed. Thus, profits for the accounting year to 31 December 1985 will be taxed as income of the following tax year, i.e. 1986/7. The tax and Class 4 NI will be due in two equal instalments; the first on 1 January 1987 and the second on 1 July 1987.

Quite apart from allowing you extra time to plan your cash flow in order to meet the tax payments on the due dates there is a greater delay in paying tax on profits with a 30 April year-end. Where profits are rising, as they generally will be in a new business, a 30 April year-end will therefore contribute positively to cash flow by causing a longer time-lag between earning profits and paying tax on the profits.

Choice of Accounting Date
Alec and Douglas both operate hamburger franchises in
Birmingham city centre. Alec's year-end is 31 March and
Douglas's year-end is 30 April. In their accounting year ending
in 1985 both have experienced bumper profits, and their
accountants tell them that their taxable profits are £35 000
each. They are also told that the total tax and NI liabilities on
those profits, after deducting all available reliefs and personal
allownces, will be approximately £12 000.

	Alec *Year to 31 March 1985*	*Douglas* *Year to 30 April 1985*
Taxable Profits	£35 000	£35 000
Year in which profits are assessed	1985/86	1986/87
Tax and NI payable	£12 000	£12 000
Due dates for payment:		
1 January 1986	£ 6 000	—
1 July 1986	£ 6 000	—
1 January 1987	—	£ 6 000
1 July 1987	—	£ 6 000

CHOICE OF ACCOUNTING DATE

Douglas's 30 April year-end allows him an additional 12-month delay in
paying Income Tax and NI on his bumper profits. He has also more time
to plan his affairs for 1986/7, and assuming his profits will attract Income
Tax at 55% he could consider paying further retirement annuity premiums
for 1986/7, or perhaps speculating in a Business Expansion Scheme investment in order to reduce his top rate of tax. As their accounts are not
finalized until late August 1985 the tax year 1985/6 is well progressed
before Alec even knows what his taxable profits for that year will be.

In reality, Douglas would probably suffer less Income Tax than Alec as
well as enjoying a greater time-lag before payment. Personal allowances
and higher-rate tax bands tend to be increased in each budget so that
Douglas' taxable income and the rates of tax applicable to it will probably
both be less than Alec's.

As a general rule it is better to get the accounting date settled in the first set of accounts. Whilst it is perfectly feasible to change the annual accounting date at a later stage this will result in some rather complicated tax calculations to arrive at your taxable profits, and may lead to revisions of assessments for earlier years.

3.2 TAXING THE FIRST TWELVE MONTHS

The standard 'preceding-year' basis of assessment can be difficult to understand at first sight, but it is simplicity itself in comparison with the rules for taxing a start-up enterprise. Special rules are needed since, obviously, a start-up business cannot be taxed on profits earned in the preceding year. The solution can lead to some complicated calculations, particularly when a tax loss is incurred in the first year. At the same time, it offers several valuable tax-saving opportunities for those who are aware of the rules and who take the trouble to plan their tax position in advance.

Remembering that Income Tax is charged for each tax year, taxable profits for the first three tax years of a start-up business are taxed as follows.

- For the first tax year the taxable profit is the profit earned in the period from the commencement of trade up to the following 5 April.
- For the second tax year the taxable profit is that of the first twelve-months' trading.
- For the third tax year the taxable profits, generally, are *again* the profit of the first twelve-months' trading. However, if there is a complete accounting period of twelve months which ends in the second tax year then it will be possible for the Revenue to apply the normal preceding-year basis to the third year of assessment (i.e. the profits of the third tax year will be those of the twelve-month accounting period ending in the second tax year).

Thereafter, the Revenue will be able to apply the preceding-year basis since, unless there is a change of accounting date, each tax year will contain a twelve-month accounting period, which will form the basis of the following year's tax assessment.

The Revenue arrive at taxable profits for years of assessment by time-apportioning the profits of each accounting period rather than by looking at when the profits actually arose. This practice, together with the rules on taxing profits in the first three tax years, can have some curious results.

The following broad principles emerge from these examples.

Taxing the First Twelve Months

(a) Joe starts trading as a butcher on 1 October 1984. He chooses a 30 April accounting date, and makes up his first set of accounts for the seven-month period to 30 April 1985. He has taxable profits for that period of £3000. For the year to 30 April 1986 he has taxable profits of £15 000. His tax assessments are calculated like this:

Tax year	Basis Period		Assessments
		£	
1984/5	1 Oct. 1984–5 April 1985		
	6/7 * × £3 000		2 571
1985/6	1 Oct. 1984–30 Sept. 1985		
	7/7 × £ 3 000	3 000	
	5/12 × £15 000	6 250	
		‾‾‾	
			9 250
1986/7	As for 1985/6		9 250
	Total Assessments		21 071

* This calculation is on a month-by-month basis, whereas in practice the Revenue would apportion the profits on a day-by-day basis.

(b) Joe's brother Jim starts trading as a baker, also on 1 October 1984. He has exactly the same profit pattern as Joe. However, he makes up his first set of accounts for the nineteen-month period to 30 April 1986. In that period his taxable profits are £18 000, but his tax assessments are as follows:

Tax Year	Basis Period	Assessments
		£
1984/5	1 Oct. 1984–5 April 1985	
	6/19 × £18 000	5 684
1985/6	1 Oct. 1984–30 Sept. 1985	
	12/19 × £18 000	11 368
1986/7	As above (first twelve months again as there is no twelve-month accounting period ending in the preceding year)	11 368
	Total assessments	28 420

Joe suffers tax on additional income of £7349 (i.e. £28 420 less £21 071), although he saves the accountancy fee for preparing a set of accounts to 30 April 1985.

- Where profits rise consistently from commencement a twelve-month initial accounting period gives the lowest taxable profit for the first three years of assessment. It ensures that taxable profits for the first twelve months are not increased by being averaged with higher profits arising after that period.
- Subject to the special rules discussed later in Section 3.6, in the unusual situation where profits fall in a start-up business the first accounting period should be longer than twelve months, and ideally should continue to the point when profits start to rise again. (Though obviously it is not practical or wise to extend this accounting period for too long.) This will ensure that the taxable profits of the first twelve months are reduced as far as possible by being averaged with profits that arise after the first twelve months of trading.
- Where profits fluctuate monthly (or quarterly) from commencement there are no overall guidelines, and it could be necessary to calculate arithmetically the optimum accounting date by trial and error. Businesses producing monthly management accounts will be in an ideal position to do so.

In practice, tax considerations are only one aspect of the choice of accounting date, although with new businesses the choice of accounting date can sometimes lead to worthwhile tax savings. It may be possible to make an educated guess at quarterly or even monthly profits from turnover figures. Your accountant may be able to help you with this by preparing regular computerized management accounts, and profits predictions, making it possible to tailor your accounting dates to achieve the best tax results.

Of course, you should never become obsessed with minimizing tax at any cost. For most businesses, particularly small ventures, an educated guess at the optimum accounting date, bearing in mind other practical and commercial considerations, is all that is required. You would not thank your accountant for applying his expensive technical skills, only to save you trivial amounts of tax.

3.3 START OF TRADING

It is clearly important that the Inspector of Taxes accepts the date on which you started to trade if you are to plan your tax affairs with any certainty. In most cases there will be no practical difficulties on this, and the Inspector will accept that the start of your first accounting period was when you began to trade.

However, if the income is derived from a part-time activity, and is small in amount, the Inspector might try to take the view that you are not trading at all, but are merely deriving income from a hobby or a casual activity. In this case he would apply the tax rules of Schedule D Case VI to the income, instead of the rules of Schedule D Case I, with the possible result that fewer expenses would be allowed as tax deductions. You would also be denied the favourable rules for taxing the first three tax years of a new business, and, perhaps most importantly, if any losses arose their utilization against other income would be severely restricted.

The Inspector might also choose to treat the income as trading income as soon as the activity became profitable, thereby inflating the tax assessments for the first three tax years.

Fortunately, there is a body of case law which can be invoked to prevent the Inspector making arbitrary decisions about the date of commencement of trading. At the end of the day, it is the facts that count in determining when you started trading. In very broad terms, a 'trade' is a venture conducted systematically with a view to profit, and the courts have evolved several 'badges of trade' which indicate that there is a trade in existence. Not all of the 'badges of trade' have to be present, but the more 'badges of trade' that mark your activity, the more likely it is to be a trade. Very often, only one of the 'badges of trade' needs to be present to demonstrate that trading exists.

'BADGES OF TRADE'

- *Profit-seeking Motive*: Where an asset is purchased with a view to resale at a profit, there is strong evidence of trading. However, an asset such as a picture or an antique might be bought also for the pleasure it gives, and in this case trading is less likely to exist.
- *Nature and Quantity of the Asset*: Some commodities by their very nature and quantity are unsuitable for personal use. In this case they are likely to be purchased for a trading purpose.
- *Way in which Assets are Acquired*: Someone who inherits a property and later sells it at a profit is unlikely to be trading. Someone who researches the property market, buys a property and then sells at a profit probably is trading.
- *Work on an Asset*: If work is carried out on an asset in order to make it more marketable, there is evidence of trading.
- *Length of Ownership*: If an asset is held only for a short time before resale, it is more likely to be sold in the course of a trade.
- *Number of Transactions*: Where a transaction is one of a series of methodically conducted transactions, there is strong evidence of trading.
- *Similar Trading Interests or Expertise*: Where a profit is made on a

transaction and the seller already conducts a similar trade, there is an indication that the profit is a trading profit.

● *Finance*: If a purchaser borrows money to make a purchase in circumstances where he will have to sell the asset to repay the loan, there is an indication that he is trading.

Whether a trade exists or not is a matter of fact, to be determined by the above tests. Inspectors tend to argue against the existence of trading where there is a part-time activity that results in a loss. Remember that it is the facts that matter and if the facts support you, it should be possible to resist the Inspector successfully.

3.4 MINIMIZING TAX LIABILITIES IN THE FIRST THREE TAX YEARS

We have seen that the trading profit of the first twelve months can form the basis of taxable profits for the first three tax years of a new venture. It follows that a low profit figure for the first twelve months is an excellent thing as far as taxation is concerned. Of course, you cannot manipulate your profit figure to achieve the best tax result. And in any case cash flow and commercial considerations are, as a general rule, at least as important as taxation. A start-up businessman will want to generate as much income as he can in his opening period of account, just as he would in any other period.

Fortunately, there are several ways of securing a lower profit figure for your first year whilst still trading with a view to maximizing income. The underlying principle is to squeeze as much revenue expenditure into your opening period as possible (subject to cash-flow requirements, of course) so that it can be relieved for tax two or three times, instead of just once. The following suggestions can all be useful in certain circumstances, but they are by no means exhaustive. You could equally well come up with planning possibilities suited to your particular venture once you appreciate the underlying principles.

EMPLOY YOUR SPOUSE OR PROSPECTIVE BUSINESS PARTNER FOR THE FIRST TWELVE MONTHS

If you are intending to trade in partnership with your spouse you can achieve worthwhile tax savings by employing him/her in the business in the first year. In fact this strategy can be applied in any situation where a new business will be run in partnership: it does not have to be a prospective husband-and-wife partnership, though in practice that is the

Employing your Spouse

Two couples — Steve and Linda and Bob and Anne — start trading as market gardeners on 1 October 1984, and make up their first set of accounts to 30 September 1985. They have a fair first year, and their accounts show a trading profit of £32 000. They share profits equally so the total taxable income for the first three years is calculated as follows:

1984/5	Total £	Steve £	Linda £	Bob £	Anne £
6/12 × £32 000	16 000	4 000	4 000	4 000	4 000
1895/86 First 12 months	32 000	8 000	8 000	8 000	8 000
1986/87 First 12 months	32 000	8 000	8 000	8 000	8 000
Total	80 000	20 000	20 000	20 000	20 000

If, instead, three of the individuals had agreed to be employed by the fourth for the first twelve months on a salary amounting to £8000 each — equivalent to their share of the first year's trading profit — a substantial sum would fall out of tax. In broad terms, the taxable profits for the first twelve months would fall to £8000 (i.e. £32 000 less three salaries of £8000 each), and a total taxable income would now be calculated like this.

1984/5	Total £	Steve £	Linda £	Bob £	Anne £
Salaries 1.10.84–5.4.85	12 000	—	4 000	4 000	4 000
Profits 6.4.85–30.9.85	4 000	4 000	—	—	—
1985/6 Salaries 6.4.85–30.9.85	12 000	—	4 000	4 000	4 000
Profits First 12 months*	8 000	5 000	1 000	1 000	1 000
1986/7 Salaries	—	—	—	—	—
Profits: First 12 months	8 000	2 000	2 000	2 000	2 000
Total	44 000	11 000	11 000	11 000	11 000

The total amount of taxable income has fallen by £36 000, resulting in a very worthwhile tax saving of £10 800 (i.e. £36 000 at 30%).

* Steve is entitled to 100% of profits in the first half of 1985/6. Thereafter Linda, Bob and Anne join him as equal partners. They each are entitled to a quarter of the profits in the second half of 1985/6.

situation in which this strategy is used most easily.

Partnerships are taxed on the trading profits of the partnership for each tax year. For example, the trading profits of Able, Baker & Co. for the year to 30 April 1985 form the taxable profits of 1986/7 on the normal preceding year basis. The taxable profits for 1986/7 are allocated between Able and Baker according to their profit-sharing ratios for the tax year 1986/7. (The fact that Able and Baker might have had entirely different profit-sharing ratios in the year to 30 April 1985 when the profits were actually earned is entirely irrelevant as far as the Revenue is concerned). The full trading profits of Able, Baker & Co. are taxed as income, whether or not the profits are actually drawn by the proprietors. Looked at another way, partners' or sole proprietors' drawings are not allowable deductions from taxable profits.

Employees' salaries are treated altogether differently. The cost of employing someone is an allowable expense which is incurred in the course of trading, and it therefore reduces taxable profits. Of course, the salary will itself be taxed as income under the rules of Schedule E, but it will be taxed only once. In a commencing business the salary cost can be relieved between two and three times, depending on the date of the commencement of trading and the choice of accounting date. It follows that if, for example, you employ your wife for the first year, and then bring her in as a partner, the cost of employing her can be relieved between two and three times for tax, whereas her salary will be taxed only once. As a further refinement, it is generally possible to purchase pension rights for an employee, and have these fully relieved for tax. You could consider purchasing pension rights for your wife whilst she is your employee during the first year of business. The employer's pension contribution could thus be relieved between two and three times for tax, so that its true cost would be reduced by perhaps 70% or 80%.

Needless to say, matters are rarely so simple in practice, and anyone thinking of adopting this strategy should talk to their accountant well in advance. In reality, employing someone will lead to a tax penalty in the form of Employers' Class 1 contributions. At the same time, the Employees' Class I contributions might well be higher than the equivalent charge to Class 4 and Class 2 contributions on self-employed earnings. You should be sure that the tax saving at the end of the day will more than match the National Insurance penalties of following this route. There is no substitute to doing the arithmetic in each case before deciding on a course of action.

The second danger point is that there must be a genuine contract of employment in force, whether written or oral, in the first year. Clearly, it will be better if it is written rather than oral, but it is also important that the underlying facts support the contention that certain individuals are

'If you are intending to trade in partnership with your spouse, you can achieve whorthwhile tax savings by employing him/her in the business in the first year.'

subject to a contract of employment rather than in partnership. In section 3.3 we looked at ways of establishing self-employed status; we are now concerned with demonstrating the existence of employment. Exactly the same considerations apply, though the Revenue has had such success in extending the case law tests of employment that it is easier as a general rule to establish employment than self-employment. It is worth stressing again that at the end of the day it is the underlying facts that count. If, in the above example, Linda, Bob and Anne act as equal partners during their period of 'employment' the Revenue could argue that they were never employed in the first place. In practice, there is little likelihood of this happening *so long as good advice is taken throughout*. Provided the groundwork is properly laid, there should be few difficulties in establishing the existence of employment in the first twelve months, and the existence of partnership thereafter. A formal partnership agreement should be signed evidencing the existence of the new partnership, just as a written contract of employment should be in force prior to the commencement of the partnership.

CONSIDER LEASING ASSETS INSTEAD OF PURCHASE

The various planning points on asset finance are dealt with later in section

4.11 and the remarks in this section relate only to the possibilities of using leasing finance to reduce the taxable profits of the first twelve months of trading. You can buy an asset outright, either by paying for it out of available cash, by borrowing or by using some form of instalment credit such as hire purchase. In all of these cases you are entitled to capital allowances on the asset so long as it is plant and machinery which will be used in your trade. However, capital expenditure can be relieved only once under the capital allowances system (discussed in section 4), and, depending on the amount of expenditure that qualifies for tax relief through 'first-year allowances', it can take several years for the bulk of the expenditure to be relieved. In fact, for expenditure incurred after 31 March 1986 no first-year allowances will be available whatsoever. Instead, an annual writing-down allowance of 25% of the residue of unrelieved expenditure will be given. In practice, it will take some eight or nine years for the bulk of expenditure to be relieved under this system.

The alternative to purchase is leasing. A lease is simply an agreement to pay for the use of an asset — a rent, in other words — for a specified period. There is no option to purchase the goods, and the capital

---

Leasing Assets in the First Twelve Months

Eileen commenced trading on 1 July 1984 as a retail florist. She leases a new van under a two-year lease, paying quarterly rentals with two rentals in advance. The quarterly rentals are £600, exclusive of VAT. In her first year of trading she therefore pays five rentals, totalling £3000. Her first year's profit, before deducting the lease rentals, is £9000. Eileen's leasing expenditure of £3000 reduces her taxable profits for the first three years of her business by £8250, calculated like this:

Year		Profit (before rentals) £		Profit (after rentals) £
1984/5 9/12 × £9000		6 750	9/12 × £6000	4 500
1985/6 First 12 months		9 000		6 000
1986/7 First 12 months		9 000		6 000
Total		24 750		16 500

The leasing expenditure in the first year had, in effect, been relieved for tax nearly three times over, which, assuming that Eileen is a basic-rate taxpayer, reduces the true cost of the leasing expenditure in her first twelve months to a trivial sum. Had Eileen bought the van outright, or used a hire-purchase scheme, the capital expenditure would have been relieved only once.

allowances go to the lessor (the owner of the equipment). The lessor in turn reflects the benefit of capital allowances in the form of reduced rentals charged to the lessee (the user of the equipment). For tax purposes, lease rentals are treated as a revenue cost rather than as capital expenditure, and they are an allowable trading expense. Whereas capital expenditure can be relieved only once through the capital allowances system, revenue expenditure in the first year of trading, as we have seen, can be relieved between two and three times. Apart from certain cash-flow benefits that leasing can offer, therefore, it can also be a very tax-efficient method of asset finance in start-up businesses. To squeeze the maximum benefit from this strategy it can be beneficial to front-load the lease payments by paying, say, rentals quarterly in advance instead of monthly in advance, or by offering the leasing company six months advance rentals, followed by monthly rentals. This will reduce the leasing charges, and will also keep the leasing company happy. After all, the larger the advance payments the lower the risk as far as the leasing company is concerned. A proposal to front-load the lease rentals might even make the difference between having your application accepted or rejected by a leasing company. Of course, cash flow planning is at least as important as tax planning, and front-loading of lease rentals should only be considered if it can be accommodated within your cash-flow requirements.

USE OVERDRAFT FACILITIES INSTEAD OF TERM LOANS

Getting the right balance of credit facilities for your business is more important than tax planning. But it can pay to remember that overdraft interest is a business cost incurred in the course of trading, and is therefore an allowable cost for tax purposes. In the first year of trading, therefore, it will be relieved several times over.

There are circumstances where you can plan your credit needs to take maximum advantage of this fact, though, obviously, you should not strain your bank manager's patience by using your overdraft for business expenditure that should properly be financed by a structured term loan.

3.5   PRE-TRADING EXPENDITURE

Tax planning begins before you even start trading. In practice, persons who are planning a new venture will incur some expenditure before trading starts — accountants' fees for preparing a business plan, travel costs for inspecting premises, costs of decorating premises, etc. It is only in recent years that such pre-trading revenue expenditure has benefited from tax relief, and there are some restrictions to the relief which are worth noting.

- The expenditure must be incurred for the purposes of a trade before the point at which you actually begin to conduct the trade.
- The expenditure must be incurred not more than three years before that point.
- The expenditure must be incurred after 1 April 1980.
- The expenditure must be revenue expenditure which would have been allowable for tax purposes had it been incurred after trading had commenced.

If your pre-trading revenue expenditure meets these criteria, then tax relief is available. (Pre-trading capital expenditure on plant and machinery can qualify for capital allowances under separate rules discussed in Section 4.3.)

Contrary to what one might expect, the relief is not given by deducting the expenditure from the trading profit, or by using it to increase the trading loss of the first accounting period. Presumably, this is to prevent such expenditure from being relieved for tax two or three times under the taxation rules for commencing trades. Instead, the expenditure must be treated as a tax loss incurred on the day trading commences. There are a variety of methods of utilizing this loss to maximum advantage, as discussed in Chapter 5. Its proper use can significantly help business finances in the first year. The immediate practical point is that as far as possible you should plan your essential pre-trading expenditure so that it meets the necessary criteria to qualify as a tax loss.

3.6   OPTION TO REVISE FIRST THREE TAX YEARS TO 'ACTUAL BASIS'

As we have seen, the first twelve months' profits generally determine the tax assessments for the first three tax years in the life of a business. Most often this is to the taxpayer's advantage, as profits in new businesses are usually on a rising trend. Where profits are rising, it is obviously better to have the profits of the first twelve months taxed several times over.

But what if profits fall after the first twelve months? In this case, the conventional rules would be to the taxpayer's disadvantage, as the higher profit of the first twelve months would be taxed several times over. With such a profit profile, the conventional rules would actually inflate the tax liabilities of a new business, and could cause it serious cash-flow difficulties. The tax liabilities on the larger first-year profits could become due when profits were falling and there was a scarcity of cash flow to meet the liabilities.

Fortunately, it is possible to elect for a different basis of assessment to be applied for the first three tax years which largely solves this problem. The taxpayer can choose that the tax assessments for the first three tax years are based on the actual profits earned in those years. In the fourth year, the normal 'preceding-year' basis of assessment applies, just as it does with the usual rules for taxing new businesses.

The election must be made in writing to the Inspector, and it must be lodged within six years of the end of the third year of assessment. In Ted's case, therefore, it must be lodged by 5 April 1993 (i.e. six years after 5 April 1987). This gives ample time for a decision to be made as to whether the election would be beneficial.

Opting for Profits to be Taxed on 'Actual Basis'
Ted starts trading as an antique dealer on 1 May 1984. His first year's profits are particularly good, due to the sale of a valuable painting which he picked up for a song. Thereafter his profits level out.

Period	Profit
Year to 30 April 1985	£20 000
Year to 30 April 1986	£10 000
Year to 30 April 1987	£10 000

On the usual rules for new businesses, Ted's tax assessments for his first three tax years (1984/5, 1985/6, 1986/7) are based on the following periods.

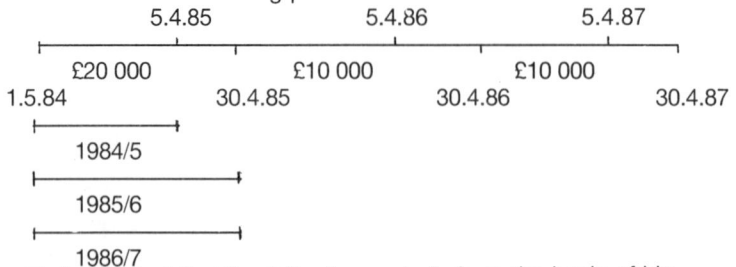

Ted can elect that the following periods form the basis of his first three years' tax assessments.

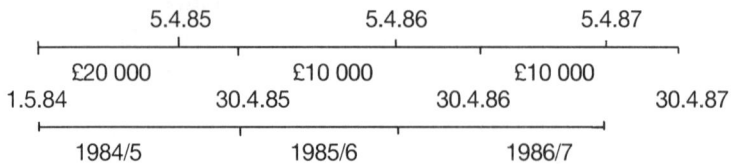

This leads to greatly reduced tax liabilities for Ted, calculated like this:

Year	Normal Basis £				Actual Basis £
1984/5 11/12 × £20 000	18 333	11/12 × £20 000			18 333
1985/6 First 12 months	20 000	1/12 × £20 000	£1667		
		11/12 × £10 000	9166		
					10 833
1986/7 First 12 months	20 000	1/12 × £10 000	£ 834		
		11/12 × £10 000	9166		
					10 000
Total	58 333				39 166

The election reduces Ted's total taxable profits for his first three tax years by £19 167 (i.e. £58 333 less £39 166) which in round terms represents a tax saving to Ted of £5750 — well worth having!

It must be remembered that the election can also affect the basis periods in which capital allowances for expenditure on plant and machinery and industrial buildings fall. Moreover, it is conceivable in some cases that reducing the overall amount of taxable income by electing for the 'actual basis' will not reduce the overall amount of tax payable. The effect of personal allowances and other reliefs for each tax year have to be considered, as do the Income Tax rates that apply to income for each tax year. An election should therefore only be considered in the context of your overall tax situation.

Chapter 4

Capital Allowances

4.1 INTRODUCTION

Trading expenses are known as 'revenue expenditure', and are generally an allowable deduction from profits for tax purposes. They are distinguished from capital items because they are incurred on a recurring basis as costs that naturally arise in conducting the trade. 'Capital expenditure' means, broadly, expenditure that is incurred *in order* that the trade can be carried on. The purchase of premises or fixed assets such as plant and machinery are items of capital expenditure, whereas recurring expenditure on, say, trading stock, repairs and maintenance, car running expenses, etc. are revenue items. Certain types of capital expenditure can benefit from tax relief through the system of capital allowances, most notably expenditure on plant and machinery which will be used in the trade, expenditure on certain industrial buildings, expenditure on agricultural buildings and works and expenditure on certain hotel buildings.

4.2 BASIS PERIODS FOR CAPITAL ALLOWANCES

Whereas the profits of an accounting period can form the basis period for several years of assessment, thereby relieving revenue expenditure two or three times over, the basis periods for capital allowances never overlap. It follows that capital expenditure can be relieved only once. However, it is possible to advance the timing of the relief by appreciating how capital-allowance basis periods operate and so improve cash flow. In certain cases it is possible to plan capital expenditure so that maximum relief is squeezed out of the remaining accelerated first-year allowances

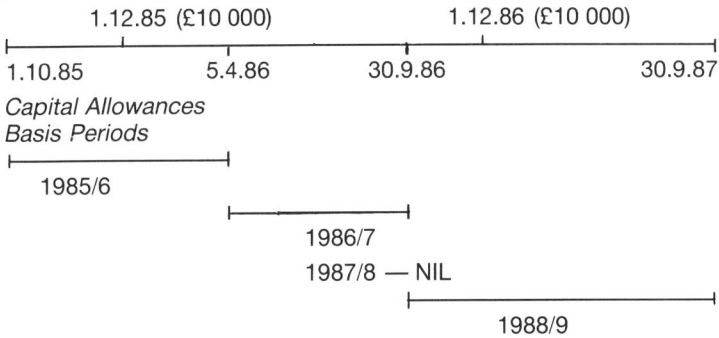

Capital Allowances in Early Years
John starts a van-hire business on 1 October 1985, and invests
£10 000 in new vans on 1 December 1985 and 1 December 1986.
He makes up accounts to 30 September annually. The basis
periods for capital allowances are as follows:

The expenditure of £10 000 on 1 December 1985 starts to
create capital allowances from 1985/6. The expenditure on
1 December 1986 does not start to create capital allowances
until 1988/9.

that are available following the phasing out of first-year allowances by the
1984 Finance Act.

For unincorporated businesses the broad rule is that capital allowances
are given for years of assessment and that each year of assessment has a
capital-allowances basis period. The capital expenditure incurred in that
basis period, or the pool of unrelieved capital expenditure which exists in
that basis period, will generate capital allowances for the relevant year of
assessment. Normally, the basis period for a year of assessment is simply
the accounting period which forms the taxable profits of that year of
assessment. For example, annual accounts made up to 30 April 1985 will
form the basis period for the 1986/7 year of assessment. Capital expenditure incurred in the year to 30 April 1985 will therefore yield capital
allowances to set against taxable profits for 1986/7.

But what happens with new businesses where the first twelve months
forms the basis period for up to three years of assessment? The rule is that
capital expenditure is only relieved once, and in commencing businesses
it is relieved in the first year of assessment into which basis period it falls.
The planning point to note is that expenditure incurred by 5 April
following the commencement of trading will start to generate capital
allowances in the first year of assessment; expenditure incurred in the
first twelve months, but after 5 April following the start of trading, will
start to generate capital allowances in the second year of assessment; but

expenditure incurred immediately after the first twelve months will not create capital allowances until the fourth year of assessment. Of course, you must balance this advantage against any commercial disadvantage of bringing forward your capital expenditure to fall in your first twelve months, but, other things being equal, it is better to incur capital expenditure within the first twelve months, rather than after.

Where the basis periods overlap, the rule for commencing trades is that expenditure will fall into the earliest possible basis period. So if the expenditure of £10 000 had been incurred on, say, 30 September 1986 it would start to create capital allowances from 1986/7.

Assuming that capital allowances on plant and machinery are available at only 25% of the residue of expenditure annually (as they will be after 31 March 1986), the following example illustrates the advantages of careful timing of expenditure.

The advantages of timing are less obvious for limited companies. Capital allowances are simply given for the accounting periods in which the expenditure is incurred. As a general rule, it is still better to incur

---

Timing of Capital Expenditure

Bob starts to trade as a self-employed farmer on 1 January 1986. By December 1986 he is ready to invest in a new combine at a cost of £24 000. If he purchases it in December 1986, he will secure capital allowances of £13 875 by 1988/9. If he purchases in January 1987 only one month later, he will only have secured capital allowances of £6000 by 1988/9.

		Capital Allowances	
Year	Basis Period	Purchase Dec. 1986 £	Purchase Jan. 1987 £
1985/6	1.1.86–5.4.86	NIL	NIL
1986/7	1.1.86–31.12.86 £24 000 at 25%	6 000	NIL
1987/8	1.1.86–31.12.86 £18 000 at 25% (i.e. £24 000 less £6000)	4 500	NIL
1988/9	1.1.87–31.12.87 £13 500 at 25% (i.e. £18 000 less £4500)	3375	£24 000 at 25% 6 000
Total Allowances		13 875	6000

In both cases Bob will get full tax relief for his combine, but by incurring the expenditure just before 31 December 1986, rather than just after, he has accelerated his tax relief and so improved his cash flow.

expenditure just before, rather than just after, the year-end in order to accelerate capital allowances. But with the abolition of first-year allowances and the fall in Corporation Tax rates this is no longer such an important consideration. However, Corporation Tax rates are still falling for companies with taxable profits in excess of £100 000 (see Appendix D), and it will still be beneficial to incur expenditure before 31 March 1986 in order that the capital allowances can be relieved at the highest rate possible.

4.3   PRE-TRADING CAPITAL EXPENDITURE

Just as pre-trading revenue expenses can be relieved for tax so can pre-trading capital expenditure on qualifying plant and machinery. The expenditure is simply treated as being incurred on the day trading commences. For unincorporated businesses, therefore, such expenditure will create capital allowances from the first year of assessment. For limited companies it will create capital allowances to set against taxable profits of the first and subsequent accounting periods.

Very often, plant and machinery is purchased and used for private purposes, and then becomes an asset of the business once trading begins — motor cars are the prime example. In this situation, first-year allowances will not be available even if the assets are of a kind which would otherwise qualify for first-year allowances. But the Inspector will allow annual 25% writing-down allowances based on the market value of the asset at the start of business.

4.4   PLANT AND MACHINERY

'Plant and Machinery' means, broadly, any asset which has an active role in the trade. In deciding whether you have purchased qualifying plant and machinery it is therefore at least as important to ask yourself 'What is the nature of my trade?' as it is to ask 'What is the nature of the asset?' Usually, there will be no problem in deciding whether the asset you have bought qualifies for plant and machinery allowances. If you are opening a restaurant, for instance, the tables, chairs, ovens, grills, etc. all have an active part to play in the conduct of your trade, and will all qualify for capital allowances. But will expenditure on pictures, murals and the like qualify for allowances?

The answer is yes, perhaps. Scottish and Newcastle Breweries Ltd successfully argued in the House of Lords that in its tied premises such items could count as plant and machinery. Customers came to enjoy the

'Plant and machinery means, broadly, any asset which has an active role in the trade.'

ambience of its hotels and restaurants, and not merely the food and drink. Pictures, statues and murals contributed actively to the trade, therefore, as market research had proven.

This is not to say that such items will always qualify for plant and machinery allowances; but they may do, depending on the nature of the trade, and their role in the conduct of the trade. The principle which emerged from the Scottish and Newcastle case can be applied to all manner of trades, and demonstrates that the concept of 'plant and machinery' is much wider than appears at first sight.

Having decided that you have indeed invested in qualifying plant and machinery, what allowances are available? Expenditure incurred on or before 31 March 1986 qualifies for a 50% first-year allowance, with the balance of expenditure being relieved by a 25% annual writing-down allowance. For expenditure incurred after 31 March 1986 no first-year allowances whatsoever are available. Instead, the expenditure will be relieved solely by annual 25% writing-down allowances. Moreover, the writing-down allowances are given on what is known as the 'reducing-balance' method: it is not 25% of the original expenditure that is relieved each year but 25% of the residue of unrelieved expenditure. In other words, a £24 000 machine (see section 4.2) will get £6000 of allowances in year one (£24 000 at 25%), £4500 of allowances in year two (£18 000 at 25%), and so on. The effect will be that it will take up to eight or nine years to get the bulk of plant and machinery expenditure relieved for tax.

Securing the 50% first-year allowance can considerably help cash flow, therefore, as the following example shows.

Maximizing First-year Allowances

Smith & Sons Ltd and Jones & Sons Ltd are both coach-tour operators making up their accounts to 30 April. Both have identified a requirement to purchase a luxury coach costing £48 000 before their year-end on 30 April 1986. Smiths' buy theirs on 15 March, and Jones' buy theirs on 15 April.

Year to 30 April 1986	*Smith & Sons Ltd*		*Jones & Sons Ltd*
First-year	£		£
Allowances:			
£48 000 at 50%	24 000		NIL
Writing Down			
Allowances:	NIL	£48 000 at 25%	12 000
Total Allowances	24 000		12 000

Smith & Sons Ltd have greatly accelerated their tax relief on capital expenditure by good timing.

4.5 INDUSTRIAL BUILDINGS ALLOWANCES

The tax system also allows relief for expenditure incurred on constructing certain new industrial buildings. These include buildings used for the purpose of a trade consisting of;

- The manufacture or processing of goods or materials,
- Maintaining or repairing goods or materials (but not where the goods are to be used by the person maintaining or repairing them in a non-qualifying trade),
- The storage of raw materials for manufacture, goods to be processed, goods manufactured or processed but not yet delivered to any purchaser, goods on arrival by sea or air into the UK,
- Agricultural contracting on land not occupied by the trader,
- A trade carried on in a mill or factory or other similar premise,
- Certain public utility, bridge or tunnel undertakings.

Buildings in use for the welfare of workers employed in qualifying trades, or as sports pavilions for workers in any trades, also enjoy relief.

In practice, difficulties can often arise over whether or not a particular activity counts as a qualifying trade, and as there can be a great deal of tax relief at stake, good advice should be sought at an early stage — preferably at the planning stage — to ensure that maximum tax reliefs are secured.

The relief is given to persons who incur expenditure on constructing *new* industrial buildings, or who buy a new and unused industrial building. The full cost of the expenditure, apart from the cost of the land, can be relieved. Present rules allow an initial allowance of 25% of cost, together with an annual writing-down allowance of 4% of cost. Unlike the writing-down allowance for plant and machinery, this allowance is 4% of the original cost (i.e. 'straight-line' depreciation). However, from 1 April 1986 the initial allowance will be abolished altogether and only the 4% annual writing-down allowance will be available. It will therefore take twenty-five years for expenditure to be fully relieved, whereas current rules allow expenditure to be relieved within nineteen years, with 29% of it (i.e. the 25% initial allowance plus 4% writing-down allowance) being relieved in year one. So far as commercial realities permit, therefore, expenditure on new industrial buildings should be incurred before 31 March 1986, rather than after. Stage-payments made before 31 March 1986 will also benefit in full from the 25% initial allowance. However, if tax mitigation is one of the reasons for making the stage-payment, then complicated anti-avoidance rules come into play to neutralize the tax advantage.

Maximizing Industrial Buildings Allowances
AB Ltd and CD Ltd are both electrical components manufacturers, making up their accounts to 30 April. In the year to 30 April 1986 both incur £50 000 expenditure on new industrial buildings, but AB Ltd incurs the expenditure before 31 March, whereas CD Ltd incurs the expenditure after 31 March.

	Capital Allowances	
Year to 30 April 1986	*AB Ltd* £	*CD Ltd* £
Initial Allowance £50 000 at 25%	12 500	NIL
Writing Down Allowance £50 000 at 4%	2 000	2 000
Total	14 500	2 000

By good timing, AB Ltd has accelerated relief on £12 500 of expenditure into year one.

In most cases an industrial building such as a factory will include office space. On modern industrial estates, the office complex and factory space are often parts of one building, and are not physically separate. In this situation capital allowances will be available on the entire costs of construction *provided* that the costs relating to the part which is not in use for qualifying industrial purposes does not exceed 25% of the cost of the whole building. Obviously, this point should be considered carefully at the design stage — it could be an expensive mistake to step over the 25% limit.

Capital allowances can also be had for the purchase of certain used industrial buildings, though the detailed rules are beyond the scope of this book. Where there is a choice of suitable used industrial buildings, the tax consequences of each option will be an important — perhaps decisive — consideration, and you should certainly seek your accountant's or lawyer's advice on this before concluding a purchase.

What allowances are available will depend on several factors, including the use to which the building was put before it was purchased, the time at which the building was constructed, the original cost of the building and the sale proceeds. If the building is more than twenty-five years old it is possible that no relief whatsoever will be available, and even if relief is available it will be restricted to the original cost of the building regardless of the price it fetches on sale. But where capital allowances can be had on the purchase of a used industrial building, it will generally be secured much more quickly than the period of twenty-five years that will be required to secure relief on new industrial buildings after 31 March 1986.

Commercial considerations are vital in the choice of whether to build a tailormade unit or to purchase an existing unit, and in the choice of which existing unit to buy. But tax considerations can also be important. In constructing or purchasing a new unit, the correct timing of expenditure can considerably help cash flow. In purchasing a used unit the tax consequences can range from there being no allowances available to allowances being available on the bulk of the expenditure and relief being granted within two or three years of the purchase.

4.6 AGRICULTURAL BUILDINGS ALLOWANCES

Currently, expenditure on agricultural buildings and agricultural works such as fencing and drainage, benefits from an initial allowance of 20% and an annual writing-down allowance of 10%. Expenditure can therefore be written off within eight years, i.e. 30% in year one and 10% for each of the remaining seven years. From 1 April 1986, however, the initial allowance will be withdrawn altogether, and the writing-down allowance will be reduced to 4%. As far as possible, expenditure on agricultural works should be timed to fall on or before 31 March 1986.

'Financial costs are more easily calculated by means of a computer program than manually.'

4.7   HOTELS

Capital allowances are available for hotel construction provided;

- The construction is of permanent buildings,
- The hotel is open for at least four months during April–October,
- It has at least ten letting bedrooms,
- It offers sleeping accommodation consisting wholly or mainly of letting bedrooms,
- Its services normally include providing breakfast and evening meals, making beds and tidying rooms.

These conditions must be satisfied in the period of twelve months ending on the last day of the taxpayer's basis period, or chargeable period for a company. Provided all these conditions are satisfied, an initial allowance of 20% is available, and an annual writing-down allowance of 4%. However, the initial allowance will be withdrawn for expenditure incurred after 31 March 1986, so careful timing of expenditure can contribute usefully to cash flow.

4.8 KNOW-HOW AND PATENT RIGHTS

Capital payments for 'know-how' can also benefit from tax relief. Broadly, 'know-how' includes information or techniques likely to assist in the manufacturing or processing of goods or materials, or in the working of oil-wells or mineral deposits, or in the conduct of agricultural, forestry or fishing operations. Current rules allow such expenditure to be written off evenly over six years. After 31 March 1986 a 25% annual writing-down allowance will be available.

The current rules allow the capital cost of patent rights to be written off evenly over seventeen years. As with know-how, relief will only be given by 25% annual writing-down allowances from 1 April 1986.

4.9 WHEN EXPENDITURE IS 'INCURRED'

Incurring your capital expenditure at the right time is obviously crucial, and you should take professional advice on this if the amounts are material. The 1985 Finance Act has defined when expenditure is incurred, and the rules are broadly as follows.

● Normally, expenditure is incurred when the obligation to pay becomes unconditional, even though the expenditure is not required to be paid until a later date.
● Where any expenditure is required to be paid at a date which is later than three months after the date on which the obligation to pay became unconditional, then the expenditure is treated as having been incurred on the date by which it is required to be paid.
● Where an obligation to pay becomes unconditional at a date which is earlier than that which accords with normal commercial usage, and the main benefit is to cause the expenditure to fall in an earlier period for tax purposes, then the expenditure will be treated as having been incurred on the date by which it is required to be paid.

4.10 ENTERPRISE ZONES

Provided your business is not sensitive to location, there are important benefits to locating in an Enterprise Zone. Most importantly, an immediate tax write-off (i.e. 100% initial allowance) is available for construction of *all* commercial and industrial buildings, including retail shops and offices. This represents a powerful inducement to locate in an Enterprise

Zone if at all possible. A company paying Corporation Tax at, say, 30% which constructs an office costing £100 000 in an Enterprise Zone will reduce its tax liabilities by £30 000. The true cost of the building therefore falls to £70 000. Other concessions in Enterprise Zones include;

- Exemption from Development Land Tax,
- Exemption from local authority rates, but not water rates, on industrial and commercial property,
- Acceleration of applications for 'inward processing relief' and certain other customs clearances,
- A much-simplified planning regime (i.e. developments that conform with the zone's published scheme do not require individual planning permission, and those that do not conform are given priority treatment),
- Exemption from industrial training levies for employers in sectors covered by industrial training boards,
- More speedy administration of remaining controls,
- Reduction in government demand for statistical information.

Details of Enterprise Zones are available from the Department of Trade and Industry, and local enterprise agencies will be pleased to supply further information. A list of Enterprise Zones is included in Part IV.

4.11 ASSET FINANCE

One financial problem facing new businesses is the question of asset finance. Having secured access to working capital, perhaps by a secured term loan for long-term capital needs, or by equity finance for limited companies, and having negotiated overdraft limits for short-term credit needs, there is still the problem of deciding how best to finance the acquisition of equipment to be used in the trade. Your objectives are to leave your existing credit lines as undisturbed as far as possible, to maximize your tax relief and to optimize your cash flow. Unfortunately, these are often competing objectives, and the final decision might well require a trade-off between them.

You might be able to finance equipment by using cash reserves or your overdraft facility, but it may not be a good idea to do so. Your cash reserves and short-term credit lines are needed as essential working capital, to help you through periods of bad cash flow. You might also need working capital to help you time sales and purchase of assets and stock to suit market conditions. So unless your business is particularly cash-rich, it can be a bad idea to tie up capital for the medium term which is needed to absorb short-term cash-flow fluctuations.

Equipment purchase is an investment of between two to seven or eight years, and what is needed is a medium-term financial tool which is tailored to fit the working life of the equipment. Despite the bewildering variety of finance plans offered by banks and finance houses, there are two basic types of medium-term finance schemes — leasing and hire purchase. Which you will choose depends largely on your tax position and on your cash-flow requirements.

Under a hire-purchase contract it is the user of the equipment who is entitled to the capital allowances on the equipment. Moreover, he is entitled to the allowances straightaway, including a first-year allowance at 50% if the equipment is purchased before 1 April 1986, even though he will pay for the equipment over a period of years, and will not legally own the equipment until he exercises his option to purchase the equipment at the end of the contract. The VAT on the cost of the equipment can also be recovered immediately, whilst the interest element in the hire charges can be relieved for tax as the charges arise. Exactly the same tax treatment applies to other types of deferred-purchase contracts, such as 'credit sale' or 'conditional sale', where at the end of the day the user of the equipment ends up owning it.

The crucial difference between a hire-purchase agreement and a leasing agreement is that with hire-purchase the user of the equipment ends up owning it. With leasing, the user of the equipment (the lessee) has no option to purchase, and instead pays lease rentals until the cost of the equipment has been met and the owner of the equipment (the lessor) has taken his profit. This does not mean that the user must do better under a hire-purchase agreement. All that he wants is an unrestricted right to use the equipment, and to get his share of any money which the equipment might eventually fetch on sale or trade-in. So long as the user gets what he wants, it should not matter to him whether he is ever the legal owner of the goods.

Because the lessee never owns the goods, as a general rule it is the lessor who benefits from the capital allowances, and whose tax liabilities are reduced as a result of purchasing the equipment. True, the lessor will suffer tax on the lease rentals as they come in, but in the meantime he has deferred his tax liabilities and so in effect has an interest-free loan from the Inland Revenue towards the cost of the equipment. Competition between lessors forces them to pass on the benefit of this tax relief to lessees in the form of reduced rentals.

Lease rentals are treated as revenue expenditure (see Section 4.1) and can be relieved for tax as they arise. The VAT on the rentals can also be recovered. In one way or another, therefore, the full costs of both leasing and hire purchase are tax-allowable. So which is preferable?

As a broad rule of thumb, hire purchase is better where the business-man has enough taxable income to absorb the first-year allowances within roughly two to three years. If it will take longer than that, it is probably preferable to lease and to get the benefit of the lessor's tax allowances in the form of reduced rentals. But remember the point made in section 3.4. In the first year of a business, lease rentals can be relieved for tax between two and three times, whereas capital allowances under hire-purchase agreements can only be relieved once. Apart from this, leasing has particular cash-flow advantages which can be important in a new busi-ness, since the benefit of tax allowances is passed on straightaway in the form of reduced rentals. For very large transactions it will be desirable to work out exactly which method gives the best result at the end of the day. But in most cases commonsense is the best guide, backed up by advice from your accountant, who will know your tax position.

Having decided what type of contract you want, you still have to shop around to get the best deal available. Unless you have a good existing relationship with a finance house, you are not likely to be offered the sharpest rate at first, and you may be able to reduce the rates on offer, particularly if you can demonstrate a good track record in the use of instalment credit. A business plan showing cash-flow projections will also be helpful if it indicates that there will be a sufficient cash flow to fund the repayments.

Hire-purchase terms vary widely, according to length of contract, amount of deposit and frequency of instalments, and the only practical way of comparing like with like is to ask for the APR (Annual Percentage Rate) being quoted. Leasing terms are generally quoted in terms of an amount of rental per £1000 of cost. There is no equivalent measurement to APR for leasing, because the lessor's yield will depend on his specific tax situation. To compare like with like, you must make sure that the quotes are based on the same investment with exactly the same rental profile. In other words, you should not compare a lease with rentals quarterly in advance with a lease which has rentals, say, monthly in arrears.

Many banks and finance houses are seeking to extend their leasing investment before first-year allowances are withdrawn, and there will therefore be downward pressure on leasing rates in the lead-up to 31 March 1986. The best rates will therefore tend to be available nearer 31 March, and on the longer contracts under which the leasing companies benefit from the falling rates of Corporation Tax on the lease rentals.

However, it is not just the cost of finance that should be negotiated. Ask yourself if the contract suits your cash-flow plans. Are you being asked to pay too much too soon? If your business is seasonal, could the payments be geared to suit your seasonal cash flow? With leasing contracts, are you entitled to the bulk of any proceeds from the eventual sale of the asset as a 'rebate of rentals', or could you negotiate a larger share? How much are the 'secondary period' rentals you will be asked to pay once you have met all the lease rentals in the 'primary period'? The leasing company will have made its profit by this time, so any 'secondary period' rentals should be trivial. Make sure that they are! Lastly, find out what penalties you would suffer if the contract is terminated early. Early termination penalties can be fearsome, and if pressurized, lessors may be willing to negotiate on early settlement terms for the larger contracts. Even if they are not, at the very least you should know what you are letting yourself in for should it turn out that the equipment must be sold early.

Chapter 5

Tax Losses

5.1   WHAT IS A TAX LOSS?

New businesses very often make losses in their early months. They may even trade at a loss for their first year or two. There is nothing wrong with this necessarily, so long as it is anticipated in the business plan and in the cash-flow forecasts. Indeed, a new business that trades profitably from the very beginning is unusual. In any event, a trading loss is not the same thing as a tax loss. Various adjustments have to be made to the profit and loss account before arriving at a profit or loss for tax purposes, and at the end of the day the tax loss might be very different from the trading loss. A trading profit might even become a tax loss, or vice versa. Capital allowances can also be used to increase losses, or even to convert a trading profit into a tax loss.

The important point for new business is that a tax loss is a valuable asset, which can in effect be converted into cash and so used to boost cash flow. For unincorporated traders and partnerships there is in fact a bewildering variety of ways in which the loss can be cashed-in with the Revenue. There can be literally dozens of routes to follow in realizing this asset. Choose the right route and you can significantly boost your cash flow; choose the wrong route and the value of the loss can be largely dissipated.

In broad terms, there are three main options for unincorporated traders, although, as we will see, there are sub-options within each main option.

- Tax losses can be set against profits of the same trade, either by carry-forward or, in commencing periods, by aggregation with profits made in the same chargeable basis period.
- Tax losses can be set sideways against other income of the trader and

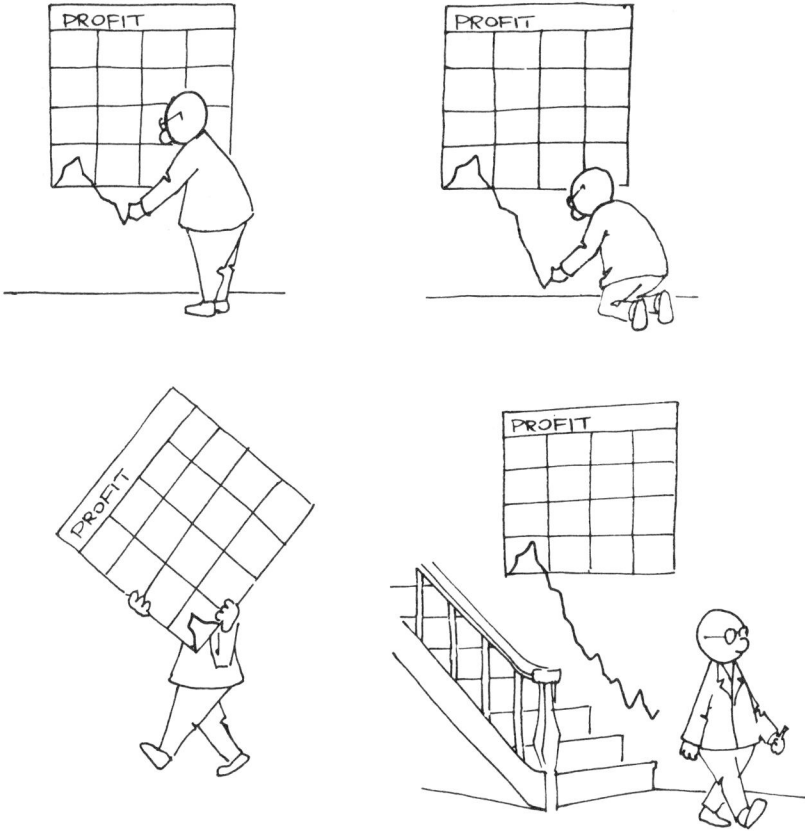

'New businesses very often make losses in their early months.'

his/her spouse in the tax year in which the loss was incurred and in the following tax year.
● Tax losses in the first four tax years can be carried-back and set against other income of the trader and his/her spouses of the three tax years preceding the year of the loss.

The following is an outline of the main choices, although in practice the use of tax losses in the early years of a trade can be very complicated indeed, and will certainly need careful consideration by your accountant.

5.2   USE OF LOSS AGAINST TRADING INCOME

The carry-forward of a trading loss for set-off against subsequent trading income is usually the simplest option, but not always the most effective.

Carry-Forward of Tax Loss

Jim and his wife trade in partnership. In their year to 31 December 1985 they incur a tax loss of £2000 and capital allowances of £1000 leading to a total tax loss of £3000. In their year to 31 December 1986 they make a profit of £10 000 and have capital allowances of £1000 again.

Year	Basis Period		Assessment £
1986/7	1.1.85–31.12.85		
	(Loss of £3000)		NIL
1987/8	1.1.86–31.12.86: Profits	£10 000	
	Capital allowances	(1 000)	
		£ 9 000	
	Less: Loss brought forward	(3 000)	
			6000

Where a loss is carried forward, it must be set against the first trading profits that subsequently arise. Moreover, the full loss must be set against subsequent trading profits. It is not possible to choose to set a portion of the loss against one year's profits and to carry forward the balance to a subsequent year.

Very often with loss claims a portion of tax losses is wasted because it is set against income which would be covered by personal allowances or other reliefs in any case. As the Married Man's allowance is currently £3455, and Wife's Earned Income Relief £2205, this can lead to total wasted allowances of £5660 in a tax year, representing wasted tax relief of £1698 (i.e. £5660 at 30%). So far as possible therefore, tax planning for loss relief should set tax losses only against income that would otherwise suffer tax. One method of achieving this, whether losses are being carried forward, set sideways or carried back, is to disclaim some or all of the capital allowances for a chargeable basis period. Just because capital allowances are available does not mean that they must be claimed. It is possible to claim any amount of capital allowances, up to the full amount of capital allowances available. Where capital allowances are not claimed, the amount that is not claimed increases the pool of unrelieved capital expenditure which can benefit from capital allowances.

Another general point to nore with loss-relief planning, again whether

Disclaiming Capital Allowances

Brian has a bad year and for his accounting period to 31 December 1985 he makes a profit of only £4500. For the same period he has capital allowances available of £1500. Apart from his Married Man's Allowance of £3455, he has loan interest to pay of £1000 annually which qualifies for tax relief. If Brian claims capital allowances of £1500 for 1986/7 a portion of his tax reliefs will be completely wasted. Instead, Brian claims only £45 of capital allowances, which gives optimum tax relief, without any waste of tax allowances.

	1986/7 (without CA disclaimer)		1986/7 (with CA disclaimer)	
	£	£	£	£
Profits (year to 31.12.85)		4500		4500
Less: Capital Allowances		1500		45
		3000		4455
Less: Loan interest	1000		1000	
Married Man's Allowance	3455		3455	
		4455		4455
Taxable Income		NIL		NIL
Wasted tax reliefs (4455–3000)		1455		NIL

By disclaiming capital allowances of £1455, Brian ensures that he eventually gets relief on this sum, rather than wasting it altogether — a simple way to save tax of £436 (i.e. £1455 at 30%).

losses are being carried forward, set sideways or carried back, is that any amount of the Married Man's Allowance which is not used can be transferred to the wife and set against her income. However, any amount of Wife's Earned Income Relief which is not used cannot be transferred to the husband and set against his income — one of the many oddities of UK taxation which helps to keep tax advisers busy. In the example above, Brian could have claimed full capital allowances and allowed the surplus personal allowances of £1455 to be transferred to his wife, thereby reducing her tax liability for 1986/7 by £436. But this would only have been worthwhile if his wife had sufficient taxable income to absorb the transferred allowances. If it had been Brian's wife, rather than Brian, who was trading, it would not be possible to transfer her unutilized wife's earned income relief to Brian.

'When no response to third letter, pass the account with full details to your lawyer.'

The broad principle which emerges is that capital allowances should not be claimed if that will lead to wasted tax reliefs. This does not mean only a waste of personal allowances; relief for qualifying loan interest and for retirement annuity premiums can also be wasted by excessive claims.

5.3   COMPLICATIONS IN EARLY YEARS OF TRADE

Special rules apply to tax losses incurred in the early years of trading. In the examples in section 5.2 the loss for an accounting period was treated as the loss for the tax year for which that accounting period formed the basis period. In other words, a loss for the year to 31 December 1985 is a loss for 1986/7, just as a profit for year to 31 December 1985 would be a profit for 1986/7. When losses are being set-off against other income of the same tax year, or are being carried back and set against income of earlier tax years, it is important to remember that with new trades the

Revenue will take the actual loss that arose in the tax year, and not the tax loss that arose in the accounting period which ends in the tax year in question. Usually, this will involve an apportionment of a loss between the tax years which are covered by the accounting period in which the loss arises. For example, a tax loss of £10 000 for the accounting year to 30 September 1986 will be split between the tax years 1985/6 and 1986/7, giving a tax loss of £5000 arising in 1985/6 and a tax loss of £5000 arising in 1986/7.

This is known as the 'strict basis' of calculating loss reliefs, and the Revenue will automatically use it in the first three tax years of a new trade. The Revenue will also use it in the fourth year of trade, if the trade incurred a tax loss in the third year. The 'strict basis' will not affect the total amount of loss which is relieved, but it can radically alter the years of

---

Losses Arising in First Twelve Months
Joe starts trading on 1 July 1985 and makes up his first set of accounts to 31 March 1986, which shows a tax loss of £3000. He then prepares accounts to 30 April 1987, showing a taxable profit of £16 000. The assessments are calculated like this, assuming that Joe does not elect for the loss to be set sideways or carried back:

Year	Basis Period	£	Assessments £
1985/6	1.7.85–5.4.86		NIL
1986/7	1.7.85–30.6.86:		
	1.7.85–31.3.86	(3 000)	
	31.3.86–30.6.86		
	£16 000 × 3/13	3 692	
			692
1987/8	As Above (First 12 months again)		692
1988/9	1.5.87–30.4.87		
	£16 000 × 12/13		14 770
Total Assessments			16 154

Had Joe elected to utilize the £3000 loss by set-off sideways against other income, or by carrying back, the assessment for 1985/6 would still have been NIL, but the £3000 loss would not have been available to reduce the assessments for 1986/7 and 1987/8. The total assessments for the first three tax years would therefore increase by £6000. Obviously, this difficulty cannot arise if the loss arises *after* the first year's trading, since in this case it can be relieved by aggregation with profits only once.

assessment into which the loss falls, and so affect the amount of tax repayable as a result of the loss claim.

Complications also arise where losses are made in the first year and have to be aggregated with the profits of another accounting period in order to arrive at the taxable profits for the first three tax years. Just as expenses can be relieved for tax several times over when they are incurred in the first twelve months, so can trading losses. However, if a loss is relieved sideways against other income of the year of the loss, or carried back, it is no longer available to be relieved in aggregation, or be relieved by carry-forward to set against other income from the same trade. There is no substitute for doing the arithmetic in each case to see which method of loss relief gives the best result.

The example above illustrates a further important point concerning losses in commencing trades. Just as the choice of accounting date can make a difference to overall taxable profits where a trade is conducted profitably from day one, so can the choice of accounting date where losses arise in the early years.

Choice of Accounting Date

The facts are the same as in the above example, except that Joe makes up one set of accounts from commencement on 1 July 1985 to 30 April 1987, a period of 22 months. The taxable profit is £13 000, which is the same net taxable profit for the 22-month period as in the above example. However, the tax assessments are considerably higher.

Year	Basis Period	Assessment £
1985/6	1.7.85– 5.4.86 £13 000 × 9/22	5 318
1986/7	1.7.85–30.6.86 £13 000 × 12/22	7 090
1987/8	1.7.85–30.6.86 £13 000 × 12/22	7 090
1988/9	1.5.86–30.4.87 £13 000 × 12/22	7 090
Total Assessments		26 588

The reason for the greatly increased assessment is that the small initial loss has been averaged with the larger profits earned after 31 March 1986, and its impact has therefore been reduced. The general rule that emerges is that where in the first twelve months losses fall consistently, and/or profits rise consistently, it is better not to have an extended first accounting period. On the other hand, if profits fall after the first twelve months, or losses start to arise, it can be better to have an extended first accounting period, so that the lower profits can be averaged out with the profits of the first twelve months.

In practice, the choice of accounting dates cannot be an exact science for new businesses. But where significant sums are involved, an intelligent choice of accounting date, drawing on data in the business plan and perhaps also on computerized management accounts, can lead to useful tax savings.

5.4 SETTING TAX LOSSES SIDEWAYS

Individuals can elect to set a tax loss against other income of the same tax year in which the loss arose, or against income of the following tax year. It follows that a loss arising in, say, 1985/6 can be relieved against other income of 1985/6, or against other income of 1986/7. Which route will be preferable will depend on your overall tax position for each of these years. And whichever course is adopted, it is important to remember that the claim must be made in writing, and lodged with the Inspector within two years of the end of the year of assessment to which it relates. Thus a claim for 1984/5 must be lodged by 5 April 1987.

In calculating the tax relief, there is a strict order of set-off which must be followed.

- First, the loss must be relieved against your other earned income.
- Second, it is relieved against the investment income.
- Third, it is relieved against the earned income of your spouse.
- Fourth, it is relieved against the investment income of your spouse.

However, it is possible to restrict the loss claim to your own income and not to extend it to your spouse's income, and this can lead to useful tax savings. As we have seen, any amount of unutilized Married Man's Aliowance can be transferred to your wife and used to reduce her taxable income. Where you wife's earnings can absorb the Married Man's Allowance there will therefore be no harm in using a loss claim to reduce your taxable income to nil.

But if the loss claim is also set against your wife's income it might reduce it to such a level that the Wife's Earned Income Relief and the transferred Married Man's Allowance will be wasted. In these circumstances it will usually be better to restrict the loss to your own income. Any amount of loss which cannot be relieved against other income of the same and of the immediately following tax year can be relieved by carry-forward to subsequent income of the same trade, or in some circumstances by carry-back to earlier years' income. Capital allowance claims can be used to create or increase a tax loss for the purposes of this claim.

5.5   CARRY-BACK OF TAX LOSSES

It may come as a surprise to many start-up businessmen to learn that, by skillful use of the existing tax rules, new businesses can often secure worthwhile tax repayments which can go some way towards relieving the financial pressures in the critical first two or three years of trading. The relief was introduced by the 1978 Finance Act, and was one of the first tax incentives to be introduced by the Thatcher government. It was brought in deliberately to encourage individuals to start in business by providing a financial cushion in the difficult opening years. There is no question of using any dubious techniques of tax-avoidance to secure the repayment, and so long as your business circumstances meet certain requirements there will be no exhausting and costly battles with the Revenue to secure your repayment. The key is to engineer your business circumstances to qualify for the relief, which is a matter of skilled planning and timing.

The general rule is that where a tax loss is incurred in any of the first four years of a business the loss can be carried back and set against total income of the three preceding tax years. A tax-repayment will then be made and, better still, the Revenue will in most cases pay interest on the tax repaid. Again, the loss can be created or increased by a capital-allowances claim, and again the loss is calculated on the 'strict basis'.

Needless to say, some complicated rules surround this relief. First, there are strict time-limits and you must take care not to fall foul of these. As with a 'sideways' loss claim, the claim must be made in writing and lodged with the Inspector within two years of the end of the tax year in which the loss arose. The same order of set-off applies as with a 'sideways' loss claim, and the same option to restrict the loss to your own income and not to extend it to your spouse's income can be exercised. Whether this will be beneficial will depend on the facts of each specific case.

Where a loss is carried back it is set first against your income of the third preceding tax year, including your spouse's income for that year. (Special rules apply if you actually got married in that year.) Any part of the loss still unrelieved is set against your income of the second preceding year, and any remaining loss goes against income of the first preceding year. So a loss for 1985/6 goes first against income of 1982/3, then against 1983/4, then against 1984/5.

The loss is used first to reduce your earned income and then your investment income. So if you suffered the 15% investment income surcharge (which is abolished for 1984/5 and subsequent years) it is possible to recover this by setting the loss against your investment income, but only after your earned income has been fully used up.

James is delighted to learn that he will be getting a tax repayment of

Carry-Back of Tax Loss

It is 1 February 1986 and James Smith, who manages a van hire outlet for a national chain, is planning to start his own van-hire business. His accountant has helped him to prepare a business plan and to secure backing from a bank, and he tells James that, if possible, he should buy the vans and start trading by 31 March 1986. With support from his bank he purchases vans costing £40 000 on 5 March, and secures first-year allowances of £20 000 (£40 000 at 50%). In his first year he makes a modest profit of £6000, so his profit for 1985/6 is £500 (i.e. for the one month from 5 March to 5 April). This is reduced to nil by capital allowances of £20 000, leaving surplus capital allowances of £19 500.

For 1982/3, 1983/4 and 1984/5 James earned £8000 annually. His wife, who is a secretary, earned £6000 in each of these years. If James elects to set the loss against both his own income and his wife's income, the tax repayment is calculated like this:

1982/3	£	*1982/3*	£
His salary	8 000	Tax Paid	2997
Her salary	6 000	Tax Due	NIL
	14 000	Tax Repaid	2997
Less: Loss	(14,000)		
Taxable Income	NIL		

1983/4	£	*1983/4*	£
His salary	8 000	Tax Paid	2826
Her salary	6 000	Tax Due	1176
	14 000	Tax Repaid	1650
Less: Balance of loss			
(£19 500 − £14 000)	(5 500)		
Taxable Income	8 500		

James would therefore get a tax-repayment of £4647 (i.e. £2997 + £1650). However, his accountant advises him that repayment will be larger if he elects to restrict the loss to his own income. The sum of £8000 would be relieved against his income of 1982/3, £8000 against his income of 1983/4 and £3500 (the balance of the loss of £19 500), against his income of 1984/5. His unused personal allowances for 1982/3 and 1983/4 would be transferred to his wife and so would not be wasted. The full £19 500 would thus be relieved against taxable income, leading to a tax-repayment of £5850 (i.e. £19 500 at 30%). James would therefore increase his tax repayment by £1203 simply by restricting the loss to his income.

£5850. He wishes now that he had been paying top-rate tax in the last three years, so that the tax-repayment would be even higher. He is even more pleased to learn that the Revenue will add interest (known as *repayment supplement*) to the tax he has overpaid in earlier years. There are some complicated rules surrounding the supplement, but in James's case, interest at 8% (simple — not compound) will run on overpaid tax from 12 months following the end of the tax year in which the tax was paid, and at 11% from 6 May 1985. So interest on the 1982/3 repayment runs from 5 April 1984, and on the 1983/4 repayment from 5 April 1985. James gets his tax repayment on 5 October 1986, and the interest is calculated like this: .

Example

Year	Tax Relief	Tax Repayment £	Period of Interest	Interest £
1982/3	£8000 at 30%	2400	13 Months at 8%; 17 Months at 11%	582
1983/4	£8000 at 30%	2400	1 Month at 8%; 17 Months at 11%	390
1984/5	£3500 at 30%	1050	6 Months at 11%	58
				1030

The icing on the cake as far as James is concerned is that the interest of £1030 is not taxable. His earlier tax payments were as good as money in the bank, and the cash-flow boost of £6880 (tax repayment of £5850 and interest of £1030) will greatly help him in his early years.

Not every business can use this strategy, but for many entrepreneurs the carry-back of start-up losses can be an extremely effective financial tool.

5.6   COMPANY TAX LOSSES

In comparison with losses for unincorporated traders, the utilization of company tax losses is a simpler affair. In broad terms, the available options are as follows:

- Set-off sideways against other income of the company of the same accounting period.
- Set-off sideways in the same accounting period against income of other group companies (i.e. where one company owns at least 75% of the

share capital of the other, or both, are under at least 75% control of another company).

- Carry-forward to set off against subsequent income from the same trade.
- Carry-back and set-off against total income of the immediately preceding accounting period, so long as the same trade was being carried on in that period. (Where the accounting period in which the loss arises is less than 12 months, then it can only be carried back and set against profits attributable to a period of equivalent length.)
- Broadly, where the loss is attributable to first-year allowances, it may be carried back and set against total income of the three years immediately preceding the year in which the loss arose, provided again that the same trade was being carried on in these periods.

This is a very broad outline of the options of relieving Corporation Tax losses, and it can be seen that the system is much less flexible than that applying to unincorporated traders, and does not offer the same advantages for start-up situations. Profits for Corporation Tax are simply the profits of the accounting period that is being taxed, so there can be no doubling-up of reliefs for losses in the first year of trade, nor can there be a doubling-up of relief for revenue expenditure in the first twelve months.

Moreover, the options to set losses against other income of earlier periods are very limited. First, the same trade must have been conducted in the period to which the loss is being carried back. Second, the facility to carry back a loss for three years extends only to losses which are attributable to first-year allowances. As first-year allowances will be abolished after 31 March 1986, even this will be lost.

Relief is available for pre-trading revenue expenditure for companies so long as the expenditure is incurred within three years of the start of trading. Similarly, pre-trading expenditure on plant and machinery by companies which are about to trade will qualify for capital allowances. However, the absence of any facility to carry back losses to periods before the trade commenced, and the inability to double up losses in the first twelve months, means that, from the tax point of view at least, a limited company is an inappropriate vehicle for commencing trades where the business plan has projected a loss in the early periods. This does not mean that a limited company will *never* be an appropriate vehicle. In Section 7 we will see that incorporation, with careful timing and planning, can be a very effective tax-saving strategy. However, remembering that a tax loss is an asset that can be realized in several ways, unincorporated traders are likely to be able to cash in their tax losses in the early years of trade for a greater amount than limited companies with equivalent tax losses. The projected tax losses of a new business are therefore a very important factor in the decision of whether or not to conduct the trade through a limited company.

Use of Company's Tax Losses
Andrew and John Brown start trading as haulage contractors through a company, Brown Brothers Haulage Ltd, on 1 March 1985. For its first accounting period to 28 February 1986 the company makes a profit of £15 000 and has capital allowances of £30 000, leading to a tax loss of £15 000. It can only carry-forward the loss within the company to set-off against trading profits of the next accounting period.

Had Andrew and John decided to trade instead as a partnership the loss could have been relieved sideways against their spouses' incomes, or carried back and relieved against their own incomes and their spouses' incomes of the three preceding years.

If you are contemplating acquiring a company which has tax losses brought forward it is very dangerous to assume that you will be able to use these losses against subsequent profits once you have turned the company round. There is a rule which prevents this use of losses where, broadly, within any period of three years there is both a change in the ownership of the company and a 'major change' in the nature or conduct in the company's trade. Where there is a dramatic reversal in the fortunes of a company in these circumstances the Inspector will almost certainly try to disallow the use of brought-forward losses. Whether he succeeds will depend on the facts and the vigour of your arguments in defence.

Chapter 6

Taxation of Companies and Directors

6.1 OUTLINE OF COMPANY TAX

A company is an entirely separate legal entity from its shareholders or directors. Whereas unincorporated traders are assessed to tax directly, a company will be charged to tax on its profits and it is the company which has the legal liability to pay the tax. Certainly company directors will be taxed, but only on the remuneration, benefits-in-kind and dividends drawn from the company. The full profits of an unincorporated business would be taxed whether they are drawn or not.

Corporation Tax is charged for accounting periods, not for tax years, as with unincorporated businesses. In broad terms this means the annual accounting period, although Corporation Tax will also be charged for an accounting period of less than twelve months. Where a company makes up its accounts for a period exceeding twelve months the profits will be apportioned between the period of twelve months and any remaining period, and both periods will be charged separately to Corporation Tax. For new companies the due date for payment of Corporation Tax is nine months from the end of each accounting period. There is no facility to pay the tax in two equal instalments as there is with unincorporated traders, nor is there any possibility of delaying the payment of Corporation Tax by careful choice of the accounting date.

The rates of Corporation Tax are summarized in Appendix D. The rates are applicable for *Financial Years* (the year to 31 March), which is *not* the same as a tax year for income tax (the year to 5 April). Where an accounting period straddles 31 March, and therefore covers two Financial

Years, the profits are apportioned to each Financial Year, and charged to tax at the appropriate rate for each Financial Year.

The full rate of Corporation Tax (which is 40% for the Financial Year to 31 March 1986) applies to companies with profits in excess of £500 000. The reduced rate of 30% applies to companies with profits of less than £100 000. Special rules, discussed in section 6.2 below, apply to companies with profits in the band from £100 000 to £500 000.

Where a company makes a capital gain on the realization of an asset Corporation Tax is charged at an effective rate of 30% on the gain, but there is no annual exempt level for gains as there is with individuals. (In 1985/6 individuals can make gains of up to £5900 before a charge to Capital Gains Tax arises.)

6.2   MARGINAL RATES OF CORPORATION TAX

Higher rates of Corporation Tax apply to companies with profits between £100 000 and £500 000. For Financial Year 1985 the marginal rate applied to profits in this band is 42.5%, and it is therefore important for companies to avoid having profits fall into this band as far as possible. Often taxable profits can be reduced in several ways with foresight and planning, perhaps by paying pension contributions for directors or by investing in plant and machinery.

Where a company's profits do fall into this band, tax is first charged at the full rate, and the liability is reduced by the formula (stated broadly):

$$(\text{Upper Marginal Limit (i.e. £500 000)} - \text{Profits}) \times \frac{\text{Income}}{\text{Profits}} \times \text{Fraction}$$

The fraction in the formula depends upon the Financial Year, and for 1985 it is 1/40. It is this formula which creates the higher marginal rate of tax for profits between £100 000 and £500 000.

MARGINAL RATE CORPORATION TAX

Smith's Ltd have profits of £150 000 for the year to 31 March 1986. Corporation Tax, which is due on 1 January 1987, is calculated thus:

£150 000 at 40% (full rate)	£60 000
Less: (£500 000 − £150 000) $\times \dfrac{£150\ 000}{£150\ 000} \times \dfrac{1}{40}$	8 750
Corporation Tax Payable	£51 250

If the first £100 000 of profits is charged at 30%, leading to a tax charge of £30 000, it follows that the remaining profits of £50 000, have attracted tax of £21 250 — an effective rate of 42.5% on those profits. For every £1 by which Smith's Ltd manages to reduce its taxable profits (down to a limit of £100 000) it will save 42.5p of Corporation Tax.

6.3   ASSOCIATED COMPANIES

As a general rule, the fewer companies that are operated, the better. Apart from anything else, more companies means more complicated accounting, more statutory obligations to fulfil and more audit fees. Moreover, there can be a significant tax penalty in operating a group of

Marginal Corporation Tax Limits for Associated Companies
Joe Fastbuck is a property developer controlling five companies. He owns the shares of Fastbuck Holdings Ltd, which in turn owns the shares of four development companies. Each of these four companies has trading profits of £25 000 for the year to 31 March 1986. Fastbuck Holdings Ltd has no taxable profits for the year. The group's Corporation Tax liability is calculated like this:

Upper Limit: £500 000 ÷ 5	£100 000
Lower Limit: £100 000 ÷ 5	£ 20 000

	A Ltd £	B Ltd £	C Ltd £	D Ltd £
Profits	25 000	25 000	25 000	25 000
£25 000 × 40%	10 000	10 000	10 000	10 000
Less: £100 000 − £25 000) $\times \frac{£25\ 000}{£25\ 000} \times \frac{1}{40}$	1 875	1 875	1 875	1 875
	8 125	8 125	8 125	8 125

The group suffers a total Corporation Tax liability of £32 500. Had Joe operated his empire under the umbrella of one limited company the liability would have been £30 000 (i.e. £100 000 at 30%). There might be good commercial reasons for Joe to operate his business in this way, but there is an annual tax price to pay for doing so, not to mention the costs of additional accounting and compliance with statutory obligations.

companies where one would do. The marginal limits of £500 000 and £100 000 are reduced where there are associated companies, so that a company with taxable profits of, say, £20 000, might still find some of its profits attracting a marginal rate of tax of 42.5%.

The marginal limits are divided by the total number of associated companies. A company is 'associated' with another company where, broadly speaking, one company controls the other one or both are under common control.

6.4   DIVIDENDS

A dividend is a distribution of profits, as distinct from a cost incurred in earning profits. The payment of a dividend does not therefore reduce taxable profits. However, when a dividend is paid the company incurs a liability to pay Advance Corporation Tax (ACT) of an amount equivalent to 3/7ths of the dividend. This is simply a payment to account towards the Mainstream Corporation Tax (MCT) liability, as the ACT, provided it does not exceed 30% of taxable profits, will be deducted from the eventual MCT liability. Any ACT which cannot be relieved in this way, either because there is no MCT liability or because the ACT exceeds 30% of the taxable profits, can be carried back and relieved against MCT of accounting periods beginning in the period of six years preceding the start of the accounting period in which the surplus ACT arose. Any surplus ACT which is still unrelieved can be carried forward and relieved against MCT of subsequent accounting periods.

When a taxpayer receives a dividend he is treated as receiving investment income which has already suffered basic rate tax. Thus a director who receives a dividend of, say, £700 will be treated as receiving gross investment income of £1000 from which tax of £300 has been deducted. So long as he is a basic-rate taxpayer, therefore, his tax liabilities on that income will have been met in full. If he is a higher-rate taxpayer a further tax charge will arise on 1 December following the tax year in which the dividend is received.

It follows from these rules that the tax effect of paying a dividend instead of a bonus or director's fees will be neutral, provided that the company pays Corporation Tax at 30% and that the rate of Corporation Tax for small companies stays at the same level as basic-rate Income Tax. But there can be a substantial saving on Employers' and Employees' National Insurance contributions.

If, for instance, a company has a taxable profit of £10 000 and decides to distribute the profits to the director/shareholder in the form of a dividend, then it will pay a dividend of £7000 to the director and ACT of

Tax on Payment of Dividends
John Brown is managing director and sole shareholder of
Brown Enterprises Ltd. In the year to 31 March 1986 the
company makes taxable profits of £50 000, and pays John
Brown a dividend of £7000 on 31 March. John Brown's top rate
of tax is 50%.

	£
Corporation Tax: £50 000 at 30%	15 000
Less: ACT Paid: £7000 × 3/7	3 000
Mainstream Corporation Tax (due on 1 Jan. 1987)	12 000
Gross dividend received by John Brown (£7000 + £3000)	10 000
Tax thereon: £10 000 at 50%	5 000
Less: Tax Paid	3 000
Higher Rate Tax (due on 1 Dec. 1986)	2 000

£3000 to the Collector of Taxes. The Mainstream Corporation Tax of
£3000 (£10 000 at 30%) will be reduced to nil by the ACT credit, so at the
end of the day the Revenue will get £3000 tax and the director a net
income of £7000. Suppose instead that the company paid the £10 000 out
as a bonus. It would have to apply PAYE to the payment, so the director
would still only get £7000 and the Revenue £3000. Corporation Tax
would be reduced to nil, as there would be no taxable profits left after
voting the bonus. The NI considerations might well make it better to pay
a dividend, however, as discussed in section 2.4.

There are also some cash-flow points to be considered when paying
dividends. First, if higher-rate income tax will be payable on the dividend
it is better to pay the dividend soon after 5 April, rather than before. The
due date for higher-rate tax is 1 December following the end of the tax
year in which the income was received. Paying a dividend on 6 April 1985
could therefore lead to a higher-rate tax charge on 1 December 1986.
Paying a dividend on 5 April 1985 would cause the charge to arise on 1
December 1985.

Second, companies paying dividends (and interest from which tax is
deducted at source, such as loan-stock interest) must account for ACT
and Income Tax retained at source each calendar quarter. (Where the
accounting year-end does not coincide with a calendar year-end there is a
fifth return period from the end of the calendar quarter up to the
accounting date.) The ACT and Income Tax returned must be paid by
the fourteenth day of the month following each return period. So if a

dividend of, say, £7000 is paid on 31 March 1986 the ACT of £3000 must be paid to the Collector of Taxes by 14 April 1986. If, on the other hand, the dividend is paid on 1 April, ACT need not be paid until 14 July, giving a three month cash-flow advantage.

The timing of dividends in relation to the year-end must also be considered. The ACT suffered in an accounting period is relieved against Mainstream Corporation Tax on the due date for payment of Corporation Tax, which, as a general rule, is nine months after the accounting year-end. It follows that the ACT on a dividend paid immediately before the company's year-end will be recovered within nine months, whereas the ACT on a dividend paid immediately after the year-end will not be relieved against Corporation Tax for twenty-one months. Therefore, generally speaking, it is better to pay a dividend immediately before, rather than immediately after, a year-end.

6.5   TAX ASPECTS OF COMPANY FINANCE

BUSINESS EXPANSION SCHEME

As an incentive to individuals to invest in young, unquoted companies the government has developed the Business Expansion Scheme, which, under present legislation, will be available for tax years up to and including 1986/7. In essence, the rules allow Income Tax relief for sums invested in certain trading companies, so providing a tax cushion for investors should things go wrong. There are now many Business Expansion Scheme funds that are actively seeking new companies with good ideas, and start-up businessmen may consider approaching these fund managers for equity capital. It must be remembered, however, that just because the capital at the fund manager's disposal is a tax shelter for investors does not mean that they will support any project. Each idea must still be evaluated on its merits, and the fund managers will take a very hard look at every aspect of a business before deciding to invest.

The Business Expansion Scheme could also be used to raise capital from friends or associates, and even from certain relatives. Providing the stringent conditions which surround this relief are satisfied, they will get tax relief on their investment. That means that a 60% taxpayer who invests, say, £10 000 in your company will reduce his tax liability by £6000. In effect, the Treasury will contribute £6000 towards his investment.

To begin with, the shares must be acquired by subscription — not purchase — and must be equity shares in a *qualifying company* for the purposes of a *qualifying trade*. The investment must also be made by a *qualifying individual*, and the shares, as a general rule, must be held for at

'The Business Expansion Scheme could also be used to raise capital from friends or associates, and even from certain relatives.'

least five years. The maximum annual investment per individual (with husband and wife being treated as one unit for this purpose) is £40 000, with a minimum investment of £500 per annum in any one company. Note that the present scheme extends only to shares issued on or before 5 April 1987. Whether it will be extended beyond that date by the Chanceller remains to be seen.

A qualifying company must, broadly, be unquoted and incorporated, and resident only in the UK. Further, the investment must be in 'eligible shares', which are new ordinary shares. Throughout the period of five years beginning with the date on which they are issued the shares must carry no present or future preferential rights to dividends, or to a company's assets on its winding up, and no present or future preferential rights to redemption.

The company must also carry on a 'qualifying trade', wholly or mainly in the UK, though a non-trading holding company can also qualify if its wholly owned subsidiaries trade wholly or mainly in the UK.

Qualifying trades do *not* include;

● Dealing in commodities, shares, securities, land or futures.
● Dealing in goods which does not amount to *bona fide* retail or wholesale business.
● Banking, insurance, financial and leasing activities.
● Legal and accounting services.

- Farming.
- Property development where the company owns the property which is being developed.

An individual qualifies for relief if he subscribes for 'eligible shares' on his own behalf, and he is both resident and ordinarily resident in the UK at the time the shares are issued. He must not be 'connected' with the company during the period beginning with the incorporation of the company and ending five years after the issue of the shares. (If the company was incorporated for more than two years before the shares were issued, then the relevant period begins from two years before the shares were issued, and ends five years after the shares were issued.)

An individual is 'connected' with a company, and will therefore be denied BES relief, where he and his associates possess or are entitled to acquire, broadly speaking, 30% of the company's share capital, 30% of the voting power or 30% of the assets on a distribution. An individual will also be connected with a company if he together with his associates is;

- An employee either of the company or of a partner of the company, or
- A partner of the company, or
- A paid director either of the company or of another company which is a partner of that company.

An 'associate' includes the individual's spouse, his business partners, ancestors and descendants. But, significantly, step-parents, step-children, in-laws, brothers and sisters are not 'associates'.

Two other tests must be passed if BES relief is to be secured. The investor must not receive any value from the company during the relevant period such as redemption of shares or loans. The value received will reduce the BES relief available. Lastly, no relief will be available if the scheme is being used for the purposes of tax-avoidance.

Despite the surfeit of restrictions the scheme has obvious attractions for certain investors and companies. For the investor, the cost of the shares is in effect subsidized by the Treasury, and there is at least a sporting chance that the shares will increase substantially in value. Any gain on the disposal of the shares at the end of the five-year period will be taxed at a flat rate of 30% (after deducting the annual Capital Gains Tax exemption, which is currently £5900, and indexation relief for inflation). The entrepreneur gets start-up capital for an assured period of at least five years. The capital can be cost-free for that period, as no dividend need be paid.

Although the investor may find that the shares are not marketable after five years it may be possible for the company to purchase its own shares from the investor at their current market value, and for the sale proceeds to be taxed as a capital gain. The Revenue will only give approval for this treatment if the arrangement in some way benefits the company's trade. But the indications are that the Revenue would view sympathetically the buy-in of company shares where an outsider shareholder has provided equity finance and is now withdrawing his shareholding. It seems, therefore, that an outside investor could subscribe for shares in an unquoted trading company and claim BES relief, and at the same time have an understanding with the company that the shares will be bought in by the company after five years if he then wishes to withdraw his investment.

VENTURE CAPITAL RELIEF

A further provision exists to encourage equity investment by individuals in unquoted trading companies, which, though not as attractive as the Business Expansion Scheme, will still be very useful should an investor ultimately realize a loss on his equity stake. The relief is also available to certain investment companies, and takes the form of allowing Income or Corporation Tax relief for capital losses incurred. The relief is available at an individual's highest rate of Income Tax or for an investment company at its full rate of Corporation Tax. If the losses are merely treated as capital losses they could only be relieved against chargeable capital gains, and only at a maximum rate of 30%.

The main qualifying requirements for venture capital relief are;

- The shares must be subscribed for — not purchased — by the individual or his spouse, or by a qualifying investment company,
- The shares must be ordinary share capital,
- The investment must be in a qualifying trading company (broadly, a UK resident unquoted trading company which has a continuous record as a UK resident trading company or as a holding company of a trading group),
- The loss must arise on a disposal either by way of a bargain made at arm's length for full consideration, or in a liquidation, or on establishing a claim that the shares have become of negligible value.

As with the Business Expansion Scheme, anyone wanting to invest on the basis of his relief being available should, of course, take independent professional advice. The detailed rules can be complicated, and it is not safe simply to assume that the relief will be available.

BORROWING TO INVEST

Where money is borrowed to invest in a business it may be possible for the borrower to deduct the interest paid on the borrowing for Income Tax purposes, so reducing the true cost of the loan. In particular, relief for interest paid may be available where money is borrowed by an individual in order to acquire ordinary share capital in a close company or in order to lend money to a close company. Unlike the Business Expansion Scheme and the Venture Capital Relief Scheme, it is not necessary for shares to be acquired by subscription — they may be purchased from existing shareholders. However, several other important hurdles must be jumped.

- The company must be a 'close' company (broadly, a company which is controlled by its directors or by five or fewer individuals together with their close family and associates).
- The company must either be a trading company, or part of a trading group, or else derive at least 75% of its income directly or indirectly from trading or from land-ownership.
- The individual must either own more than 5% of the company's ordinary share capital (together with his close family and associates) *or* own ordinary shares in the company and have worked as a manager or director of the company for the greater part of his time between the application of the loan and the payment of interest.

Director/shareholders should therefore generally secure tax relief for such borrowing's. At the end of each tax year they, or their accountants, should ask the lender for a certificate of loan interest paid in the tax year. The claim should be entered in the tax return under the section for qualifying loans, and the certificate should be forwarded to the Revenue along with the tax return. The Inspector will then give relief for the interest at the taxpayer's top rate of tax.

Following the 1983 Finance Act a similar relief is now available for borrowings to invest in an employee-controlled company, this being an unquoted company in which, broadly, at least 50% of the issued ordinary shares and voting rights are owned by full-time employees. The relief is available where a loan is applied to acquire up to 5% of the shares of the company, and is intended largely to facilitate management buy-outs of existing shareholders.

6.6   EQUITY OR LOANS

Whether equity shares or loans or a mixture of both should be used to finance a company will depend on whether one is looking from the investor's point of view or from that of the director/shareholder. As far as the investor is concerned, it is generally easier to extract loan capital from an unquoted company than to realize shares. However, the tax incentives of Venture Capital Relief and the Business Expansion Scheme apply only to equity investments.

From the company's point of view the issue of shares carries a tax penalty of 1% capital duty. Moreover, professional fees and other costs associated with raising equity finance are not tax-deductible. The incidental costs of raising loan finance can be allowable, however, provided the loan is not convertible into shares of securities within three years of obtaining the loan or the issue of loan stock. Even where a loan is convertible in this period, tax relief for costs of raising the loan will still be available providing the loan is not *actually* converted within the three-year period.

Another important consideration is whether it would be better for the company to pay dividends or interest to outside investors. As the following example shows this question is largely tax-neutral under current Corporation Tax rules, providing the company is paying Corporation Tax at only 30%. As soon as Corporation Tax is paid at rates in excess of 30%, then loan finance is preferable, as far as taxation is concerned. However, in structuring a business's capital base, due weight must be given to a variety of factors, of which taxation is only one. How to secure capital at the lowest possible cost, and how to secure capital without losing control are usually more important questions than the tax results of specific types of finance.

TAX CONSIDERATION OF EQUITY VERSUS LOAN FINANCE

A Ltd borrows £50 000 at 12% for a 10-year period from a venture capital fund. B Ltd issues £50 000 £1 12% preference shares, redeemable after 10 years, to the same fund. In the year to 31 March 1986 both companies make profits of £30 000.

	A Ltd £	B Ltd £
Profits	30 000	30 000
Less: Interest: £50 000 at 12%	(6 000)	NIL
Taxable Profits	24 000	30 000

Corporation Tax at 30%	7 200	9 000
Less: ACT on dividend at 3/7 at £4200	NIL	(1 800)
Mainstream Corporation Tax	7 200	7 200

	A Ltd	B Ltd
	£	£
Profits	30 000	30 000
Less: Interest	(6 000)	NIL
Less: Dividend		(4 200)
Less: ACT Paid		(1 800)
Less: Mainstream Corporation Tax	(7 200)	(7 200)
Retained Profits	16 800	16 800

In both cases the Mainstream Corporation Tax is £7200, and in both cases the gross yield on the £50 000 invested is £6000. (For B Ltd, the yield comes as a dividend of £4200 and an accompanying tax credit of £1800). Both companies have retained profits of £16 800, so in this case the choice of equity or loan finance is tax-neutral. If B Ltd was paying Corporation Tax in excess of 30%, however, loan finance would be preferable assuming ACT stays at the same level.

6.6   REMUNERATION STRATEGIES

We have already seen the savings in NI contributions that can be achieved by paying dividends instead of bonuses and by remuneration through benefits-in-kind. More tax can often be saved by a well-thought-out remuneration policy.

The overall object for a controlling director should be to minimize the Revenue's overall 'tax-take' from both the company and himself. Assuming that his company's taxable profits are less than £100 000, the company will suffer a flat rate of 30% Corporation Tax. For every £1 of remuneration drawn, therefore, the Corporation Tax bill will fall by 30p. But at the same time, for every £1 of remuneration drawn an Income Tax liability will arise. As soon as the Income Tax liability exceeds 30p per £1, the payment of remuneration is 'tax-inefficient' — it simply leads to an Income Tax liability which is greater than the Corporation Tax saved. Setting the correct level of remuneration for director/shareholders is therefore a balancing act between taking out as much remuneration as possible without increasing the overall tax charge.

Appendix C gives Income Tax rates for 1985/6, which show that the higher-rate charge arises as soon as taxable income exceeds £16 200. Note that this is *taxable* income, after deduction of personal allowances, mortgage interest, superannuation payments and any other tax reliefs that might be available for 1985/6. Suppose a director is married, and pays gross mortgage interest of £3000 in 1985/6. His total reliefs for 1985/6 are £6455 (mortgage interest of £3000 and a Married Man's Allowance of £3455). He will need total income of at least £22 655 before his taxable income exceeds £16 200 and starts to attract higher-rate tax.

The same considerations apply to dividends paid to controlling directors. So long as the tax credit carried by a dividend satisfies the director's basic-rate tax liability on any dividend he receives, and so long as he is a basic-rate taxpayer, then paying a dividend will not increase the Revenue's overall 'tax-take' from the company and the director.

Paying one's wife can also take profits out of tax altogether. The Wife's Earned Income Relief of £2205 can be used to set against earnings, which will therefore be shielded from tax. Where both spouses are directors and are drawing £25 361 or over in salaries between them in 1985/6, it might also be possible to reduce the overall Income Tax charge by lodging a Wife's Earnings Election. The effect is that husband and wife will be taxed as separate individuals. The husband will therefore lose his Married Man's Allowance of £3455 and get instead a Single Person's Allowance of £2205. However, the salaries will not then be aggregated for the purposes of calculating higher-rate tax and, providing the joint income is over a certain level, a tax saving will result. As the basic-rate band is now £16 200, and the Single Person's Allowance £2205, both partners could draw £18 405 each (£36 810 in total) before higher-rate tax is attracted; and more if there is mortgage interest or other tax reliefs available. Of course, the salaries have to be paid genuinely as remuneration for services if they are to be an allowable expense for the company. Thus a wife who drew £20 000 as an employee for part-time secretarial duties would not impress the Inspector of Taxes as being remunerated solely for the purposes of the company's trade. But if she was a director who was expected to represent the company, meet clients and participate in policy-making for the company, the Inspector would be hard-pushed to disallow her salary. Everything depends on the facts of each case, and it goes without saying that professional advice should be sought if this strategy is to be adopted.

Paying one's children for part-time duties which they are legally allowed to undertake can also take profits out of tax. Each child has a Single Person's Allowance, which can be used to shelter income of £2205 in 1985/6, though again the Inspector may require to be satisfied that the remuneration is not excessive in relation to the work undertaken. Care should also be taken with older children that one does not walk into the National Insurance trap discussed in section 2.2. As soon as wages exceed £35.49 weekly an NI charge on the employee of 5% of wages is triggered, and a further 5% on the employer — a total charge of 10%.

Fortunately, it is comparatively easy to set the correct level of directors' remuneration. The normal practice is to vote the directors' remuneration at the company's annual general meeting following the accounting year-end. The directors' bonuses or fees are provided in the accounts and reduce the Corporation Tax liability for that accounting period, even though the bonuses or fees are not paid until some time after the accounts' year-end.

To complicate matters, directors' total remuneration for each year-end can be taxed in two separate ways. Most commonly, directors are taxed on the 'accounts basis' of assessment. This treats a director's income for a tax year as being remuneration for the accounting year which ends in that tax year. For instance, suppose that a director of a company with a 30 September year-end has total remuneration, including salary and bonuses, of £20 000 for the year ended 30 September 1985. If he is being taxed on the accounts basis his remuneration for 1985/6 will be his remuneration for the year to 30 September 1985, that is, £20 000.

The alternative to the accounts basis is the 'earnings basis', which is the statutorily correct method and is now generally imposed by the Revenue on new directors, whether they want it or not. (Directors on the accounts basis can insist on being put on to the earnings basis, but directors on the earnings basis can only request to be put on to the accounts basis.) Where a director's remuneration is taxed on the earnings basis, his remuneration for each accounting period will be apportioned between the years of assessment in which it was actually earned. Suppose that a director has remuneration of £20 000 for the year to 30 September 1985 and £16 000 for the year to 30 September 1986. His taxable remuneration for 1985/6 will be calculated as follows:

	£
Year to 30 Sept. 1985	
£20 000 × 6/12	10 000
Year to 30 Sept. 1986	
£16 000 × 6/12	8 000
	18 000

The earnings basis will *always* be applied:

- For the first tax year in which emoluments are earned,
- For the second tax year if the company's accounting period ending in that year is shorter than twelve months,
- For the tax year in which the emoluments ceased, *and* the preceding tax year.

The accounts basis is generally easier to administer for both the Revenue and the director's accountant. Moreover, where earnings are on a rising trend, the tax assessments are based on lower earnings than were actually received by the director, so delaying tax payments and giving the director a cash-flow advantage. On the other hand, where earnings fluctuate, the accounts basis can lead to a heavy tax charge for a year in which the actual earnings are low. In this situation, the earnings basis will tend to smooth out the profile of taxable remuneration and, perhaps, prevent higher-rate tax applying in high-income years.

6.7   BENEFITS-IN-KIND

As a general rule, employees earning less than £8500 can only be assessed to tax on benefits in kind if the benefit can be converted into money. Thus, the *gift* of a company car to an employee earning less than £8500 would be a taxable benefit, since the employee could convert the car into cash by selling it. However, making a car *available* to an employee earning below £8500 will not create a taxable benefit (unless the scale charge for the car in question when added to the remuneration exceeds £8500), as the employee cannot convert the benefit into cash.

However, special rules apply to 'higher-paid employees' (employees earning over £8500) and to directors. The general principle is that directors and higher-paid employees are assessed to tax on benefits-in-kind whether or not the benefits can be converted into cash. The value of the benefit for tax purposes is the cost to the company of providing the benefit. So if a company rewards its director by buying him a £500 video recorder he will be treated as receiving a taxable benefit of £500. Nor can this charge be sidestepped by the company buying the machine and merely making it available to the director. In this case the benefit is 20% of the market value of the machine when it was acquired for each tax year in which it is made available to the director. Needless to say, there are provisions to ensure that benefits made available to a director's family or household are also caught.

It follows that gifting an asset to a director will normally have no tax advantage. A £500 video recorder gifted to a director will lead to a £500 tax charge; the same charge as would have arisen if the director had received a £500 bonus. Lending the recorder to him will lead to a tax charge on £100 (20% of £500) each year. But it is worth noting that cash remuneration will attract employees' and employers' NI contributions at a combined rate of 19.4% on the rates in force to 5 October 1985, assuming that total remuneration is below the NI Upper Earnings Limit of £13 780. The transfer of a video recorder does not create an NI charge, so where directors are below the £13 780 NI threshold there is scope for making some useful NI savings by remuneration through benefits-in-kind. After 6 October 1986 this strategy will also save the 10.45% employers' NI contribution on remuneration in excess of £13 780.

COMPANY CARS

The above rules are simply an outline of general principles, and special rules apply to certain benefits. Most important, the benefit-in-kind charge on company cars, which is now almost a universal perk for directors, is still quite generous. The actual charges for car and fuel are set out in Appendix F, and a little consideration shows how tax-effective the provision of a company car can be.

The total cost of providing and running a modest car is, let us say, £3000 annually. If the company bears this cost and it is a small company paying tax at 30%, the tax saved by the company will be £900 (i.e. £3000 at 30%). The scale charge on the director for a typical 1600-cc saloon will be £1050 (i.e. car and fuel benefits at £525 each), leading to a tax charge of £315 (£1050 at 30%) if he is a basic-rate tax payer. The overall saving would therefore be £585 (£900 tax saved less £315 tax charged), without even looking at the saving in employees' and employers' NI contributions. (In fact, the position is rather more complicated than this, since the director would obtain tax relief for running costs and depreciation attributable to business use if he owned the car. But unless there was little or no private use there would still be a substantial tax saving by the company providing the car.)

Where a second car is provided, perhaps for the use of the director's wife, the scale benefit is increased by 50%. Even so, there is still a significant tax benefit in the company providing the car instead of paying the director a further salary of, say, £3000 annually so that he can provide the car himself.

Several other planning points on company cars are noteworthy:

- The scale benefit is usually related to the car's cylinder-capacity. It is obviously better to acquire a car that is just below the higher benefit thresholds of 1300 cc and 1800 cc. Cost becomes a factor when total retail cost, including VAT, exceeds £17 500, at which point the annual benefit leaps to £1200 for 1985/6, regardless of the car's engine size.

- The scale charge falls for cars over four years old. Where a director is provided with a prestige car, the provision of a second-hand vehicle, which has an original cost below £17 500, will greatly reduce the scale charge.
- The scale charge reduces by 50% where the business use of the car exceeds 18 000 miles in the tax year. However, it increases by 50% where the business use is less than 2500 miles in the tax year. Obviously, directors with low mileage should try to cover more than 2500 business miles, and directors with high mileage should try to cover more than 18 000 business miles. Home-to-work travel is *not* business mileage for this purpose, unfortunately.
- The scale charge reduces proportionately for periods where the car is incapable of being used, usually because of repairs, but only if the car is unavailable for thirty or more consecutive days. The scale charge is also reduced where the user cannot actually use the company car, perhaps because he is abroad for long periods. In this situation a board minute could be drawn up, withdrawing authority for the use of the car for such a period.

FUEL BENEFITS

A scale charge also applies (see Appendix F) where an employer provides fuel for private motoring by an employee in a company car. The charge is normally the same as the charge for the use of the car, which is another reason for thinking carefully before acquiring a car costing over £17 000, or a car with an engine capacity in excess of 1800 cc. However, there is no 50% uplift in the fuel benefit where a second car is provided.

Despite the scale charge, it is still usually beneficial for the company to supply fuel for private motoring. Suppose that a director has a 1600-cc car, leading to a fuel benefit of £525. If the director covers 10 000 private miles in a year in a car capable of 30 m.p.g., and with petrol at £2.00 per gallon, the fuel will have cost the company £666. But the taxable benefit-in-kind will only be £525. On the other hand, if the director covered only 2000 private miles the private fuel would cost only £133, but the taxable benefit would still be £525. In this situation the director is better off paying for private fuel personally, ignoring the impact for PAYE of drawing additional salary to pay for the private fuel.

To avoid the scale charge on fuel benefits it is essential that the director pays for *all* private fuel. If the company has paid for private fuel the scale charge can be wiped out, but only when the director makes good to the company the *whole* cost of private fuel. The full scale charge will still stand even where 90% or more of the cost is reimbursed to the company.

Chapter 7

Incorporation

7.1 CHOICE OF TRADING VEHICLE

A trade can be conducted through the medium of a company or through an unincorporated partnership or sole proprietorship. The trading medium you choose is a fundamental business decision. Choosing the correct medium can have important long-term benefits: choosing the wrong one can seriously harm your business's prospects.

The taxation treatment of incorporated and unincorporated businesses is one of the most important factors in the choice of trading vehicle, but there are many other aspects to be considered. The most important non-tax point is that incorporating a trade will confer limited-liability status, so that the directors cannot be held personally liable for the company's liabilities. In some trades, such as building, this will be a vital consideration, though in others it will be almost irrelevant. Often limited liability is rendered useless by bankers and other lenders requiring personal guarantees from directors, and sometimes security by means of a mortgage over directors' homes.

The following are some of the other advantages of incorporation:

- Owning shares in a company, as distinct from owning the assets of a trade, can make Capital Transfer Tax planning easier. Shares can be put into trust for minor children or grandchildren, and their value will, hopefully, increase through time outside the estate of the donor. Shares can also be gifted in small tranches annually in order to utilize the annual £3000 Capital Transfer Tax exemption.
- It may be easier for a company to raise capital from banks and other lenders. For instance, a company can give a floating charge over all of

its assets whereas an individual cannot. Lenders might also insist on an equity stake, which an unincorporated business could not offer.

- Whilst the combined employers' and employees' NI contributions are much higher than NI contributions levied on unincorporated businesses, the social security benefits available to an employee are much better. The additional benefits which are *not* available to self-employed persons include unemployment benefit, earnings-related additions to the state retirement pension, widow's pension and invalidity pension. A self-employed person can always buy these benefits in the insurance and pensions markets, but at a much greater cost.
- Shares in a limited company can often be realized more readily than the assets of a trade. Companies are now permitted to buy back their own shares, and this has helped to extend the market in private company shares to outside investors who need no longer be 'locked-in' to the company indefinitely.

The following are some of the general disadvantages of trading through a company:

- Additional time and trouble is involved in maintaining minutes of directors' meetings and general meetings. Various statutory filing requirements must be satisfied, such as notifying changes of directors and filing accounts and annual returns.
- A company's accounts must be audited leading, often, to higher accountancy fees.
- The accounts of a limited company are available for public scrutiny. However, small companies need not file a profit and loss account.
- Loans to directors are prohibited by the Companies Act. Loans to shareholders make the company liable to pay tax equivalent in amount to the Advance Corporation Tax that would have been payable had the loan been a distribution.
- Directors' salaries and bonuses are subject to PAYE immediately they are made available to the director. This leads to a cash-flow disadvantage, since tax on profits of unincorporated traders can be delayed for up to twenty-one months.

7.2   TAX CONSIDERATIONS

Often the most important question to be asked is 'Which trading vehicle will pay less tax, a company or an unincorporated business?' Unfortunately, the answer is far from simple, and there is no substitute for totalling the tax pros and cons for each individual case. The answer will vary with the personal finances of the would-be sole traders/partners/ directors, with their projected profits, and with the Income Tax and Corporation Tax rates that are currently in force. One approach is to take a projected profit for an accounting period, to calculate the total tax and NI charge on these profits if the trade is conducted through a limited company and compare this with the total tax and NI charge on an unincorporated business with an identical profit.

Company versus Partnership

John and Harry operate a travel agency as partners sharing profits 50:50. For their year to 31 March 1985 the taxable profits are £40 000. Both men are married and their wives draw £1500 in salary for secretarial services, which is covered by the Wife's Earned Income Relief. Would they be better off trading through a limited company, and drawing, say, £15 000 each in salary anually?

Unincorporated Business	£
Taxable Profits	40 000
Less: Married Man's Allowances (2 × £3455)	6 910
	33 090
Income Tax: £32 400 at 30%	9 720
£ 690 at 40%	276
Class 4 NIC (6.3% × £9630) × 2	1 213
Class 2 NIC ((£3.50 × 26) × 2) + ((£4.75 × 26) × 2	429
Tax Relief on 50% of Class 4 NIC: £606 at 40%	(242)
	11 396

Incorporated Business	£	£
Profits	40 000	
Less: Salaries: £15 000 × 2	30 000	
	10 000	
Less: Employer's NI (£15 000 × 10.45%) × 2	3 135	
Profits subject to Corporation Tax	6 865	
Corporation Tax £6865 at 30%		2 059
Employer's NI		3 135
Taxable Salaries: £15 000 × 2	30 000	
Less: Married Man's Allowances: £3455 × 2	6 910	
	23 090	

Basic Rate tax: £23 090 × 30%	6 927
Employee's NI: (£13 780 × 9%) × 2	2 480
Total Tax and NIC	14 601

On these figures John and Harry would be worse off
annually by £3205 by operating through a limited company
largely because of the additional NI charges. Their annual
taxable profit would need to be considerably higher, so
attracting higher rates of Income Tax, before there would be a
good tax reason to incorporate.

Footnote: this example assumes that the profits of the incorporated business
remain at 40 000 in 1985/86. The employer's NI calculation is for illustration and
special rules (not available at the time of writing) may apply to directors in
1985/86.

This is only one approach to the problem, and there are other tax points
to consider. Incorporation will have the following advantages, which are
not available to partners and sole traders:

- Car benefits and fuel benefits may be taxed on a more favourable basis
for directors than for partners.
- Self-employed individuals, as a general rule, can only fund pension
premiums of 17.50% of profits (technically, 'net relevant earnings').
Companies can usually fund much larger amounts depending on the
director's age, salary and length of service, and hence they can often
shelter larger amounts of profits from taxation. The reason is that
companies' pension contributions are restricted only if they would fund
more than the maximum retirement benefits allowed by statute. The
maximum benefits are generous, and allowable premiums can often be
very high in relation to the director's salary. However, self-employed
retirement annuity premiums are limited to 17.50% of 'net relevant
earnings'.
- A company can attract capital in return for shares qualifying for
Business Expansion Scheme relief.
- Where an individual, including a director, subscribes for shares in
certain companies and the company is subsequently liquidated or the
shares become of negligible value, the capital loss can be relieved
against taxable income and hence lead to an Income Tax repayment.
- Where a loan to a company becomes irrecoverable in certain circumstances a capital loss can be crystallized which can be used to offset any
chargeable capital gains.

There are also important tax reasons to remain unincorporated, however, particularly in the early years of trade, when profits are likely to be low and losses may occur.

- An unincorporated trader will be able to set tax losses arising from the trade against his other income. Losses in the first four years of trade can be carried back and set against total income of the preceding three tax years, leading to a tax repayment augmented by repayment supplement.
- Unincorporated traders have a favourable basis of assessment for the first three tax years in that the profits of the first year of trading can form the taxable profits of the first three years of assessment. Expenditure can be timed to minimize the profits in this period.
- There can be a twenty-one-month delay in paying Income Tax and Class 4 NI on self-employed profits. Corporation Tax is payable within nine months of the accounting year-end, and PAYE and employers' and employees' NI contributions on directors' salaries are payable immediately.
- Funds can remain in a company having suffered Corporation Tax at 30% instead of suffering Income Tax at perhaps higher rates in an unincorporated business. But it can be very difficult to make these funds available to directors/shareholders without incurring a tax penalty. If the retained profits are distributed they will be taxed as income in the hands of the recipients. If the company is liquidated and the share capital repaid, there could be a substantial capital gain subject to Capital Gains Tax.

7.3 PLANNING FOR INCORPORATION

Despite these disadvantages, in many unincorporated growing businesses there will come a point where the higher-rate Income Tax charge on profits becomes too great, and a significant tax-saving will result from incorporation. In this situation the planning and timing of incorporation is vital since, if done correctly, it can lead to useful tax savings. There are so many opportunities and pitfalls that this is certainly an area where traders should take good professional advice well beforehand.

Apart from tax planning, there are a host of other points to bear in mind on incorporation.

- Agreements between the owners of the business and the company must be drafted.
- Customers and suppliers must be notified.
- Hire-purchase and leasing companies must be notified and their agree-

'It is useful sometimes, if the product is not too cumbersome to take a sample to your meeting with the bank manager.'

ment obtained to the assignment of contracts.
● The Inland Revenue and Customs and Excise must be informed, and a VAT registration number obtained for the company.
● Alterations must be made in telephone and trade directories.
● Invoices, stationery, business cards, etc. must be changed.

Whilst these, and other points, must be observed, the tax-planning of incorporation is perhaps the most important concern.

TIMING OF INCORPORATION

Just as a special basis of assessment applies to the first three tax years of a new business, special rules also apply to the last three years. The rules for ceasing businesses work in the Revenue's favour, but careful timing of incorporation can minimize their effect. As we have seen, unincorporated businesses are taxed on the preceding-year basis; i.e. the profits for a tax year are the profits for the accounting year ending in the preceding year of assessment. On cessation, however, the rule is that the profits for the period from 5 April up to cessation form the taxable profits for the tax year in which cessation takes place. So if a business is transferred to a company on 30 September 1986, the 1986/7 assessment will tax the profits arising between 5 April 1986 and 30 September 1986.

However, the Revenue then has the option to revise the assessments of the two tax years preceding the year of cessation, and to tax the actual profits which arose in those years. Where profits are on a rising trend — and they usually are where a young business is being incorporated — this will lead to an additional tax charge for the two tax years prior to the year of cessation.

Income Tax Assessments on Incorporation
Bill is a computer consultant whose taxable profits are accelerating rapidly. For the years to 31 March 1984, 1985, 1986 and 1987 his profits are £35 000, £45 000, £55 000 and £60 000. If he incorporates on 31 March 1987 his tax bill will increase for 1984/5 and 1985/6 as follows:

	Original Assessment (Previous-year Basis) £		*Revised Assessment (Actual Basis)* £
1984/5:			
Year to 31 March 1984	35 000	Year to 31 March 1985	45 000
1985/6:			
Year to 31 March 1985	45 000	Year to 31 March 1985	55 000
Total	80 000		100 000

The Revenue would exercise its right to assess 1984/5 and 1985/6 on the actual basis, and additional income of £20 000 would suffer tax.

Timing of Incorporation
Suppose that Bill postponed incorporation until, say, 10 April 1987. In that case it would be the tax years 1985/6 and 1986/7 that the Revenue could revise (the two tax years preceding the year in which incorporation took place), and not the tax years 1984/5 and 1985/6. Instead of suffering revised assessments of £100 000, Bill would suffer revised assessments of £115 000, calculated like this:

	Original Assessment (Previous-year Basis) £		*Revised Assessment (Actual Basis)* £
1985/6:			
Year to 31 March 1985	45 000	Year to 31 March 1986	55 000
1986/7:			
Year to 31 March 1986	55 000	Year to 31 March 1987	60 000
Total	100 000		115 000

Nevertheless, for the final 3 years Bell would pay tax on profits of £150 000 instead of £160 000. He should therefore delay his incorporation.

On incorporation it is obviously important to take account of such an additional tax charge in planning cash flow. The additional tax on £20 000 would obviously be a heavy burden. But just as important is an awareness that good timing of incorporation can reduce the tax penalty significantly, depending on the business's profit profile in the years before incorporation.

CAPITAL ALLOWANCES AND STOCK RELIEF

When the assets of a business are transferred to a limited company there can be a clawback of tax relief previously given on plant and machinery and industrial buildings. In the past there could also be a clawback of relief given under the stock-relief provisions, up to the abolition of stock relief in March 1984. Fortunately, so long as the trade will remain under the same control after incorporation as before incorporation there need be no such clawback. Instead, the limited company will stand in the shoes of the unincorporated business's proprietors as far as capital allowances and stock relief are concerned. To achieve this, joint elections must be lodged between the limited company and the unincorporated business's proprietors, and it is essential that this point is not overlooked.

There are circumstances in which a 'balancing charge' on plant and machinery on which clawback capital allowances were previously given will be beneficial. The balancing charge could, for instance, be used to mop up an individual's tax losses of the same year. The company would then acquire the assets at market value for tax purposes, and get annual writing-down allowances on the market value thereafter.

While first-year allowances are still available there can be merit in buying new plant and machinery immediately prior to incorporation, rather than after. The first-year allowances could create a tax loss. Because the loss arises in the year of cessation, it is a 'terminal loss' and special rules apply. Broadly, the terminal loss can be carried back and set against taxable profits of the trade in the three preceding tax years, so leading to a useful tax repayment on incorporation. If, instead, the new assets are bought by the limited company, the capital allowances will eventually be relieved against trading profits, but it will take much longer for the benefit of the relief to be felt: it could take twenty-one months (i.e. nine months following the end of the first accounting period). The relief might also be given at a lower rate, and repayment supplement (interest on tax overpaid in earlier years) will not be available.

WITHDRAWAL OF FUNDS PRIOR TO INCORPORATION

If all the assets, including cash, of a business are transferred to a company, it will be impossible for the director/shareholder to draw the cash from the company without incurring a tax charge. If it is drawn as salary it will be taxed under PAYE; if it is drawn as a dividend it will be subject to Advance Corporation Tax, and perhaps also to higher-rate tax in the director's hands. However, the director might very well need the cash to meet any additional Income Tax liabilities on incorporation. It is therefore common for partners/sole traders to withdraw capital from the business immediately prior to incorporation, and lend the funds to the company a few days later. This has the added benefit of reducing Capital Duty on the formation of the limited company.

CAPITAL GAINS TAX

The transfer of a business to a company is a disposal of the assets of that business for Capital Gains Tax, but, providing proper steps are taken, no Capital Gains Tax will be payable. The sort of assets that are most likely to give rise to a capital gain are;

- Goodwill (broadly, any value of the business over and above the value of its net assets),
- Land and buildings,
- Investments.

Where the company is controlled by the previous owners of the unincorporated business the capital gain will be the difference between the market value of the assets on incorporation and their original cost. If a business is profitable and is expanding rapidly the value of goodwill can be substantial, leading to a large gain on incorporation. Large gains can also arise on business premises. It is therefore vital to ensure that proper advantage is taken of the reliefs from Capital Gains Tax on incorporation. Two types of relief are possible, both of which in effect defer the chargeable gains on assets. Which route is chosen is an important tax-planning point.

First, the charge to Capital Gains Tax on incorporation can be deferred, provided;

- The *whole* of the assets of the business are transferred to the company (though cash can be retained if desired),
- The business is transferred as a going concern, and
- The business is transferred wholly or partly in exchange for shares issued by the company to the person transferring the business.

Where the consideration for the assets is wholly in shares, the entire gains are deferred ('rolled over'). In effect, the gains on assets are deducted from the market value of the shares on incorporation for Capital Gains Tax purposes, and the chargeable gain will be crystallized if and when the shares are sold or the company liquidated.

Rollover of Gains on Incorporation
Bob transfers his rapidly expanding printing franchise to a limited company. The assets are as follows:

Asset	Historic Costs	Market Value	Gain
Premises	20 000	30 000	10 000
Goodwill	NIL	20 000	20 000
Plant & Machinery	20 000	10 000	NIL
Capital Gain			30 000

Bob transfers these assets to the company in return for 100 ordinary shares. The market value of the shares is then £60 000 (the total value of the business assets), but this is reduced for Capital Gains Tax purposes by £30 000 (the 'rolled over' gains). Capital Gains Tax will be charged on the 'rolled over' gain if and when the shares are sold or the company liquidated. The chargeable gain will be the difference between the value received for the shares and £30 000, which is their CGT base cost. (If the shares realize less than £30 000 there will, of course, be a capital loss.)

The disadvantage with this route is that *all* the business assets must be transferred to the company. This maximizes the Stamp Duty and Capital Duty payable on incorporation. Moreover, it prevents possible tax-saving by leaving assets outside the company altogether. For example, a double charge to tax can arise where a company sells an asset — its premises, for instance — and suffers Capital Gains tax at 30% on the gain. The funds cannot then be put into the hands of the shareholders without incurring a second tax charge.

It can therefore be desirable to leave certain assets outside of the company, particularly land and buildings, and to lease them to the company after incorporation. But how can this be done without incurring Capital Gains Tax on other assets transferred to the company?

This brings us to the second route to incorporating a trade. Instead of transferring the entire assets of a business in return for shares, individual assets can be *gifted* to the company. The capital gain arising at the transfer of each asset to the company can then be rolled over by a joint rollover election between the company and the proprietors of the unincorporated business. With this method it is the capital gain on each asset that is rolled over, so reducing the Capital Gains Tax base cost of each asset in the company's hands. With the first route, however, the assets are taken over by the company at their market value, and the gain is rolled over by reducing the Capital Gains Tax base cost of the company's shares.

Which route is better will depend on the assets and circumstances of individual businesses, and is certainly a matter for experienced professional guidance.

STAMP DUTY

Wherever the title to property must pass by means of an instrument rather than by physical delivery, Stamp Duty is payable at 1% of the consideration for the transfer. On incorporation and the transfer of assets to a company, therefore, Stamp Duty will become payable on:

- Land and buildings (including fixtures and fittings which are part of a building),
- Goodwill,
- Debtors,
- Bank deposit accounts (but not current accounts), and
- Stocks and shares, and other marketable securities.

It will be immediately apparent that useful savings in Stamp Duty will arise by leaving certain assets outside of a limited company and following the second route to incorporating a trade outlined above.

Other planning points should be noted, however:

- An agreement for the sale of an interest in land in certain circumstances is not a conveyance on sale, and Stamp Duty may be avoided if the legal estate is not conveyed to the company. On any later sale by the company to a third party, the legal estate in the property can then be conveyed directly to the third party. The effect is to avoid Stamp Duty on the transfer of the property to the company.
- The market value of goodwill will be a matter of negotiation with the Stamp Duty office, and skilled negotiation can considerably reduce the value for Stamp Duty purposes.
- To avoid Stamp Duty on the transfer of stock and work in progress, title should pass by their delivery and should not pass under a contract for sale of the business.
- Stamp Duty is payable on the transfer of debtors to a company. To avoid this, the owners of the unincorporated business should retain title to the trade debts, and appoint the company as its agent to collect

the debts. In this case, not all of the assets of the business will have been transferred to the company, so the second route outlined above must be followed to ensure that capital gains on transfer of assets are rolled over.

● It will be helpful in negotiations with the Stamp Office to draw up a vending agreement between the unincorporated traders and the company, apportioning consideration to the various assets transferred.

CAPITAL DUTY

Capital Duty becomes payable on both the formation of a limited company and on an increase in the share capital of a limited company by the contribution of assets. The rate is 1% on the greater of:

● The nominal value of the shares issued or allotted, and
● The value of the assets contributed (less any liabilities assumed or discharged by the company).

Two planning points are worth noting. First, withdrawal or capital by partners/sole traders will reduce the value of the assets contributed to the company and so reduce Capital Duty. Second, unlimited companies do not suffer Capital Duty on their share capital. Since the Corporation Tax treatment of an unlimited company is identical to that of a limited company, consideration should be given to incorporating an unlimited company wherever limited liability is not required by the shareholders.

VAT

VAT is charged where there is a supply of goods or services by a taxable person made in the course or furtherance of his business, and the legislation specifies that the disposal of a business is such a supply. However, where a business is transferred as a going concern to another taxable person (the company) and the transferor then ceases to be a taxable person, the transfer is *not* treated as being a taxable supply and there is therefore no need to charge VAT.

The situation is more complicated where a person who carries on two or more separate businesses incorporates one of his businesses. As he will not usually cease to be a taxable person by incorporating one of his businesses, the general rule that the transfer of a business to a company which is itself VAT-registered need not carry VAT does not apply. Fortunately, further special rules exist which will take the transfer outside the scope of VAT, provided:

- *All* the assets of the business, or any part of the business, are transferred as a going concern,
- The business is transferred to a taxable person, or to a person who immediately becomes a taxable person as a result of the transfer, and
- The business or part of the business which is transferred has been run as a separate concern with separate accounts.

The requirement that *all* the assets must be transferred should be noted. If this provision is not satisfied, it will be necessary to charge VAT on the value of all the assets transferred, including goodwill. True, the company will recover this as input VAT when its first VAT return is lodged, but this will cause a cash-flow hiccup which the new company could do without. Furthermore, if the company makes exempt supplies as well as taxable supplies (see section 1.15) it is possible that not all of the input VAT will be recovered.

Good advice should be taken to ensure that, as far as possible, incorporation is structured so that VAT is not a cost and does not create a cash-flow disadvantage.

IV Sources of Finance

1.1 RAISING FINANCE

It is wrong to underestimate the difficulties which can be involved in raising finance. Many potential investors have been put off by the lack of awareness of the individuals seeking assistance to raise the finance, and the period of time required can be far longer than many new businesses realize. The delay involved can make the original costings obsolete.

Before approaching a source it is essential to have considered certain points:

- Why are you looking for external funds? Nothing puts an investor off more quickly than the realization that the entrepreneur is not prepared to invest his own money!
- What sort of finance are you looking for?

    Short term   1 to 3 years
    Medium term   3 to 10 years
    Long term   10 to 25 years
    An amount repayable on demand.

    Short-term finance or amounts repayable on demand generally cover the following requirements:
    (a) Day-to-day fluctuations in working capital
    (b) Seasonal fluctuations
    (c) Acquisition of minor fixed assets (e.g. photocopiers, but *not* significant capital items such as vehicles or sophisticated machinery)
    (d) Bridging situations
    Medium-term finance covers:
    (a) The acquisition of fixed assets, apart from buildings
    (b) Working capital, i.e. the capital which is required regardless of cash-flow fluctuations.
    Long-term finance is concerned with:
    (a) Buildings
    (b) Other assets with long lives
    (c) Permanent working capital
    (d) In the case of a new business the initial cash injection.

- Do you want a loan or are you prepared to give an equity stake (shares)?
- Are you hoping to obtain a Government Grant?
- Are you looking for technical assistance and guidance?
- What level of finance are you looking for in rough terms? £1000, £50 000, £1 000 000?

Having answered these questions you are in a better position to decide which of the many sources of finance available is suitable for you, and to impress an investor with your analysis of your financial requirements.

1.2   SHORTFALL IN THE PROVISION OF FINANCE

Although financial facilities for the small business have improved dramatically in the past few years, there are still significant problems in finding finance for this sector. Particular problems can arise for:

- Risky ventures; or those in which are perceived to be risky, such as publishing.
- Ventures requiring more than, say, £15 000 and less than £50 000.
- Unproven businesses.
- Unproven businessmen.

Small businesses should recognize this and put greater thought and energy into the pursuit of finance.

The government is anxious to encourage the growth of the smaller business but there is mounting concern about the number of start-ups which fail. If you have limited knowledge of business methods and finance, consider taking advantage of the business courses run by the extramural departments of universities and colleges. They may well improve your business acumen and help you to prove to your astute bank manager that you are a good risk.

In spite of their variety, sources of finance all have certain points in common:

- They are able to pick and choose their investment.
- Their interest in different forms of investment will vary from time to time.
- The conditions they impose are subject to change.
- They will all look askance at investments where the work has already started. This is particularly true of the various government bodies.

The lesson is that if you are looking for finance you should prepare your arguments well, supporting them with a business plan which is appropriate to the enterprise and to the finance sources which you intend to approach. Most important, you should approach the potential lender at the earliest possible moment.

(1) THE CLEARING BANKS

The clearing banks are one of the principal sources of finance open to the smaller business. They offer loans to finance both working capital and the acquisition of assets.

Loans for working capital normally take the form of an overdraft. This can be a relatively cheap form of loan. However, the interest payable is subject to fluctuation, and the loan is repayable on demand. Once an overdraft facility has been acquired it will be subject to an annual review.

Loans for the acquisition of fixed assets generally take the form of a term loan repayable over a number of years. Interest will normally be charged quarterly at a variable rate. Sometimes, however, personal loans will be given, in which case capital and interest will be spread throughout the period.

Initially, you should approach your own bank manager. However, it should be borne in mind that the 'counter limit' — the amount which the manager is allowed to advance to any one person — varies according to the size of the branch and the seniority of the branch manager. Amounts above the counter limit have to be referred to head office.

This system is very dependent upon the branch managers. If the branch manager dislikes your proposition, it is unlikely to be accepted by head office. However, if one bank turns down a project it could be worthwhile going the rounds of the other banks. It can be surprising how projects turned down by one bank can be accepted by another. Listen to what the bank managers are saying — it may help with the presentation of your case. A good bank manager can apply some creative thinking which will help convert an unacceptable risk into a credible proposition.

In addition to the standard loans available through any branch the clearing banks have set up special schemes for long-term loans aimed at the small business. Details of these can be obtained from the clearing banks. These schemes usually involve a capital-repayment holiday of up to two years, but interest payable is generally higher in these two years.

There are drawbacks, of course. Most of the banks will require some form of security for a loan, although not necessarily for an overdraft. This security may take the form of a charge over some or all of the assets of the business, life assurance policies, or may be the dreaded directors' personal guarantee. This last, which involves the company directors' guaranteeing the loan to the bank and removes the protection of limited liability, should be avoided if possible. However, for many new businesses it will be the only way in which finance can be acquired. In some cases the problem of security can be alleviated by the Loan Guarantee Scheme, discussed under the assistance section below.

(2) OTHER BANKS

Do remember that other banks exist apart from the clearing banks. They offer similar services and are interested in extending their market share. Their principal drawbacks can be the delay in having transactions cleared once an account is in use, and the limited number of branches. Some of these banks are American in origin and may have a slightly different approach to that expected by the British public. Examples are Standard Chartered, Hong Kong and Shanghai, Citibank, etc. Money shops are also opening on high streets, some of which will listen to start-up propositions.

(3) MERCHANT BANKS

This sector covers the merchant banking arms of the clearing banks, together with recognized merchant banking houses and merchant banking companies. They all provide some medium-term finance but the merchant banks, rather than those controlled by the clearers, are generally looking for a maximum investment of eight years. They are all interested in equity investments, and may well look for a seat on the board. Usually they are not interested in the bottom sector of the small businesses market, certainly in nothing under £50 000, but they will invest in new businesses and management buy-outs above this level. They will often be looking for an easy exit through the USM, for example, and this may not be a feasible step.

If you are looking for this type of finance the easiest way to approach the source would be through your accountant. Local firms quite often have links with the larger national firms which have some expertise in this field.

(4) INDUSTRIAL AND COMMERCIAL FINANCE CORPORATION (ICFC)

ICFC is part of the Investors in Industry Group plc, a company 85% owned by the clearing banks. Since its establishment in 1945 this has become one of the major sources of private finance in the UK. It is active in the small to medium-sized company market. It is interested in providing both loans and equity. In addition to its own funds it has access to European Community monies. It offers both variable and fixed-interest loans, covering periods from 5 to 20 years. Generally, it will ask for a charge over the assets of the company. Sometimes penalty clauses for early termination of the loan will be inserted into the agreement. Consider this provision carefully if you have any reason to think that the loan will not run its term.

ICFC will also take an equity stake in a company, frequently by way of preference shares which yield a dividend at a percentage. It seldom wishes to be represented on the board of a company but may suggest that non-executive directors known to it are present on the board. One valuable condition can be the requirement to submit management accounts. This should not be looked upon as an additional burden but rather as good management practice. It is worth noting that ICFC is particularly interested in management buy-outs.

ICFC has a number of offices throughout the country and can be approached direct or through your professional advisers.

(5) VENTURES DIVISION

This is another section of Investors in Industry which is primarily interested in new-technology businesses. It is only interested in equity investments. Its office is in London but contact can be made through any ICFC office.

(6) EUROPEAN INVESTMENT BANK

The European Investment Bank is part of the EEC structure. It offers loans to small companies to assist with capital-investment projects. These loans bear competitive fixed-interest rates and are available to manufacturing industries and some service industries in areas qualifying for Regional Assistance.

These loans fall in the range of £5750 to £2m and cover a maximum of 50% of the cost. They are available through the Regional Support, Inward Investment and Tourism Division, certain banks and ICFC.

(7) OTHER EEC LOANS

Special loans are available in areas of steel and coal industry closures. New community instrument loans are available to small businesses in non-assisted areas. Such schemes are changing all the time, and new schemes are being introduced. Information about these can be obtained from the government or from ICFC.

The Regional Development Fund also sets up schemes to assist under-developed areas from time to time. Details of these are generally available locally. A first source might be the library or local paper!

(8) DEVELOPMENT AGENCIES

The government development agencies are all empowered to invest in businesses. These include the Scottish Development Agency, the Welsh Development Agency, the Northern Ireland Office, the Department of Economic Development, the Highlands and Islands Development Board and the Council for Small Industries in Rural Areas. They are prepared to advance either loans or equity.

Loans are authorized for the acquisition of buildings and equipment and for working-capital requirements. Loans to small businesses are usually restricted to a maximum of 80% of the project cost or £150 000. The interest rates and terms relating to the loan will vary according to the area involved, the type of company and the object of the project. Generally, some form of security will be required, but again the exact nature will vary from case to case.

The terms for equity investment are considered as cases arise. The agencies differ in their approach from the banks and other private-sector finance sources in that they actively consider job opportunities, development prospects and export potential. Consequently they may invest in projects turned down by more profit-orientated organizations. Any offer from these agencies will take into account money raised by the proprietor from other sources such as the bank. Since they are handling public money their response can be slow at times. During the period of their involvement they will require management accounts together with annual accounts, and one of their officers will make periodic visits. These visits can be quite helpful, as the officer will give advice and point out any problems he discovers.

(9) BUSINESS EXPANSION FUNDS

Some of the funds set up to pool private investors' business-expansion scheme money are prepared to invest in unproven businesses. They are looking for investments in excess of £50 000. Partly because of their short life-span and their tendency to charge management fees they are considered a mixed blessing. This is the type of institution which is probably best approached through your financial advisers. In addition, certain third parties may invest through the Business Expansion Scheme and secure tax relief on the investment.

(10) VENTURE-CAPITAL FUNDS

Some of these institutions are prepared to invest in new businesses, particularly those involved in new technologies. Again they are looking for more substantial investments and are best approached with professional help.

(11) LOCAL GOVERNMENT

Local government is now empowered to give assistance to local industry, which they generally do through grants and loans. The amounts involved are small and the criteria applied are, as one would expect, social in nature. However, they can be of considerable importance to the one- and two-man businesses. They are unlikely to give assistance if they believe that their contributions will add little to the viability of the project. Applications are usually made by filling in forms obtained from council offices.

(12) THE FAMILY

It may be that your family are able to provide financial aid. Before embarking on this course it is essential to consider whether or not the relationship can withstand the frictions that are generated between persons involved in the same venture. If you do not wish to have family interference, do not use this source. Also consider what would happen if the venture failed. Can your mother bear the loss?

A properly drawn-up contract setting out the terms of a loan will help to prevent future 'disagreements, and remember that tax relief may be available to the investor through the Business Expansion Scheme if the investment is handled correctly.

(13) HIRE-PURCHASE

There are very few businesses which can afford to purchase fixed assets outright. The majority are forced to arrange some sort of loan. Hire-purchase falls into this category. Many individuals have an in-built distrust of this method of acquiring finance, but provided the contract is clearly understood at the time it can be a valuable tool to the small business.

The majority of the finance houses are controlled by the clearing banks but act independently of them. They offer loans under a variety of term, with the loan period varying with the type of asset being purchased. Hire-purchase can be expensive, but it does offer a solution to the problems faced by small businesses in raising finance. The terms vary from institution to institution and it can be well worthwhile shopping around.

If purchasing a vehicle, do point out that it is for business use, as the business schemes are frequently better than those offered to the general public. Contact can be made either by approaching the local branch office or through the dealer selling the goods. Addresses can be found in the *Yellow Pages* under 'Credit and Finance Companies'. If you have had no previous dealings with a particular company they will probably ask for a bank reference and run a credit check.

(14) LEASING

This is a method of acquiring the use of assets which has been growing in popularity. Title to the goods remains with the leasing company: but this should not matter so long as you have unrestricted right of use. This can be the most sensible method of acquiring equipment which is subject to frequent improvements. Computer equipment, for instance, rapidly becomes out of date. The companies involved in this field are essentially the same as those involved in hire-purchase. As with hire-purchase, the terms and conditions vary. An approach is made in the same way as for hire-purchase, and shopping around is certainly worthwhile.

(15) TRADE CREDIT

Trade credit is not always available to new businesses. Use it where it is available, but be wary. It can often be withdrawn without notice, causing a major hiccup in cash flow. If you obtain trade credit, abide by the terms and do not be tempted to abuse the privilege. Remember, you need the supplier — the supplier may not need you. Trade credit is obtained by a direct approach to the supplier, who may ask for a bank reference and run a credit check.

(16) DEBT-FACTORING

Under this system the right to collect the debt is passed over to another party in return for early payment at a discount, though it is not normally available for new businesses. It can be a tempting option, but, once commenced, it can be difficult to return to a more standard approach, nor is it necessarily beneficial for your public image.

1.3 SUMMARY OF SOURCES OF FINANCE

Loans Institution	Term	Amounts from	Security	Approach	Conditions
Clearing banks	On demand Short term Medium term Long term (through specific schemes)	0 0 0 Varies	Possibly not Yes Yes Yes	Local branch	Frequently none — but will not object to regular accounts
Other banks	Same as the clearing banks	—	—	—	
Merchant banks	Medium term Long term	£50 000	Varies	Through professional advisers Companies only	Seat on the board. Regular accounts
ICFC	Medium term Long term	0	Varies		Regular accounts Possible penalties for early withdrawal
Ventures Division	Long term/ permanent	Varies	N/A	Via local ICFC office	Only interested in equity
European Investment Bank	Medium term	£5750 £2m	NO	Via gov. dept or ICFC	Regional Assistance Areas only. Social conditions

Development Agencies	Short term Medium term Long term Equity	Up to £150 000	Yes N/A	Through agency offices	Regular accounts Regular check-ups Social criteria Take into account assistance to other sources
Business expansion funds	Medium term	From £50 000	Varies	Through professional advisers	Management charge
Local government	Short term Medium term	0 Say, £50 000	No	Council offices	Social criteria
Hire purchase	Short term Medium term	— —	Goods may be repossessed Sometimes also directors' guarantees	Via local office or dealer	

1.4   SOURCES OF ASSISTANCE

'Assistance' encompasses both monetary aid and guidance. Many of the principal sources are, of course, the government and local authority agencies, but the private groups should not be ignored. Any application for aid will be subject to the same rigorous testing that applications for loans receive. In particular, it is virtually unknown for aid to be given to projects which have commenced at the time of application.

SUPPORT FOR BUSINESS

The government has just reorganized the ways in which it gives assistance to industry. Previously there were a great many separate schemes run by different departments and subdepartments. In an attempt to rationalize these schemes they have been brought together under one umbrella known as 'Support for Business'. This is then divided into four separate areas:

- Support for Business and Technical Advisory Services.
- Support for Innovation.
- Support for National and Regional Investment.
- Support for Exports (not dealt with here).

Initial contact is made through the Department of Trade and Industry Information Service.

SUPPORT FOR NATIONAL AND REGIONAL INVESTMENT

(1) Regional Investment Support

The centrepiece of the government's aid programme is the regional development system. In recent months this has undergone a fundamental change. Most important, the map of regional assistance has been changed and the emphasis has swung in favour of job-creation and away from capital projects. There are complex transitional provisions and the old system will terminate on 28 November 1985, the new system having commenced on 29 November 1984.

Regional assistance falls into two categories — Regional Development Grants and Regional Selective Assistance. This assistance is only available in specified areas of the country classified either as development areas or as intermediate areas.

(i) Regional Development Grants

Regional Development Grants are available in *Development Areas* to *eligible persons* in respect of *eligible projects* relating to *qualifying activities*.

Development areas. Development areas are those parts of the country which are defined by the government to be in need of special social assistance (see page 00). The government has decided on these areas on the basis of unemployment statistics, such statistics being drawn up from information gathered in Travel to Work Areas (TTWAs).

Eligible persons. Basically any company, partnership or sole trader may apply.

Qualifying activities. The RDG guide is very helpful on this point. Manufacturing industries have always qualified. Now, however, certain service industries will also qualify, such as data-processing and other business services. However, businesses involved with the repair of consumer goods will not qualify. If a service is provided of which the major part consists of qualifying activities, then the overall service activity will qualify. The Secretary of State has discretion to treat as qualifying a project which, although desirable, does not meet these criteria.

Eligible project. An eligible project must be carried out by an eligible person and relate to qualifying activities. It must provide assets and/or create jobs in a development area and it must:

- Create new productive capacity, or
- Expand existing productive capacity, or
- Result in a material change to a product or service, or
- Result in a material change in the process of producing a product or providing a service.

The grant. The grant is the greater of:

- 15% of eligible capital expenditure subject to a limit of £10 000 per net new job created, or
- £3000 per net new job created, provided that part of the expenditure relates to capital assets and subject to a maximum of 40% of capital investment for manufacturing industries.
- For firms spending less than £500 000 and employing less than 200 people, the £10 000 per job limit does not apply.

Eligible expenditure. This is the net of VAT cost of new plant and machinery and the cost of constructing buildings required for the project. The cost of carriage and installation work is also included. Where part of the work is carried out by the recipient of the grant the DTI will allow the relevant costs, but will naturally scrutinize them more carefully.

New companies may purchase second-hand equipment. So if a management buy-out is envisaged it is important to ensure that the original company actually ceases to trade. Modernization costs are not normally eligible but companies employing less than 200 people may qualify.

How to apply. There are two stages to the process. First of all, approval for the project has to be obtained and then an application made for the payment of the grant. Applications for approval can be made up to twelve months after the date on which the first assets or job is provided. However, it is likely that the majority of applicants will look for the grant at an earlier date. If the project is approved a letter detailing the terms and amount will be sent to the applicant. This letter forms part of a legally binding contract.

The second stage is to apply for payment of the grant. The application must be received within twelve months of the completion of the project, and must be accompanied by an auditor's certificate. The grant will be determined in accordance with the conditions ruling at the qualifying date.

The qualifying date. This is the earlier of the date when:

- The capital expenditure was first defrayed, i.e. when the obligation to pay has been met, or
- The first asset was provided, i.e. received or completed, or
- The first job commenced, or
- The application for project approval was received by the DTI.

The completion date. This has to be notified to the Department at the time of the application for project-approval. It is very important that this should be estimated accurately, as expenditure incurred after this date will not qualify.

The contract. A legally binding contract covering the conditions of the grant will be drawn up. Under this contract the grant may be recovered if the project ceases within three years and the grant is asset-related, and 18 months if the grant is job-related. The purpose is to ensure that the government's aim of encouraging development is not used to finance other activities.

What to do. If RDG assistance is sought the matter should be discussed with your financial advisors and the RDG office at the earliest possible moment.

(ii) Regional Selective Assistance

This is available in both development areas and intermediate areas and is, as its name suggests, more discretionary than Regional Development Grants. To qualify, a project must secure or lead to the creation of jobs. In addition, it must be shown that the RSA is essential to the viability of the project. If work commences before the application is made it will be hard to claim that RSA is essential. It is worth noting that modernization work will continue to qualify for RSA.

If a grant is awarded it will be between 10% and 15% of the eligible expenditure. Eligible expenditure is basically capital costs but may include such items as relocation and training costs. Each individual project is subject to negotiation. Exceptionally, loans at reduced rates might also be available.

(b) National Investment Support

(1) Small Firms Finance

(i) The loan guarantee scheme. This scheme now falls within the heading of Support for National and Regional Investment. It exists to assist small businesses to obtain bank loans. Effectively, the government acts as a guarantor for 70% of the loan. Experiences to date under this scheme have not been encouraging, and as a result the regulations have been tightened up considerably. In future it seems likely that a business plan plus subsequent management accounts will be required. Where an individual is unwilling to pledge personal assets, e.g. his house, he will be unable to obtain assistance.

The scheme is not cheap. The government charges 5% of the outstanding guaranteed amount, payable quarterly in advance, and the bank may also charge an arrangement fee. The interest rate charged by the banks is usually between 1.5% and 2.5% above base rate, since the banks take the view that a loan might not otherwise have been available. The maximum loan available under the scheme is £75 000.

The principal parties involved are ICFC and the clearing banks, from whom further details can be obtained.

(ii) New technology. Grants are available to manufacturing firms to assist with the implementation of advanced manufacturing systems. They are

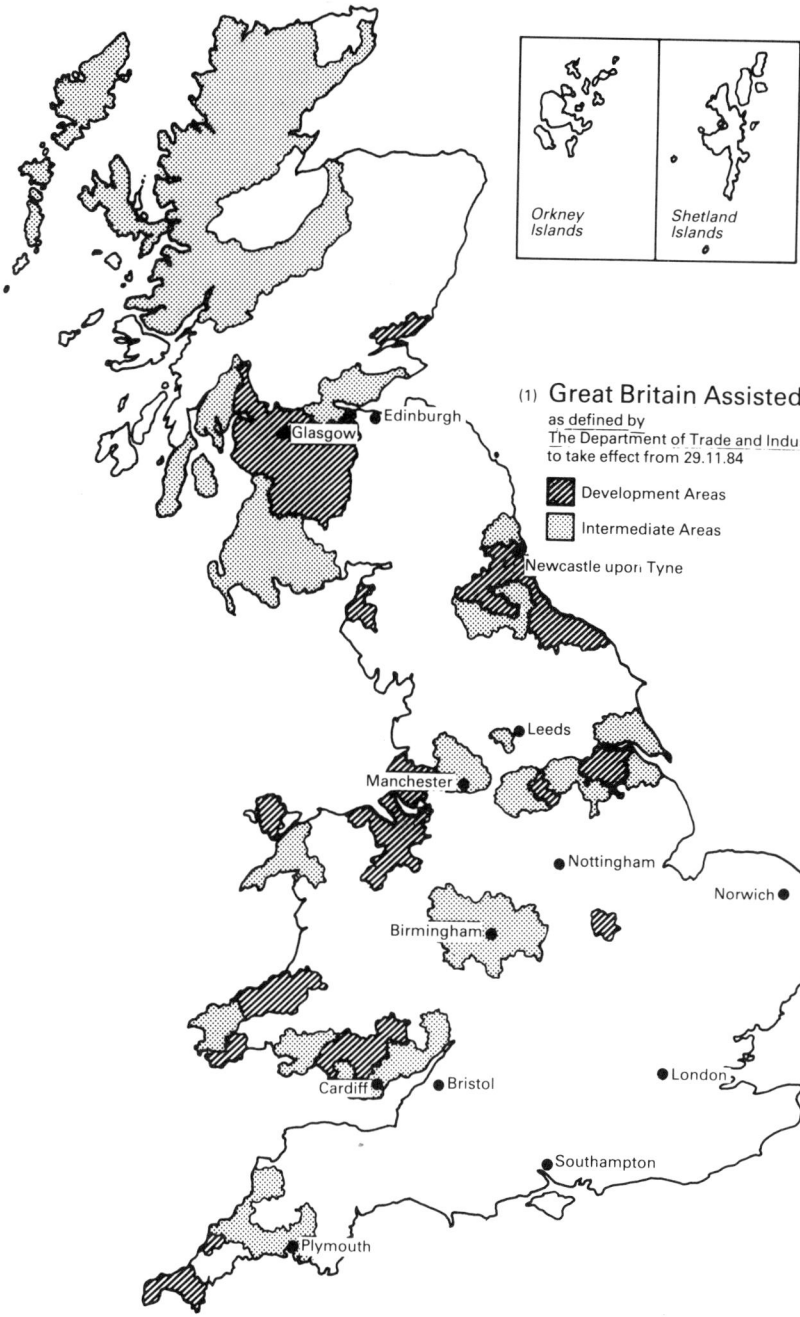

(1) **Great Britain Assisted Areas**
as defined by
The Department of Trade and Industry
to take effect from 29.11.84

Development Areas

Intermediate Areas

Orkney
Islands

Shetland
Islands

also available to assist with the costs of capital-investment projects relating to advanced micro-electronic, fibre optics, opto-electronics components and related activities. The maximum grant is £2500 or 75% of the eligible costs. It is essential to liaise with the DTI before the project commences.

(iii) Quality assurance. Grants are available to firms employing up to 500 people to assist with the cost of implementing a consultant's recommendations about how the product may be improved to meet British Standards Requirements. The maximum grant is 25% of the cost or £25 000, whichever is lower.

(2) Business and Technical Advisory Services

(i) Advice. A free advice service which covers all aspects of business is operated through the Small Firms Centres. (In Scotland and Wales these are operated by the development agencies on behalf of the DTI.) The advice is strictly confidential. Free consultancy from experienced businessmen may also be available. The department will pay for up to three sessions, and thereafter a charge of £30 per session applies. In addition, a series of helpful leaflets are available. The service is available to all small and medium-sized firms and to those setting up in business.

(ii) Products and process consultancy. Manufacturing firms employing up to 500 people may obtain assistance with the costs of consultancy aimed at improving the quality and design of their products or their manufacturing methods.

(iii) Grants for new technology feasibility studies. Grants are available towards the cost of feasibility studies aimed at assessing the viability of new production methods. The maximum grant of £2500 is available to all manufacturing firms.

(3) Accommodation

The government provides small workshop units, some of which can be occupied free of charge or at reduced rates by new businesses for a number of years. Initial contact should be made to the relevant Development Agency or to 'English Industrial Estates'. Certain local government agencies also provide accommodation, particularly the new town corporations. Occasionally British Rail can be a source of cheap accommodation.

(4) Better Business Service

The Better Business Service (presently available only in Scotland) offers guidance through a pool of consultants for a range of problems besetting the smaller business. The service covers management, finance and marketing. Thus the preparation of a business plan may qualify for assistance. The service is operated by the HIDB, the SDA and the Industry Department Scotland. It is partly funded by the EEC.

A grant of 55% of the cost of a report or a maximum of £550 is available. To be eligible a manufacturing firm must employ less than 200 people. Firms in other fields will only qualify if they employ less than 25 people. The initial step is to contact the agency involved. Work should only commence once approval has been obtained.

(5) Better Technical Services

This is an extension of the BBS and is only available in Strathclyde, Dundee, Arbroath, Blairgowrie and Kinross. Grants may be available to assist with marketing, research and development and computer applications.

(6) Enterprise Allowance Scheme

The enterprise allowance scheme is aimed at increasing the number of self-employed individuals, and particularly at helping the unemployed become self-employed. To qualify, an individual must have a reasonable project, e.g. setting up as a mechanic, hairdresser or craftsman. The individual must have been unemployed or under notice of redundancy for at least 13 weeks and must be able to contribute £1000. (This can often be raised from the bank.)

The proposed business must not employ more than 20 people. If an individual is accepted he/she will receive £40 per week for a year whilst the business gets off the ground. This allowance is taxed like any other business receipt. It is usually paid fortnightly in arrears into the business bank account.

Initial applications should be made through the local job centre, which will arrange for you to attend a one-day course run by the Manpower Services Commission, at which further details are available. Partnerships and co-operatives also qualify for this scheme.

(7) Employment Incentives

The government runs a number of schemes to encourage employers to take on additional employees.

(i) Young workers scheme. This offers subsidies to employers who take on young people between the ages of 16 and 18 in their first full-time permanent job. If the employee will earn less than £50 a week a subsidy of £15 per week may be given for up to one year.

(ii) The community programme. This relates to firms involved in work of benefit to the local community. If it can be shown that an eligible person could not otherwise be employed to carry out the proposed project a subsidy may be given.

(iii) Job-splitting scheme. This was set up to encourage employers to provide more part-time jobs. However, it is unlikely to be of benefit to the new business since it is a prerequisite that an existing job be split into two.

(iv) Youth training scheme. The Youth Training Scheme provides trainees with work experience of 9 months plus 3 months' further education. Many start-up businesses will be unable to provide the necessary experience, but since the cost to the employer is nil it may be worth enquiring.

(v) Job-related training programme. Under this new scheme assistance with training costs may be available. Initial enquiries should be at a job centres or to the Manpower Services Commission.

(8) Enterprise Zones

In recent years the government has set up a number of enterprise zones. There are a number of benefits to be obtained in these areas, the principal benefit being that they are rate-free. Further details can be obtained from the Department of the Environment.

    The Enterprise Zones in operation at the time of writing are:

Name	Operative Date
(a) Clydebank/Glasgow, Strathclyde	3 August/18 August 1981

(b) Newcastle/Gateshead, Tyne and Wear	25 August 1981
(c) Belfast, Northern Ireland	21 October 1981
(d) Hartlepool, Cleveland	23 October 1981
(e) Wakefield (Langthwaite Grange), West Yorkshire	31 July 1981
(f) Speke, Merseyside	25 August 1981
(g) Salford/Trafford, Greater Manchester	12 August 1981
(h) Corby, Northamptonshire	22 June 1981
(i) Dudley, West Midlands	10 July 1981
(j) Swansea, West Glamorgan	11 June 1981
(k) Isle of Dogs, London	26 April 1982
(l) Delyn, Clwyd	21 July 1983
(m) Wellingborough, Northamptonshire	26 July 1983
(n) Rotherham, South Yorkshire	16 August 1983
(o) Londonderry, Co. Londonderry	13 September 1983
(p) Scunthorpe, Humberside	23 September 1983
(q) Wakefield (Dale Lane and Kinsley), West Yorks	23 September 1983
(r) Workington, Cumbria	4 October 1983
(s) Invergordon, Highland	7 October 1983
(t) North-West Kent	31 October 1983
(u) Middlesbrough (Britannia), Cleveland	8 November 1983
(v) North-East Lancashire	7 December 1983
(w) Tayside (Dundee and Forfar)	9 January 1984
(x) Telford, Shropshire	13 January 1984

(9) EEC Aid

Strictly speaking, this forms part of the Regional Investment Support Programme, but as it is often thought of as something apart it is mentioned here separately. From time to time the EEC runs development programmes in selected areas. Exceptional levels of assistance may be available under such schemes which are generally well reported in local papers. The European Social Fund is also involved in certain projects and EEC assistance can also be obtained for feasibility studies.

A number of agencies have access to European Regional Development Fund monies, this money being used to supplement the amounts available from the UK government. Firms employing up to 200 people or setting up business in steel, shipbuilding and textile closure areas may obtain help. Further information can be obtained from leaflets held by the Development Agencies or from the Department of Trade and Industry.

(10) Local Trusts

A number of local trusts have been set up in recent years by concerned local organizations to give advice on business matters. They may also have funds available for grants and accommodation for lease at non-commercial rates. Information may be available in the local library or through council offices.

(11) Local Authorities

In addition to making loans the local authority may be willing to give grants towards suitable local businesses. Further information can be obtained from council offices.

(12) Support for Innovation

This area of support is primarily aimed at large firms but projects costing less than £100 000 will also be considered. The principal aim is to encourage research and development leading to new products and processes.

(13) Science Parks

The universities and other institutions have established a number of centres from which the assistance of experts is available. This is an attempt to bridge the gap between industry and academics.

(14) Tourist Boards

The tourist boards offer grants and loans to businesses in the tourist sector. Full details of the range of assistance can be obtained by writing to the appropriate authority.

(15) Chamber of Commerce

Do not forget the local Chambers of Commerce. They have been in the advice business for years and have particular knowledge of local conditions. They can be found through the telephone directory.

1.5 USEFUL ADDRESSES

Co-operative Development Agency

Broadmead House, 21 Panton Street, London SW11 4DR
  or
The Scottish Co-operatives Development Committee, Templeton Business Centre, Templeton Street, Glasgow
The Design Council
28 Haymarket, London SW1Y SSU
Tel: 01–839 800

THE DEPARTMENT OF TRADE AND INDUSTRY

DTI Regional Offices

North-East
Northumberland, Tyne & Wear, Cleveland and Durham

Stanegate House, 2 Groat Market, Newcastle NE1 1YN
(0632 324722)

North-West
Cheshire, Lancashire, Merseyside, Greater Manchester, High Peak, District of Derbyshire and Cumbria

Sunley Buildings, Piccaddilly Plaza, Manchester M1 4BA
(061 236 2171)

Yorkshire and Humberside
North, South and West Yorkshire and Humberside

Priestley House, Park Row, Leeds LS1 5LF
(0532 443171)

East Midlands
Nottinghamshire, Derbyshire, — except for High Peak District, Leicestershire, Lincolnshire and Northamptonshire

Severns House, 20 Middle Pavement, Nottingham NG1 7DW
(0602 56181)

West Midlands
Shropshire, West Midlands Metropolitan County, Staffordshire, Warwickshire, Hereford and Worcester

Ladywood House, Stephenson Street, Birmingham B2 4DT
(021 632 4111)

South-West
Cornwall, (incl. Scilly Isles) Devon, Somerset, Wiltshire, Gloucestershire, Avon and Dorset

The Pithay, Bristol BS1 2PB
(0272 291071)

South-East	Edbury Bridge House, 2/18
Greater London, Kent, Surrey,	Edbury Bridge Road,
East and West Sussex, Hampshire,	London SW1W 8QD
Isle of Wight, Bedfordshire,	(01 730 9771/9713)
Berkshire, Buckinghamshire,	
Essex, Hertfordshire,	
Oxfordshire, Cambridgeshire, and	
Norfolk	

Other Departments acting for the DTI

Scotland   Industry Department for Scotland,
                      Alhambra House, 45 Waterloo Street,
                      Glasgow G2 6AT
                      (041 226 3949)

Wales   Welsh Office Industry Department,
                      Government Buildings, Cathay Park,
                      Cardiff CF1 3NQ
                      (0222 825111, Ext. 4183/4058)

Northern Ireland   Industrial Development Board,
                      IDB House, 64 Chichester Street,
                      Belfast 1
                      (0232 233233)

REGIONAL DEVELOPMENT GRANT OFFICES

These all fall under the DTI except that enquiries from certain areas are
not handled by the Regional Offices:

(i)   *Merseyside*
      Graeme House
      Derby Square
      LIVERPOOL L2 7UJ
(ii) *South Western*
      Phoenix House
      Notte Street
      PLYMOUTH
      Devon PL1 24F
(iii) *Scotland*
      The Industry Department for Scotland
      Magnet House

59 Waterloo Street
GLASGOW G2 7BT

English Industrial Estates
Kingsway, Team Valley, Gateshead, Tyne and Wear, NE11 0NA (0632 878941)
European Regional Development Fund
Kingsgate House, 66–74 Victoria Street, London, SW1E 6SJ (01–212 0400)
European Community Loans
Inward Investment and Tourism Division, Kingsgate House, 66–74 Victoria Street, London, SW1E 6SJ (01–212 0400)
Export Credit Guarantee
Aldermanbury House, Aldermanbury, London, EC2P 2EL
Highland and Islands Development Board
Bridge House, 27 Bank Street, Inverness (0463 234171)
Investors in Industry Group plc
Ventures Division, 91 Waterloo Road, London SE1 8XP
ICFC
38 Carden Place, Aberdeen AB1 1UP (0224 638666)
112 Colmore Row, Birmingham B3 3AG (021 236 9531)
47 Middle Street, Brighton BN1 1AL (0273 23164)
Pearl Assurance House, Queen Square, Bristol BS1 4LE (0272 277412)
Cambridge Science Park, Milton Road, Cambridge CB4 4BH (0223 316568)
Alliance House, 18/19 High Street, Cardiff CF1 3TS (0222 394541)
8 Charlotte Square, Edinburgh, EH2 4DR (031 226 7092)
9th Floor, Pegasus House, 375 West George Street, Glasgow G2 4AR (041 248 4456)
Headrow House, The Headrow, Leeds LS1 8ES (0532–430511)
Abacus House, 32 Friar Lane, Leicester LE1 5QU (0533 25223)
Tithebarn Street, Liverpool L2 2LZ (051 236 2944)
91 Waterloo Road, London SE1 8XP (01–928 6600)
Virginia House, 5 Cheapside, Manchester M2 4WG (061 833 9511)
Scottish Life House, Archbold Terrace, Jesmond, Newcastle Upon Tyne NE2 1DB (0632 815221)
38 The Ropewalk, Nottingham NG1 5DW (0602 412766)
43/47 Crown Street, Reading, RG1 2SN (9734 861943)
11 Westbourne Road, Sheffield S10 2QQ (0742 680571)
Capital House, 1 Houndwell Place, Southampton SO1 1HU (0703 32044)
Northern Ireland Office
Department of Economic Development, Netherleigh, Massey Avenue, Belfast, BT4 2JP (0232 63244)

Patent Office
25 Southampton Buildings, London, WC2A 1AY
PERA
(Producing Engineering Research Association) Melton Mowbray,
Leicestershire LF13 OPB (0664 64133)
Scottish Development Agency
120 Bothwell Street, Glasgow G2 7JP (041 248 2700)
Haymarket House, Edinburgh (031 337 9595)
Small Firms Centres
Dial 100 and ask for FREEPHONE Enterprise; or
Contact the DTI Regional Office; or
The SDA; or
The WDA; or
The Northern Ireland Office, Department of Economic Development.
Support for Business
Phone 01–215 4021
or any of the following regional numbers:
North-East
Newcastle Upon Tyne 0632 324 722

Yorkshire and Humberside
Leeds   0532 433 171

West Midlands
Birmingham   021 632 4111

South-West
Bristol   0272 272 666

Wales
Cardiff   0222 825 111

North-West
Manchester   061 236 2171

East Midlands
Nottingham   0602 506 181

South-East
London   01–730 9678

Scotland
Glasgow   041 248 2855

Northern Ireland
Belfast   0232 233 233

Welsh Development Agency
Treforest International Estate, Pontypridd, Mid-Glamorgan CF37 5UT
Tourist Boards
English Tourist Board
4 Grosvenor Gardens, London SW1W ODU
Scottish Tourish Board
23 Ravelston Terrace, Edinburgh EH4 3EU
Wales Tourist Board
Branch House, 2 Fitzalan Road, Cardiff CF2 1UY
Northern Ireland Tourist Board
River House, 48 High Street, Belfast BT1 1DR

1.6   SOME USEFUL PUBLICATIONS

Money for Business, published by the Bank of England.
The Banks and Small Firms, published by the Banking Information
Service.
A wide range of leaflets produced by the Small Firms Service.
Leaflets produced by ICFC.
Pamphlets produced by the banks, e.g. Barclays/Bank of Scotland
Guides for Businessmen.
The Business Start Up Guide, produced by the SDA.
Booklets on sources of assistance produced by the large firms of
Chartered Accountants.
The Investment and Innovation Handbook, produced by the Department
of Trade and Industry. (If reprinted!)
Marketing: An Introductory Text by Michael J. Baker, published by
Macmillan.
Foundation in Accounting, by Richard Lewis and Ian Gillespie,
published by Prentice-Hall.
Tolleys Tax Guide 1984–85 and *Practical Tax Advice for the Non Expert*,
by Arnold Homer, FCA ATII, and Rita Buncers, MBA ACIS ATII,
both published by Tolleys Publishing Company Ltd.
A Tax Guide to Pay and Perks, by Bill Packer and Elaine Burker,
published by Macmillan.
VAT Guidance notes and leaflets, produced by HM Customs and Excise.
National Insurance guidance leaflets, produced by the DHSS.
Tax and PAYE guidance leaflets, produced by the Inland Revenue.

Appendix A. National Insurance Contributions

Class 1

	Employee rate		Employer rate	
	Not contracted out	Contracted out	Not contracted out	Contracted out
Rates to 5 October 1985				
Earnings below £35.50 per week	NIL	NIL	NIL	NIL
Where earnings reach £35.50 but are below £265	9%	6.85%	10.45%	6.35%
Excess earnings over £265	NIL	NIL	NIL	NIL
Rates from 6 October 1985				
Earnings below £35.50 per week	NIL	NIL	NIL	NIL
Where earnings reach £35.50 but are below £55	5%	2.85%	5%	0.9%
Where earnings reach £55 but are below £90	7%	4.85%	7%	2.9%
Where earnings reach £90 but are below £130	9%	6.85%	9%	4.9%
Where earnings reach £130 but are below £265	9%	6.85%	10.45%	6.35%
Where earnings reach or exceed £265	£23.85 per week	£18.92 per week	10.45% on all earnings	£18.28 per week plus 10.45% of earnings over £265

Class 2 (Self-Employed)
Weekly contributions are £4.75, reducing to £3.50 from 6 October 1985.
No contributions are levied where profits are below £1925 in the 1985/86 tax year.

Class 3 (Voluntary)
Weekly contributions are £4.65, reducing to £3.40 from 6 October 1985.

Class 4 (Self-Employed)
For 1985/6, 6.3% on profits between £4150 and £13 780.
50% of contributions are tax-deductible.

Appendix B. Personal Allowances 1985/6

	£
Married Man	3455
Single Person	2205
Wife's Earned Income Relief	2205
Age Allowance: Married	4255
Single	2690
Income Limit	8800
Additional Personal Allowance (largely for single parents)	1250
Widow's Bereavement Allowance	1250

Appendix C. Income Tax Bands 1985/6

Up to £16 200	30%
£16 201–£19 200	40%
£19 201–£24 400	45%
£24 401–£32 300	50%
£32 301–£40 200	55%
£40 201 upwards	60%

Appendix D. Corporation Tax

	Year to 31 March 1986	Year to 31 March 1987
Full rate	40%	35%
Small Companies Rate	30%	30%
Lower Relevant Amount	£100 000	£100 000
Higher Relevant Amount	£500 000	£500 000
Small Companies Fraction	1/40	1/80
Capital Gains reduced by	1/4	1/7

Note
Companies with taxable profits below £100 000 suffer Corporation Tax at 30%.
Companies with taxable profits in excess of £500 000 suffer Corporation Tax at
the full rate. Where taxable profits fall between £100 000 and £500 000, the
taxable profits are charged to Corporation Tax at the full rate, and the liability is
then reduced by the product of the formula:

$$(\text{£500 000} - \text{Profit}) \times \frac{\text{Income}}{\text{Profits}} \times \text{Small Companies Fraction}$$

('Income' and 'Profits' have technical definitions for these purposes.)

Capital gains are reduced by the fraction shown in the table above and then
charged to Corporation Tax at the full rate. The effect is to apply a flat rate
charge of 30% to capital gains.

Appendix E. Capital Allowances

	14 March 1984—31 March 1985	1 April 1985—31 March 1986	1 April 1986 onwards
Plant & Machinery			
First-year allowance	75%	50%	NIL
Writing-down allowance (Reducing balance)	25%	25%	25%
Industrial buildings (excluding Enterprise Zones)			
Initial allowance	50%	25%	NIL
Writing-down allowance (Straight line)	4%	4%	4%
Agricultural buildings			
Initial allowance	20%	20%	NIL
Writing-down allowance (Straight line)	10%	10%	4%
Hotels			
Initial allowance	20%	20%	NIL
Writing-down allowance (Straight line)	4%	4%	4%

Patent rights
For expenditure incurred up to 31 March 1986, capital expenditure on acquiring patent rights is relieved evenly over 17 years. For expenditure incurred on or after 1 April 1986, relief will be given by 25% annual writing-down allowances (reducing-balance method).

Know-how
For capital expenditure incurred up to 31 March 1986, relief is given evenly over 6 years. For expenditure incurred on or after 1 April 1986 it will be relieved by 25% annual writing-down allowances (reducing-balance method).

Appendix F. Summarized car and fuel taxable benefits 1985/6

Car benefits	Less than 2500 miles business use		2500–17 999 miles business use		18 000 or more business miles	
	Under 4 years £	4 years or more £	Under 4 years £	4 years or more £	Under 4 years £	4 years or more £
Original market value up to £17 500						
1300 cc or less	615	412	410	275	205	137
1301–1800 cc	787	525	525	350	262	175
Over 1800 cc	1237	825	825	550	412	275
No cylinder capacity						
Under £5500	As for 1300 cc or less					
£5500 to £7699	As for 1301 to 1800 cc					
£7700 to £17 500	As for over 1800 cc					
Original market value over £17 500						
Over £17 500 to £26 500	1800	1200	1200	800	600	400
Over £26 500	2850	1905	1900	1270	950	635

Fuel benefits						Taxable benefit £
Cylinder capacity	
1300 cc or less	410
1301 cc to 1800 cc	525
Over 1800 cc	825

Index

Accommodation, 236
Accountant, 7–8, 24, 28, 63, 69, 75, 108
Accounting date, choice of, 148, 151
Accounting system, 77
Accruals, 30
Administration costs, 25, 35, 44
Advance Corporation Tax (ACT), 137, 138, 192, 193, 194, 214
Advertising, 15–16, 55–56
Agricultural buildings allowances, 169–170
Allowable expenses
  for earnings, 140
  for trading profits, 140
APR (Annual Percentage Rate), 174
Asset finance, 156–158, 172–175
Assistance to industry, 229
Associated companies, 191–192
Assumptions, 64, 72, 83, 92–96
Attitude, 8

Bad debts, 36
Badges of trade, 152–153
Balance sheet, 46–50, 69
Bank loan, 45, 63, 70, 75
  security for, 223
Bank manager, 70, 223
  approaching, 71
  initial meeting, 72
  second meeting, 73
Bank overdraft, 37, 45–46, 62, 63, 70, 75, 158, 223
Benefits in-kind, 200, 203–205

Better Business Service, 237
Better Technical Services, 237
Borrowing to invest, 198
Business and Technical Advisory Services, 236
Business description, 52–54
Business Expansion Scheme, 194–197, 209, 226, 227
Business plan
  object of, 7
  presenting the case, 7
  reason for, 7
  synopsis, 81, 89
Buying, 53–54

Capital, 72
Capital accounts, 49
Capital allowances, 162–175, 251
  basis periods for, 162–165
  limited companies, 164–165, 213
Capital base structuring, 199
Capital Duty, 217
Capital expenditure, 157, 162
  pre-trading, 165
  time of incurring, 171
Capital Gains Tax, 196, 214–216
Capital Taxes Office, 139
Capital Transfer Tax, 138–139, 206
Cash flow, 35–46, 68, 146, 159, 160
  and VAT, 128
  forecast, 27, 40–46, 77
  monitoring, 77–80
Cash outflow, 78–79

Cash payable, 42
Cash receivable, 42
Casual activity, 152
Casual employees and PAYE, 143–145
Clearing banks, 223
Commercial vehicles, 58
Company cars, 204–205, 252
Company finance, tax aspects of, 194–198
Company secretary, 63
Company tax outline, 189–190
Competitors, 9, 15, 17, 54
Computer, 58, 60–61
Computer package, 69
Computer program, 28, 29
Computer spreadsheet, 29, 50
Contract of employment, 139, 142, 155–156
Contract of service, 141
Corporation Tax, 28, 137, 138, 187, 200, 250
    due date for payment, 189
    full rate of, 190
    marginal rates of, 190–191
    rates of, 189
    rules, 199
Cost of sales, 22, 34, 68
Costing, 10
Counter limit, 223
Credit control, 35–40
Credit limit, 39
Credit sales, 78
Credit terms, 20, 37, 39–40
Creditors, 30
Creditworthiness, 38

Debt collecting agency, 39
Debt factors, 39, 228
Debtors, 31, 38–39, 40, 49, 68, 69
Department of Trade and Industry, 241–242
Dependence on any one purchaser, 55
Development agencies, 226
Directors, 90
    accounts basis, 202
    annual earnings period, 136
    earnings basis, 202
    remuneration, 28
Discounts, 10
Distribution costs, 13, 24, 35, 43

Dividends, 192–194
    instead of salary, 137–139
Drawings, 28

Employees
    numbers and grades, 18
    salaries, 155
Employment
    incentives, 238
    terms and conditions, 60
    versus self-employment, 140, 141
Enterprise allowance scheme, 237
Enterprise Zones, 171–172, 238
    concessions in, 172
Equity, 63
    versus loan finance, 198–200
Equity investment, 197
European Investment Bank, 225
European Regional Development Fund, 239
Expenses, 140

Factory costs, 22, 34
Factory space, 18
Family loans, 227
Finance, acceptance of, 75–76
Finance costs, 26, 35, 45, 75
Finance houses, 227
Finance package, 62–64, 74
Finance sources, 70–76
    identifying, 70–71
Financial control, 91
Financial projections, 83, 92–96
Financial shortfall, 222
Finished goods, 31, 33
Fixed assets, 46, 69
Fixed costs, 12
Forecasting, 8
    capacity to provide services, 17
    cash flow, 27, 40–46, 77
    employee numbers and costs, 18
    essential, 50
    manufacturing capacity, 17
    market size and share, 17
    preparation of, 30–51
    stockholding facility, 18
Forecasting period, 50–51
Fuel tax benefits, 205, 252
Funding, 82
    future, 64
    short-term, 63–64

Grants, 63
Gross profit, 13, 23
Gross profit percentage, 23, 24, 35

Hire purchase, 45, 173, 174, 227
Hobby, 152
Hotel construction, 170

Income receivable, 42
Income tax, 22, 28, 43, 138
  due dates for payment of, 147
income tax assessment
  first tax year, 149
  option to revise first three tax years,
    159–161
  preceding year basis of, 146–147, 149
  second tax year, 149
  third tax year, 149
Income tax bands, 249
Income tax liabilities, minimizing in
  first three tax years, 153–158
Income tax planning, 146–161
Incorporation, 206–218
  advantages, 209
  disadvantages, 207
  planning for, 210–211
  tax considerations, 207–210
  timing of, 211–213
  withdrawal of funds prior to, 213–
    214
Industrial and Commercial Finance
  Corporation (ICFC), 224–225
Industrial buildings
  allowances, 167–169
  used, 169
Inland Revenue, 60
Interest, 158
Investment Income Surcharge, 137

Know-how, capital payments for, 171

Labour costs, 22, 34, 43
Leasing, 44, 228
  vs. purchase, 156–158
Leasing agreement, 173
Legal duties, 63
Limited company, 28, 60, 63, 115
  capital allowances, 164–165, 213
  case study, 89–96
  see also Incorporation
Loan finance, equity versus, 198–200

Loan Guarantee Scheme, 224, 234
Loans, 49, 63, 227
  see also Bank loans
Local government assistance, 227
Location of premises, 56
Loose tools, 57

Machinery selection, 17
Mainstream Corporation Tax (MCT),
  137, 138, 192, 193
Manufacturing capacity, forecasting,
  17
Market début, 53
Market image, 53
Market research, 9, 10, 54
Market review, 82, 90
Market sector, 52
Market size and share, 17, 55
Market strategy, 82
Marketing, 14–15
Married Man's Allowance, 178, 179,
  183, 201
Merchant banks, 224
Money shops, 224
Monitoring, 8
Monthly earnings period, 135

National Insurance contributions, 11,
  22, 43, 44, 45, 68, 130–145, 207, 246
  applicability, 131–134
  benefits in kind, 134
  Class 1 contributions, 135, 139, 142,
    145
  Class 4 contributions, 147
  minimizing, 134–136
  part-time staff, 132–133
  threshold, 132, 133, 134
Net profit, 28–29
Net sales, 21, 23

Offer document, 75–76
Office equipment, 57
Overdraft, see Bank overdraft

Packaging costs, 43
Packing materials, 61
Partnership, 28, 45, 49, 153
Part-time staff, NIC savings, 132–133
Patent rights, capital cost of, 171
Pay-As-You-Earn, see PAYE
PAYE, 43, 44, 130–145, 193

and casual employees, 143–145
applicability, 131–134
threshold, 133
Pension contributions, 43, 44
Pension premium, 209
Personal allowance, 248
Personality, 8
Personnel, 59–61
Planning points, 132
Planning possibilities, 153
Plant and machinery, 57, 157, 164–167
Premises, 55–57, 82, 91
Pre-payments, 30
Present market, 54
Pre-trading expenditure, 158–159
Pricing policy, 12, 15
Product details, 81
Product knowledge, 15
Production costs, 22
Products, 8, 53
Profit and loss account, 30–35, 68
Profit figure for first year of trading, 153
Promotion, 15–16
Publications, 245
Purchase vs. leasing, 156–158

Qualifying company, 194–195
Qualifying individual, 194
Qualifying trade, 194, 195

Records, 60
Regional Development Fund, 226
Regional Development Grant Offices, 242–245
Regional Development Grants, 232
Regional development system, 229
Regional Selective Assistance, 234
Remuneration policy, 200–203
Rent reviews, 57
Repayment supplement, 186
Reservation of title, 62
Retail business, 53, 61
Retail schemes, 123–124
Revenue reserves, 49
Romalpa clause, 62

Salaries, 67
dividends instead of, 137–139
employees', 155
Sales costs, 22, 34, 68

Sales estimates, 20
Sales ledger, 38
Sales outlets, 55
Sales target, 29
Salesmen, 16, 25, 39
Schedule D Case I, 140, 152
Schedule D Case VI, 152
Schedule E earnings, 139, 142
Security for bank loan, 223
Self-employed labour, 139–140
Self-employment
and employment, 140, 141
hallmarks of, 140–143
income tax planning for first year, 146–161
Selling, 16
Services industry, 11, 17
Share capital, 63
Share schemes, 60
Single Person's Allowance, 201
Small firms finance, 234
Sole trader, 28, 45, 49
case study, 81–89
Sources of assistance, 229
Sources of finance, 219
Spouse, employment of, 153
Stamp Duty, 216–217
Start of trading date, 151–153
Statutory Sick Pay, 143
Steel and coal industry closure areas, 225
Stock categories, 31
Stock control, 61
Stock valuation, 31
Stockholding facility, 18
Student employment, 145
Subcontractors, 139
Superannuation contributions, 134
Suppliers, 61–62
Support for Business, 229

Tax losses, 176–188
against trading income, 177–180
aggregated with profits, 182
carry-back of, 184–186
company options, 186–188
definition, 176–177
incurred in early years of trading, 180–183
setting against other income of same tax year, 183

setting against total income of three preceding tax years, 184
setting sideways, 183
Tax planning, 105
Tax reliefs, 146
Tax rules, 139, 152, 199
Tax year, 146, 148
Taxable benefit, 203
Taxation, 28
Timing of supplies, 128
Trade credit, 228
Trading medium, 206

Value added tax, *see* VAT
Variable costs, 12
VAT, 21, 22, 23, 26, 33, 35, 42, 64, 107–129, 217
  accounting period, 122
  acquiring goods for personal use, 120
  activities outside scope of, 110
  and cash flow, 128
  business as going concern, 121
  choice of registration, 115–118
  definition, 109
  de-register voluntarily, 120
  de-registration, 119–120
  disallowance on petrol, 126
  exempt outputs, 109, 110, 127
  free supplies of services, 125
  gifts, 125
  hidden supplies, 124–125
  incurred on supply of goods, 114
  incurred on supply of services, 114
  input, 65, 109, 110, 112, 114, 125–127
  intending trader-registration, 112–113

  interest charge on late payments, 123
  lease rentals, 173
  output, 65, 109, 110, 123–124
  partial exemption, 127
  pre-registration input, 113–115
  registration, 111
  returns and records, 118, 121–123
  sources of information, 108
  subsistence expenses, 127
  tax point, 128
  taxable persons, 111, 112
  taxable sales, 21
  taxable turnover, 111
  turnover of taxable supplies, 115
  voluntary registration, 112
  who is registered, 118–119
  zero rates, 109
VAT assessment, 108
VAT compliance, 108
VAT payable/repayable, 66
VAT returns, 128
VAT threshold, 9
Vehicle costs, 44
Venture-capital, 63, 74, 227
Venture-capital relief, 197
Ventures-division, 225

Wage-related costs, 11
Wages, 11, 67
Warehouse costs, 26
Weekly earnings period, 135
Wife's Earned Income Relief, 133, 135, 178, 179, 183, 201
Work in progress, 31, 35
Workforce, 59–61